for a
friend,
Acts 29+

for Charmaine
in Christian love
and appreciation

Lauren Hammond

Isaiah 43:2
I Cor. 15:13
Gal. 6:9

# Beyond Love

# Beyond Love

**Laurence Hammond**

Creation House
Carol Stream, Illinois

Published by Creation House, 499 Gundersen Drive, Carol Stream, Illinois 60187
In Canada: Beacon Distributing Ltd., 104 Consumers Drive, Whitby, Ontario L1N5T3
In Australia: Oracle Australia, Ltd., 18-26 Canterbury Road, Heathmont, Victoria 135

Biblical quotations from the *New American Standard Bible* are used with permission from the Lockman Foundation.

ISBN 0-88419-000-5
Library of Congress Catalog Card Number 76-14542
Printed in the United States of America

For Merikay whose gay and loving heart beat as one with mine for nearly twenty-four years.

And in deep thanksgiving to all those whose prayers for us both over the years rose as incense before the throne of God.

And for the glory of that same great God who breathed the breath of life into each of us . . . that all His children—black and white, brown, yellow and red—may in this life come to know His only Son, Jesus as Savior, Great Physician and Baptizer in the Holy Spirit.

# CONTENTS

## TO BE READ

This book will be controversial. Many will ask, "How can God use an alcoholic—or anyone involved in questionable activities?"

This is not a new question. However, it may be one of the few times it surfaces in the publication of a book.

We do not pretend to know the answer. God, it would appear, has His reasons, based on His great grace and love for mankind.

By the publication of this book, we do not endorse these practices. Rather, we believe this book illustrates the fact that God often uses imperfect means by which to draw men and women to His Son, Jesus Christ, who said, "Let him who is without sin cast the first stone . . . "

The Publishers

Some of the names in this book have been changed to avoid embarrassing the real people.

# 1

# Love Song

Down the staircase and into my heart she twirled, with her golden hair and sea-green eyes. She was bursting with life, so radiant my heart hurt just to look at her. I didn't dare touch her for fear that, like some beautiful bubble, she might suddenly disappear.

"So," she laughed up at me, "what took you so long?"

It had been a fifteen mile taxi trip from the Drake Hotel in Chicago to Winnetka. About to catch a plane to keep a tight radio schedule, I had phoned to thank her parents for their hospitality the night before. I had met with them to present a public relations project. Then, over the line, came this throaty voice, like the touch of velvet on a night made bright by the full moon.

Her mother had told me how beautiful her only daughter

was. As a wise widower, skilled in ducking lionesses with homely, buck-toothed cubs, I had discounted that 100 percent. But now . . . the roof fell. I had the helpless feeling I was drowning.

The minutes sped into hours. The hours turned into days. Merikay and I sunbathed and swam. We walked through woodsy places, hearts in hand. We danced on clouds and hoped the nights would never end. When my hungry arms encircled her she was curving soft and pulsing warm. We kissed as if there'd be no tomorrow.

At breakfast one morning her father drily asked her mother about the strange young man he'd seen in various parts of the house during the past week. "LB," as her husband always called her, explaining it was short for "Le Boss," passed it off with a laugh.

"Oh, he came for dinner, and he stayed for life," she said prophetically.

Finally business put a period to that first heady chapter of our romance. Merikay drove me to the airport and we kissed a breathless goodbye.

Flowers I sent her. And letters I wrote. But the days dragged emptily by until late one night as I was going to bed in my lonely Manhattan Tower, that same throaty voice floated over the long distance wires from Chicago. Seven of what the world calls hours turned into fleeting seconds as we talked and laughed and cried and shared the night away.

"Tell me all about you as a little girl. What did you like?"

"Rabbits. Until they caused a population problem. And you?"

"Guinea pigs were my thing. Mother thought it a good way to learn the facts of life."

"Was it?"

"I learned all about guinea pigs. Never applied it to people."

12

"And horses. I loved horses. Liked to ride and jump. Even won some ribbons. And loved to gallop over wild western prairies. Still do. The soft feel of the air washing your face in the hot sun."

"And gallop right on into tomorrow."

"Laurie." A sigh. "Let's."

"What do people you love call you?"

"My parents call me 'Merikay,' my college friends all call me 'Mac,' and my Uncle Bubba calls me 'Mimi.' Take your pick."

Question after question, hurled with love's soft eagerness. Sharing our joys, our sorrows. What are you really like deep down inside? It was the tender trust of one soul opening itself up to its long-sought mate. So our love unfolded all our deepest thoughts . . . the never before revealed yearnings of our hearts . . . two hungry hearts which on that velvet, timeless night melted into one.

As dawn broke, setting the sky aflame to match our hearts, my young son stumbled sleepily into the living room and began to operate his electric train. Introductions took only a moment. Soon he was again busy with his train, being engineer, fireman, passenger, signalman, lost in his childish world.

So Merikay learned for the first time that I was a widower with a son named Lance. Also I learned that she planned a trip to Europe with her cousin Caroline. They would be coming through New York within the week. My heart leaped with joy.

Those precious few days with Merikay were filled with the hustle and bustle of sharing the places I loved, doing the things we both loved, but mainly being alone together and loving each other. Too soon I was watching the plane rise into the sky like some huge, pregnant guppy. As it disappeared into the clouds, part of my heart went with it.

In my new-found loneliness, I wondered. I had avoided a quick remarriage, wanted to be so sure the girl would make the best substitute mother for my little son. Was Merikay the right one? They had liked each other on sight. The night I took him back to the friends with whom he was living in rural New Jersey, he had said shyly, "If you really like her, Dad, then I like her, too."

But would it work out really? I had made so many mistakes during the five years since his mother had died. Again, for the thousandth time, I heard that childish voice, "Daddy, where's Mommy?"

Again I relived the horror of that moment when I stumbled sleepily into the kitchen and found her slumped forward, her head cradled in her arms across the open door of the gas oven. Even as my heart burst into a soundless cry, my fingers ran swiftly across the gas jets. They were all closed. I sighed with relief. Now the oven. It was turned on. But the breeze through the partly opened window at her side had blown out the flame. The smell of gas was strong.

I snapped off the oven, threw the window wide on that sub-zero morning, dragged her limp figure to the window, and propped her there, face full in the chill breeze.

The helmeted rescue squad from the fire department clumped in on the shrill echoes of the fire siren. They slapped her cheeks, bent for what seemed hours above her stretched-out form. Speedily, with surprising tenderness, they placed the oxygen mask over her face.

*Now*, I thought, *it will be all right. Surely they've come in time. Maggie can't have been unconscious that long. Dear God, don't let it be too late! Oh, God!*

But was there a God? There must be a God somewhere! I had been raised by devout Christian parents, had sung in the choir, had served as an altar boy in the Episcopal church. I had grown up, loving the idea of God. But I had never had a real, personal relationship with Him. Jesus had always seemed way off there in space and time and history. Slowly, as I listened to unbelieving professors in the universities I attended, the idea of God had become old-fashioned, almost mythical. I had stopped attending church.

But now I needed Him! I needed God . . . I cried out in my heart silently, agonizingly. Meanwhile I tried to distract and comfort my son. In desperation I gave him the Sunday paper. He buried his face in the comic section. Then the firemen shook their heads, the lines etched deeper in their stubbled faces.

"Too late. Did our best. If only we'd got here a few minutes sooner . . ." Their voices trailed away as they began dragging out the oxygen mask and cylinder. "If only . . . "

If only . . . if only I had sensed something wrong and had awakened before Lance had tugged at my arm. If only I had not wasted time looking all around the apartment . . . If only I had run right away to the kitchen . . . I remembered how Maggie's habit had been to rise early Sunday morning and wash her hair. How she always dried it by opening the oven door and resting her head upon her arms on the door. How she had persisted even though I had often warned her about the danger of passing out in the warmth. And what if the oven should somehow blow out? What then?

But Maggie, full of life and self-confidence, laughed me out of my fears. And now . . . apparently the breeze had blown out the flame this one time. Oh, God, why did You let that breeze spring up? Why on such a cold morning did she open the window at all? Or why didn't she throw it wide open, instead of just a crack? A crack big enough to let the wind blow out the oven. Oh, God . . . why, God?

Over the now painfully quiet sound of the firemen shuffling out, suddenly came a burst of childish laughter. My blood froze. Over and over again during that endless morning of my

15

spiritual crucifixion came burst after burst of that same laughter. Deeper and deeper each burst drove into my hands and my feet the torturing nails of self-condemnation and remorse.

*My little boy! Doesn't even know his mother is dead, that he'll never see her again. Oh, God! He mustn't know she is dead yet. I have to get him out of here before he finds out. Have to have time to think clearly. There'll be doctors. And, yes, the undertaker. Lance mustn't know. Not yet. Oh, God, give me strength. Give me wisdom. I've got to break the news slowly, give him time to adjust to not having her around. I'll tell him she's gone on a trip. And the trip will be longer and longer as the weeks go by. Then some day when he's older, I'll tell the truth. When he's able to understand.*

If I had only known then that *not knowing* is the worst of all.

So I made my first mistake. Instead of being honest, I lied to my boy. I took him across the street to his friend Tommy's house. And all that afternoon he and the other children played. And played. And it seemed as though I'd never heard laughter so loud.

It was a horrible, totally unnecessary accident. But Maggie was Margaret Montague, an internationally famous fashion designer. And I was a well-known radio writer and director, and a member of the board of directors of the Authors' League. It was good copy for the newspaper reporters. They came like buzzing hornets ready for the kill . . . the "scoop."

"How about a picture, bud? One little picture won't hurt. Well, if you won't let us photograph the body, how about a recent still? How about that one in the frame by the bedside? Why'd she do it, man?"

"It was an accident, I tell you." I brushed them away wearily. No use making them mad. You couldn't tell what horrible possibilities they might think up. I'd been a reporter myself. "Just

16

an accident," I repeated emphatically.

"Yeah. Sure. An accident. You two have a fight or something?" A knowing leer.

Through a nearby friend who was a medical doctor, a kindly coroner came, trying to make it as easy as possible. But, of course, the police had to be notified. In they came, full of accusations. The night before, in a strange quirk, my wife and I had been aroused late by a noisy argument in front of our open second-story window. I asked the man and woman to please go away. They just began to yell louder and shriek obscenities at me. So I had phoned the police. They took their time coming over, although the precinct office was just a couple of blocks away. By the time they came, the fighting couple had completely disappeared. So apparently the investigating officer had entered it on the police blotter as a "family quarrel."

"There'll have to be an inquest," said the officer grimly. "Looks like foul play to me." His tone was the kind police use to known criminals. "Yes, we'll have to check into this. Something fishy about it. You and she all alone in the apartment with a little kid . . . we better have a few words with him alone."

I lunged toward him. "Why, you . . . you let that child alone. Why, he doesn't even know his mother's dead yet."

"Well, it's high time he did." The policeman backed out the doorway, pad in one hand, pencil stub clamped in his mouth like a cigar. As his other hand caressed the butt of his .38, sudden peals of childish laughter came from across the street.

So another agony. Now accused of murdering Maggie. Gay, laughing Maggie whom I had loved for five years. Maggie, my wife. Maggie, the mother of my son. Maggie, my love. Oh, God, is there no end to suffering? No end? Oh, God!

Further investigation convinced the police that their suspicions were unfounded. With that burden removed, I turned my efforts to the task of adjusting. Like thousands of other wifeless fathers, I found being both father and mother too much. I tried. Oh, how I tried! And my friends helped. Matt Crowley left his own dear wife, May, to spend those first fierce nights with me, while Lance was loved by the neighbors across the street. My associate on the Committee for Economic Development, Tex Faught, made the identification after the autopsy at the morgue—a task I found beyond me.

Tex and his lovely, warm-hearted wife, Patricia, opened their apartment and their hearts and took us both in for the next few months. Their chubby son, Douglas, and Lance became fast friends. We were one big happy family, except—having no other spiritual resources—I sought forgetfulness in the bottle. Oh, I managed to continue producing network programs satisfactorily. Never missed any on account of drinking. But I often operated at a woozy 85 percent instead of 100 percent. One night while waiting in a friend's apartment for him to get ready to go out for dinner, I casually flipped through a book *How To Know if You're an Alcoholic.* Smugly I began checking the questions at the end. *Some people,* I thought proudly, *might not be able to handle their liquor, but I sure could. And do my work, too.*

Then I turned the last page. "If you have checked 'yes' to half the questions," it said right there in big black print, "then *you* are an alcoholic, and need help." I had checked every one of them. I tore the covers off that little book and threw it into the log fire.

Some weeks later, lying in bed in the Faughts' Tudor City apartment, I reached down where I kept a bottle of liquor. It was easier to start the day off by taking a swig right out of the bottle.

*Some people start the day off,* I thought, *by brushing their teeth. But I . . .*

Suddenly a shaft of sunlight shot across the bed. Into my mind came the thought, *What kind of a father are you, starting the day off with booze when that motherless boy in the next room is depending on you?*

Even then God must have been speaking to me, though I didn't realize it was His voice. I had just opened a brand new bottle of Southern Comfort. I got out of bed, went to the kitchen and poured the whole gurgling bottle down the sink. And that was the end of that. I never had a desire to drink again.

Through the years since then I had tried desperately to carry on my work and care for my boy. It seemed impossible to keep him in New York City, so I sent him to one boarding school after another, each a worse mistake than the one before. Finally I had found a couple with two boys of their own in Harrington Park, New Jersey. During those years I had become "gun-shy" of women interested in almost anyone alive.

Some were attractive to me. But always the thought recurred, *were they interested in me, and my son? Or were they interested in spite of him? What kind of mothers would they make?* Desperately wanting to be sure, perhaps I had waited too long.

Now, busy as I was, preparing to produce a new Broadway play by Eric Hatch, a dense fog seemed to hang over all my thoughts and actions. After such close bliss with Merikay, such emptiness, such separation. Gradually, as the days dragged by, I realized I really could not—in fact did not want to—live without this lovely creature. Whether she would make a good mother for my boy or not, I was hopelessly, helplessly in love with Merikay.

Suddenly a dark thought. *A girl fourteen years younger than I? Stories about older men and younger wives came to my mind. Was I asking for trouble? Double trouble?*

19

# 2

# One Bong Extra

Letters were not fast enough. So I cabled.

HOW MANY RAINDROPS IN A SHOWER . . . HOW
MANY SNOWDROPS IN A STORM? HOW MANY
GRAINS OF SAND ALONG THE SEASHORE? COUNT
THEM ALL AND MULTIPLY THEM A MILLION TIMES
A MILLION . . . AND YOU'LL KNOW HOW MANY
HEARTBEATS IN MY LOVE FOR YOU . . . .

Some days later came back an answer referring to the bad-
tempered swan I had asked Merikay to look up for me at Lake
Windermere.

SIGHTED SWAN. SWATTED SAME. LOVE YOU AL-
WAYS. MERIKAY.

By the painfully slow trans-oceanic telephone I tried to reach my darling that night. In the early morning hours I fell asleep waiting for the report of the overseas operator. Suddenly the ringing phone jarred me out of my slumber.

It was my old friend, Pamela, the Marchioness of Huntley, in Aberdeen, Scotland, inviting me to fly over for the Highland Games. My only interest was in the whereabouts of Merikay who had volunteered to bear a bottle of Pamela's favorite bourbon to Scotland.

"Oh, the little American," said the Marchioness silkily. "Oh she's gone off in the moors in the moonlight calling sheep, baa, baa, baa."

Suddenly I was overwhelmed with bitter-sweet memories. Her lilting laugh. Like half-heard, half-forgotten music of the wind it swept from nowhere and as quickly faded away. Her pert and saucy sense of humor.

With the dawn I sent a cable to the Savoy Hotel in London, which had been expecting Merikay's arrival daily for more than a week (it seems she and cousin Caroline had become so enamored of the great Edinburgh Festival that they kept retracing their steps, returning to it night after night):

PREPARE RING FINGER. ARRIVING PAN AM TO-MORROW AFTERNOON. LOVE ALL WAYS AND AL-WAYS. LAURIE

For several days before sending this cable I had researched all the possibilities of arranging a marriage ceremony in Europe. It seemed that Merikay's travel schedule would not permit us to qualify anywhere. But I knew I had to marry this enchanting creature with the curling blond hair and deep green eyes and soft, velvety voice.

Besides I had discovered that she was unofficially engaged to two other men. The one in Chicago with the big, black cigar would tenderly entrust her by plane to New York, where a timid type with Granny glasses who raised tropical fish would take over. In due time he would return her safely to the moustache with the big, black cigar. It seemed wise to go to Europe where the competition was not so tough. Besides, as a good redblooded American, I owed it to my country to prevent this rich little gem from being gobbled up by some sleazy gigolo with a phony title.

Suddenly inspiration came. Why not be married in the air, returning from Europe? If a ship's captain could marry passengers at sea, why not the captain of an airship? So I discussed this with the vice president in charge of legal affairs for Pan Am Airways. Finally he consented reluctantly, based on my permission to allow them to publicize this first-time marriage in the air over the Atlantic.

Meanwhile, my money was all tied up in the Broadway play. At the bank I found a friendly ear in the vice president. He had recently succumbed to matrimony after forty years of bachelorhood. He thought the whole idea romantic enough to loan the necessary funds on my signature alone, something he had never done before.

As I was preparing to leave, the Pan Am vice president telephoned to say that the board of directors had refused to give their approval.

But, he continued, I could go ahead unofficially.

"Only," he cautioned, "make sure that there is a Bible somewhere." That was not standard issue on their airline. Also I should caution the pilot not to perform the wedding ceremony over any island or there might be international complications.

With these warnings ringing in my ears I flew to London for

a joyful reunion with Merikay at the Savoy Hotel. There followed a kaleidoscopic blur of sight-seeing in London and Paris while I interviewed ingenues for the Broadway play. We swirled in the traffic around the Place de l'Etoile with its majestic Arc d' Triumph, revelled in the splashing fountains of Versailles, the hidden country restaurants.

Days were filled with the quaint bistros and art shops of Montmartre. Nights with the velvet darkness and twinkling lights of the boats on the river Seine. The rush of violin strings in the night clubs as we danced and danced and danced. Maxim's . . . Les Seigneurs . . . especially Les Seigneurs where the singing strings swept us higher ever higher into realms of ecstasy.

All too soon we were back in London on the very day set to return to the United States. Getting seats during that mid-September tourist rush had been difficult. Finally I had obtained three on the assurance to the public relations official that we would allow them to publicize this first wedding in the air.

But now as I walked into his office, he told me there had been a reversal of the decision by the Big Brass. They absolutely refused to have anything to do with this wedding ceremony. I could still have the three seats for Merikay, cousin Caroline and myself. But please get out of his life and not complicate it any more.

So there I was at about ten in the morning of the very day we were due to leave, Friday the thirteenth. Originally I had picked that day thinking that many people would cancel their reservations and we'd be able to get our seats. I was right.

But how could I return home without marrying my love? Between us millions of words had been said about love. But nothing about marriage. If we waited until we returned home, there were the two unofficial fiances, plus parental objections. There would be all the complications of a big social wedding. In the end we might be too tired of each other even to want to be married.

What to do?

I tried the American ambassador, only to find there is no extra-territoriality for something as unimportant as a wedding. But why not talk with the U.S. consul? So I asked the consul if there was any possible exception to the general marriage laws of England?

"Banns must be said three consecutive Sundays," he chortled. "No other way."

Banns are public announcements of a proposed marriage.

"There must be exceptions," I protested. "Let me see the marriage laws and see what the fine print says."

Fifteen minutes later I found it. In case of certain emergencies and with the consent of the faculty of Westminster Abbey, and if a local parish priest would agree to perform the ceremony, the matter of banns could be waived. I called Westminster Abbey who informed me that Claridge's, where Merikay was staying, was in the parish of St. Martin in the Fields.

The rector was enjoying an early tea. "Which month do you wish to be married?"

"This month."

"Which week?"

"This week."

"Which day?"

"Today," I said with as much urgency as possible. "It's an emergency. We fly back to the States tonight."

The rector cleared his throat. "That presents a problem. According to British law there can be no valid marriage ceremony after six o'clock in the evening."

My watch said it was then a quarter after four.

"However," he continued in that suave British way, "if you and the young lady can be here by half-past five, I will do my best. But be sure not to be late, because it takes half an hour for the ceremony."

Excitedly I phoned Merikay at Claridge's. She was resting after a session with the hairdresser. "Hurry up and get dressed," I urged. "I'm picking you up in fifteen minutes and we're going to be married."

Witnesses? A young lady in the social welfare department at the embassy offered to be one witness. The cabbie could be the other. But I wanted my friend, Bill Procter, director of Bass' Ale, to be my best man.

Over the phone he reminded me that London rush hour traffic was as sticky as molasses. It was impossible for him to get from one side of London to the other by five-thirty. But he would try. He and his black Bentley and veteran chauffeur.

Taxiing to Claridge's, I dashed up to her second floor apartment, grabbed Merikay by the wrist before she could even finish putting on her shoes and stockings, and swept her down the stairs two at a time.

"Where to, sir?" asked the imperturbable, top-hatted doorman.

"Westminster Abbey. We're going to get married."

"Yes, sir," Old Stony Face replied, closing the taxi door with a flourish, as if we were royalty. "Very good, sir."

As we chugged off I realized suddenly that he hadn't even held out his hand for a tip. Not quite sure yet what was going on, Merikay struggled with her shoes and stockings. Then she fully realized what was up. She sat bolt upright. "I will *not* get married," she exclaimed, her sea green eyes snapping. "I will *not* get married. I will not *get married*!"

For emphasis she twirled her long eyelashes with one of

those weird little curling instruments. There was beauty even in her fury. My heart melted with the love of her. In just a few minutes, that is if we made it before the six o'clock curfew, she would be my wife.

At Westminster Abbey a small potbellied official in a brown derby interrupted his afternoon tea to affix the necessary stamps, seals, and long red ribbons. The cost was only a few shillings and I was pleasantly surprised until he suggested, "What about something for the expedition?"

Asia? Africa? What is he talking about?

"After all, sir," he explained, "my afternoon tea's been interrupted . . . so . . . there should be some minor consideration." He coughed.

Anticipating my evening departure I had changed most of my money back into dollars. All I had was a ten shilling note and a one pound note.

I held out one in each hand. "Which would seem appropriate?"

"That will be quite satisfactory," he replied, taking them both.

Papers in hand, red ribbons streaming behind, I dashed back to the taxi. It was now five-fifteen. "Full speed ahead!" I urged. But the more I urged the driver, the slower he went. It was like a nightmare. All this time, under the disapproving eyes of Miss Godding, the welfare worker, Merikay kept repeating in a crescendo that approached hysteria, "I will *not* get married, I will not *get married*."

Our black antique taxi squirmed its painful way through the rush hour traffic. Finally we turned into Trafalgar Square. Blue and grey and white, the pigeons strutted around the splashing fountain. Gay red and yellow balloons slipped upwards out of childish hands and floated heavenward. High atop his sky-splitting pedestal, Lord Nelson peered at distant horizons. The smell of gunpowder was in his nostrils. The thunder of distant cannon blotted out the squawling, squawking traffic beneath him. His eyes were filled with the memories of writhing wooden ships and toppling sails of the famous battle at Trafalgar.

"Better think it over, guv'ner," the cabbie called over Merikay's chant, "I'm a married man. With six kids. Look wot 'appened to me."

Merikay's green eyes glared. The cabbie pointed up toward Lord Nelson, perched atop his pillar. "And look at Lord Nelson," he continued, "and 'im a British 'ero. 'e gets married and loses an arm and a leg, that's wot 'appens."

Merikay's glare became violent. "No cab driver is going to tell me what to do," she exploded. "I will *too* get married."

As the cab crawled up before the dainty jeweled spire of St. Martin's, Bill's Bentley gleamed up behind us. The cab driver's beaming expression faded when I told him his services as a witness would not be needed. He even offered to turn the meter off. His expression faded further when I told him I had no money.

But Bill peeled off the proper bills and the cabbie disappeared muttering.

The three of us puffed up the steep, stone steps. Just before we left Claridge's, cousin Caroline had phoned from the airport. She had just flown in from France and wanted us to hold the ceremony until she arrived. But no Carolyn in sight. And no time to wait.

Inside the darkened church the organ was playing softly while a handful of old ladies in black knelt over their whispered prayers. Never having been in the church before, I didn't know how to reach the crypt where we were to meet the vicar. I tapped one old lady on the shoulder gently and whispered, "Where is the crypt?" She gasped and began to pray all the faster. The same thing happened with the next old lady and the next. We were running out of time.

So I strode into the center aisle, raised my voice and cried, "Where is the crypt?" The organ jarred into sudden silence. From behind a distant pillar a black robed acolyte leaped out and gestured frantically.

We followed him down the winding stone stairs into the crypt which had been used as an air raid shelter during World War II. Deep in that candle-flickering darkness there were still sandbags. Waiting for us was a white-haired, ruddy-faced man, perfectly cast for his priestly role. He identified himself as the Rev. Mervyn Charles-Edwards, the vicar.

"You're cutting it a bit close, young man," he chided. "After all, it does take nearly half an hour to perform a proper ceremony." So with friend Bill at my side and the lady social worker at Merikay's side, the beautiful marriage ceremony of the Anglican church began. The measured tones paraded slowly through my mind. Meanwhile the minutes ticked speedily away.

Suddenly Merikay swayed. I put an arm around her to steady her. "Darling," I whispered. She gave me that familiar sharp elbow in the ribs.

"It's all right," she murmured. And I realized her voice was beautiful even in a whisper. "I was just trying to see the birthdate on the slab in front of me." She pointed towards the marble slab containing the remains of Lord and Lady Romaine.

The vicar's beautiful tones flowed slowly onwards. Far too slowly. I began to get nervous. The minute hand on my wristwatch was approaching the 6 p.m. deadline. Outside nearby the deep, sonorous tones of Big Ben began to strike the hour of six. One *bong* . . . two *bong* . . . three . . . four . . . And still the marriage ceremony droned on. Five . . . *bong!*

"I now pronounce you man and wife," said the vicar, binding our wrists together with the white silken sash. *Bong* went Big Ben for the sixth time. Merikay and I clung to each other in our first marital embrace. As we came up for air a few minutes later, the vicar smiled.

"You see," he said, "there was no need for alarm."

Merikay's laughter bubbled up. "We beat the *bong*."

The vicar nodded judiciously. "Yes," he echoed. "We had one *bong* extra."

Always—the rest of our lives—there was one bong extra. All our life together there was a love song, from the first swift surge of passion through the sometimes painful task of learning to give . . . to live . . . and then receive. How hard a lesson. And to forgive.

No wonder this wise, unflappable priest was shortly after this elevated to Bishop of Worcester. Merikay and I signed the parish register. She a young widow from the war, and I a not-so-young widower, but young in heart. So we became the 250th couple to be married at St. Martin's in the Fields. I breathed a sigh of relief. We had made it, even if just by a few seconds.

Sniffling from her cold, Merikay looked up at the vicar plaintively. "Now can I go back to bed?" she asked. The vicar smiled gently.

"Don't be so precipitate, my child," he reassured her. "The rush hour is now over."

I turned to the priest. "Tell me, how did you happen to agree to perform a ceremony on such short notice for persons you had never met before?"

The vicar smiled again. They had just returned from a most enjoyable trip to the United States, he explained. They had been treated so royally by the Americans that, as he had told Mrs. Charles-Edwards, he intended to repay this kindness by doing any favor within his power for the first American who called upon him for anything.

"And you," he finished, patting me on the back, "are the very first American to ask me a favor."

He unwound the silken scarf with which he had bound our wrists together in a symbol of the new unity of our souls. Then he cautioned us not to give any statement to the press. Otherwise he would be besieged by others seeking quick marital relief. So ended the fastest marriage off the record in England.

The four of us descended the stone steps outside, dodging the aggressive starlings overhead who were doing their best to make up for the absence of rice. At the bottom of the steps was wide-eyed Caroline, panting from the rush from the airport. She didn't have any money either. So good old Bill paid off her taxi and ushered us all into his gleaming limousine. Off we sped to Claridge's for a champagne celebration.

Several bottles of champagne later, it was time to leave for our midnight plane. At the airport all was confusion. Suddenly everybody had realized it was still Friday the thirteenth until midnight. Hurriedly the officials reshuffled the departure time so that the plane would leave at five minutes past midnight. Everybody heaved a sigh of relief.

So the three of us, my new bride, glowing in spite of her cold, cousin Caroline, and I spent our bridal night on an airplane with the romantic name of Robin Hood. But the air conditioning was not working. The plane seethed with wild-looking passengers of many colors and races enroute from the Middle East to the United Nations in New York City. Some apparently had never seen modern plumbing before. Merikay emerged from the rest room to inform me that the sinks were all stopped up with the leavings from hair washing.

At an emergency comfort stop in Shannon, Ireland, we fortified ourselves with some Irish coffee with white, rich cream. Later I discovered that the Irish had already fortified that coffee with whiskey. It helped us get through the rest of the trip.

So the bridal night passed with both of us sitting upright in adjoining seats, clasping hands like any staid married couple celebrating their fiftieth wedding anniversary.

At the International Airport cousin Caroline taxied off to Westchester to meet her waiting fiance. Merikay and I wearily taxied up to my smart bachelor apartment and burst into a scene of utmost confusion. Outside was a large, red fire engine. Firemen were running in and out with hoses and hatchets. Police were blowing shrill whistles and pushing ropes to keep the crowd back. Inside there was no way to my second floor apartment except by the stairs. The elevator was jammed. It seemed that the bachelor above me had been entertaining a friend of uncertain sex. The friend had become angry and cut the elevator cable, thus locking himself and it between floors. For a hectic half hour firemen swung axes and chopped away. Finally they freed the elevator cab. Then the police handcuffed the culprit and sirened him away in the paddy wagon.

Inside my apartment we found chaos of another kind. Before flying to Europe I had taken pity on a husbandless friend with a little child and let them stay during my absence. However, I hadn't known the lady was an alcoholic. She had gotten into all the various liquor bottles, kept for entertaining my clients. Empties were strewn all over the floor. Papers were tossed everywhere, even in the fireplace. All my files were torn open and scattered. Not exactly the type of homecoming one would plan for a bride.

Only the canaries seemed happy. They burst into lilting song at my arrival. But then these little yellow troubadors sang on little or no provocation, even when I picked up the telephone. Barely had we entered the apartment when the landlady, Mrs. Deutsch, came knocking frantically on the door, face bathed in tears.

"Papa, papa," she cried, clutching her fat husband's fat arm.

"What are we going to do? Where are we going to sleep? The only way up to our penthouse is by the elevator. And the elevator is ruptured!"

Could they, they pleaded, spend the night in my apartment? Hardly the ideal beginning for a new marriage. But an hour later we were rescued when the elevator was put back in service. The landlady and her husband went off to their penthouse and their own bed.

"And so," as the famed diarist, Pepys, was wont to say many years before, "to bed." It had been a long day. Merikay giggled as we collapsed. "Oh well, cheer up," she murmured sleepily. "The first day of marriage is the hardest."

# 3

# The Birdcage

Life spins like a great golden wheel in New York. Faster and faster. Everybody's afraid to get off. You might not be able to climb back on. Or you might even get run over. So you keep on going around and around.

Friends called my studio apartment "The Birdcage." A large, sunny room held my desk, my secretary's desk, a file cabinet, several guest chairs, a studio couch—and several cages of canaries in full song. Mostly they chirped and chattered. But whenever a visitor entered or I picked up the telephone, they would burst into a full-throated, deafening serenade. Often my callers would think I was speaking from some tropical night club.

In the back was a small bedroom with a bed that had been big enough for me, but as Merikay brightly said, "Two in love may be able to live as cheaply as one. But they surely can't sleep as well in a single bed." She slept next to the wall, so I would not disturb her as I was an early riser. Fall turned into winter. Her back got colder and colder until one frosty morning she said with a forced smile, "Laurie, my back's to the wall." As we both suddenly realized the double truth of that statement, we burst into laughter. But we knew, romantic as the studio apartment was, we would have to get a larger place. Often Merikay became a prisoner in that back bedroom, unable to sneak in her pajamas through my business conferences to the bathroom on the other side.

Then there was Lance. He had come in from Harrington Park the first weekend after we flew back.

"Daddy," he said with all the excitement of a ten-year-old facing a new adventure, "Can I come home for good now?" My heart hurt. How many times since his mother's death had he asked the same question. I yearned to say yes. But there was a marriage to be built. To be fair to Merikay, she and I needed some time alone, to get used to each other, to work out personality wrinkles. I knew, from being married before, that a good marriage doesn't just happen. It takes work. Then there was his schooling. I pointed to the studio couch. "Not enough room here, son."

"I don't mind, Dad," he said eagerly. "It'd be fun sleeping out here with the birds. Besides I could have my electric train . . . "

His childish squeal trailed off as he read my face. Every weekend Lance had spent with me we'd slept in the same bed, arms around each other. I was his security blanket. And then later in the night when he was peacefully asleep, I'd carry him to the studio couch. But first we'd talk about his school and his friends, and what fun it was to climb a tree by the railroad tracks and watch the train chug by with its lonesome whistle. And we'd breathlessly plan our next canoe trip, or hike through the rolling Ramapo Mountains. And we'd read *Wind in the Willows* and make up new stories continuing the thrilling adventures of Pooh and Eeyore, until the excited whispers, "And then what happened?" lapsed into yawns and heavy breathing.

But now . . . there was someone else in that bed. It was hard to take. But he was gallant.

"It's okay, Dad," he'd say bravely. "I know you've been lonely," a big gulp, "cause I have, too. But now," his lip would quiver just the least little bit as his blue eyes searched mine hopefully, "we're not going to be lonely any more, now that there are three of us . . . are we?"

He was so eager to have a mommy again. But Merikay was so young, too. She was not really ready to have a noisy, busy ten-year-old share her own personal love. She didn't feel comfortable being called "Mother" by this little stranger. So he called her "Merikay," which is what the treatment girls at Elizabeth Arden's, salesclerks, delivery boys, everybody called her at first sight. My darling was just that open and friendly. Like a sunflower, I often thought, stretching out towards the sunshine of attention.

Neither of us meant to shut Lance out of our life. But we were so in love. Madly, passionately, insanely.

Mostly Merikay treated Lance like some friendly tail-wagging puppy to be patted on the head when she felt like it, and to be brushed off when she didn't. For months she descended to his childish level and competed with him for my time and attention. Both my dearest love and the son of my heart struggled to be first with me. So needlessly. It was not a case of either or, but *both*.

After the first weekend Merikay and I flew to Chicago to share the news personally with her family.

"I knew it," quipped my fashion-plate of a mother-in-law.

"You did come for dinner. Now I suppose you hope you'll stay for life." A disapproving glance. "A widower with a ten-year-old son (as though that were the crime of the century). Why you're old enough to be her father!"

*Not quite*, I thought, biting my tongue.

"Well! *My* daughter could have married any one of several millionaires. All crazy about her." Those sharp brown eyes searched me suspiciously. "Obviously you don't have plenty of money. No writer ever does. I don't suppose you even have a job. The Howards will have to support you, too."

"Not quite," I answered. "I've managed to earn a good living for many years. Right now I'm producing a national radio series featuring sports announcer Bill Slater and leaders in industry . . . "

"What's it called?"

" 'Americans, Speak Up' "

"Never heard of it." She shot me down.

"Well I've written and produced shows like 'We the People,' and 'America's Town Meeting of the Air.' " Still that blank stare. " 'Mr. District Attorney?' " I faltered hopefully.

"Is that all?"

"Well, I . . I'm producing a new Broadway show. Eric Hatch play. Wrote the big hit *My Man Godfrey* and . . ."

"You'll lose your shirt. That is, if you have another one."

"Stop it, Mother!" Merikay, green eyes flashing, came to my rescue. "He's one of the very top TV-radio writers and producers. Besides if you'd ever stop talking long enough to read a book, you'd know he's the coauthor of that best seller, *The Care & Feeding of Executives*. Everybody's reading it, that is, everybody who can read. Or have you been out of Wellesley so long you've forgotten how?"

Love and hate. How very close they are. Merikay and her mother, I thought. Like a battle between a tank and a butterfly.

I sighed. More competition. The Silver Chord. Invisible. But was it invincible? Time alone would tell. Like so many mothers, Lydia Belle Howard was trying desperately to live her life over again through her only daughter. A handsome, wealthy, devoted husband, she had. A famous Ivy League sports star son. Yet she was consumed by the desperate need to be number one in the life of her daughter, a former debutante of the year.

*Why can't people,* I thought, *why can't parents love by letting go, setting free?*

"We like the same things, same people, same places. We do everything together," bragged her handsome mother. "Why we even wear the same size. We can wear each other's clothes."

*With some alterations,* I thought, mentally comparing my slim darling to my matronly mother-in-law.

My rating rose slightly from zero when at the Glenview Country Club that night LB discovered I was an accomplished dancer. And she ran into important friends who had previously bought copies of my book and thought I was something like famous. Anyway they sought my autograph. And that raised my rating another couple of points. LB imperiously summoned the waiter.

"Merikay and I love champagne. And Scotch. The best of course. Which will you have?"

I declined, explaining I didn't drink alcohol any more.

"Humph!" she snorted. "You're as bad as my son. He doesn't drink or smoke."

Well, at least I smoked, too much of nearly everything —cigars, pipes, cigarets. I was a walking furnace. LB hated smoke of any kind, although her husband Tex fancied long Havana cigars. Well, at least Merikay and I shared something she didn't like—the same brand of cigaret.

Back in New York I plunged into my neglected radio

productions. Merikay it seemed had had musical comedy experience and had helped produce a couple of radio quiz shows. She thrust herself joyfully into my work. Then there was the Broadway play, *Kelly*. In spite of its name it was not lucky for me. We previewed it for financial angels on the "Kraft Music Hall" TV show. But money was tight. And personal problems took priority. Merikay began to show abrupt personality changes.

She would be gay and laughing, then in an instant become rude and say nasty things without any apparent reason. Friends became offended, avoided our dinner invitations. Sometimes she would burst out crying for no cause. I found she was a night person. Afflicted with insomnia she would roam around our little apartment all night long. Then when dawn came, she would collapse in exhaustion and sleep most of the day. It was hard for me, trying to live a normal life and carry on my business. Then I found she had forgotten to give me important messages. For the first time in my career, I missed a broadcast. We began to quarrel, violent arguments, then the bliss of making up again.

Sometimes when her quarterback brother, Gene, was playing for Dartmouth, we'd drive out to Princeton, or Columbia or Hanover, New Hampshire for the game. There were bright golden-leaved autumn days with the smell of apple cider. And there was the hurricane. Suddenly it whirled upon us. It came when Lance was home for the weekend and playing with his "brother," as he thought of Douglas Faught. It was the Faughts who had so compassionately taken us into their Tudor City apartment after Maggie's fatal accident.

Through marital musical chairs Doug now had a foster mother. The kids thrilled to the wild storm outside, piled boards and chairs into a shelter and giggled out the storm. When it was time to leave, Doug crawled into my arms. "Larry," he begged, "can't I stay and live here always with you and Lance and Merikay? After all, we're really brothers—even if we do have different last names." Lance leaped at me, "Please, Daddy, please?"

I glanced at Merikay. She nodded. Today she was her real self, loved the children, was in fact a child right along with them in all their games. We'd been to the circus, too—Ringling Brothers at Madison Square Garden. Merikay especially liked feeding peanuts to the long curving trunks of the elephants.

"Merikay," Doug had said seriously as we finally dragged her away, "you're going to marry an elephant when you grow up, if you don't be careful."

Merikay and I would have adopted Doug in a minute, but his father loved him too much to part with him. Memories flowed through my mind, the lazy summer days on Southampton Beach, teaching Doug to overcome his fear of water. Romping through the twisting, leafy paths of Central Park. Hill & Hollow Farm where his parents and I had placed them both as pre-school kids to grow up on a working farm, close to nature. The way in which they'd clung together in their mutual loneliness away from home for the first time. How they loved each other. Really just like brothers. That was the last time we were physically close to Doug. His father moved to Connecticut and we saw him less frequently over the years. But I always thought of him as my second son.

One night soon after our return from England Merikay came with me to the important election where we were choosing new officers for the Radio Writers' Guild. As with so many unions, while most of us were away fighting in World War II, radical elements had gotten in and, through illegal tactics, taken over control. Always on the lookout for new attractive recruits, Peter, the leader of the pro-Communist group which had usurped control, spied my beautiful Merikay, and immediately played up to her. Later when he found out she was my wife, he developed a hatred that nearly cost her life.

Strange phone calls began to upset Merikay at night. There were many meetings of the AWARE group as we called ourselves. Every time I'd leave the apartment, within five minutes a strange voice over the phone would warn her to get me to stop my opposition or I'd end up run over by a truck at 1st Avenue, or in a cement overcoat in the East River. Sometimes there would just be heavy, ominous breathing, sometimes just silence. Calls like these often woke her out of sound sleep. Her nerves became strained, how badly I never knew. But I do know one mature woman member who suffered this sort of persecution for twenty-four hours and became so shook up that for months the very sight of a telephone set her to shaking uncontrollably.

Even when we visited her parents in Winnetka that Christmas, the anonymous phone calls pursued us. Often Merikay begged me to cease my opposition. But I knew my only chance of safety from their threats lay in continued public opposition. Then if some "accident" happened, it would get public attention, and there would be investigations.

In the spring, Patricia Faught, now a Conover model and married to Allen Marks, moved out of my old apartment at 455 East 51st Street, and Merikay and I moved in. There was a beautiful view of the East River, and on one side we looked down over the United Nations headquarters. Now we would have bedrooms enough for Lance when school was over. We could be a real together family at last. That's what I thought.

But I hadn't counted on Merikay's strange condition which would come upon her from time to time unexpectedly. Sometimes her eyes would get a wild look and she would suddenly become irrational. Sometimes she would just sit and shake. Sometimes her eyes were red and face mysteriously swollen. There were emotional explosions at the least word. I couldn't figure it out.

In the long talks we'd have in bed, which were often monologues, the reasons for her bitterness towards her mother finally came out. Early during World War II Merikay had fallen in love with a young man living in Winnetka. His moustache must have helped, and his uniform certainly did. He came of a good family. But his mother was a widow and had to work. The family had no money, as LB pointed out, and besides she had decided her only daughter, as the granddaughter of the chief executive of the Santa Fe Railroad, should marry a millionaire like the son of the president of Bethlehem Steel. The steel executive was a business associate of her husband, Tex.

But Merikay loved Whit Duncan, loved him truly. She followed him out to the southwestern desert sands where he trained in tanks as part of General George C. "Blood & Guts" Patton's famous 5th. Against her mother's solid opposition, Merikay single-handedly arranged the wedding. One last desperate effort as LB sent obedient, great-hearted Tex, her husband, out to the military camp at Indiantown Gap to "have it out with Merikay. The poor child doesn't know what she's doing marrying a man who will probably never come back. Or if he does, will come back in a wheelchair, a life-long invalid."

"Are you bound and determined to marry this young man?" Tex asked.

Merikay's green eyes sparkled defiantly, "Yes."

So her father, cigar back in his mouth, took the next train back.

And the midwinter wedding at Christ Church, Winnetka, made them man and wife. More army camps, then silence as the Army poised to ship out. A frantic call. Liberty for just a couple of hours before departure. A weary Merikay training in

43

from Ossining where she had been waiting in suspense, to the Commodore Hotel. A hurried farewell embrace. Then a khaki blur as the Lieutenant rushed down the rail platform. A turn of the head. A quick wave. And he was gone.

The ladies were having cocktails at the country club. Friends asked LB, "Where's your daughter's handsome husband?"

"Overseas. And it would be a blessing if he never came back."

Shocked silence even in the midst of liquor-loosened tongues. And when the yellow telegram came soon after, a hard kernel of bitterness developed in Merikay. How many thousand times LB must have regretted those careless words. Estranged, Merikay had moved away from her family, refused their help, carefully set aside the widow's pension for his mother, went to work. Far worse, the secret sealed within her heart that only a few weeks before this news, Merikay had fallen down a steep flight of stairs and lost the child she'd hoped to have. She had never been able to forgive her mother.

Then, too, Merikay was tortured by the thought of an afterlife. "If there is a heaven, as the Bible says," her green eyes clouded, "and Whit is there and you are there, what will I do? How can I choose between you?" It was the heartsick cry of many who do not know, as we did not, that all is different there. No marriage or giving in marriage. The problem tortured my dearest one, and thus her torture was mine, too.

To celebrate her birthday we dressed up and went to a fashionable nightclub. All I drank was wine those days. But the Dubonnet I ordered turned out to be a cocktail. After two I found myself dancing with a pillar and inviting everyone there to share in the tiny candle-lighted birthday cake. When we got out, there were no taxis to be had. We wandered unsteadily,

Merikay supporting me by one arm. Suddenly I needed a smoke worse than anything. But the crumpled package in my pocket was empty. At that moment I'd gladly have traded the soul I wasn't sure I had for one good drag of nicotine.

So at 1st Avenue and 51st Street, in my rumpled tuxedo I got down on my knees and searched in the garbage in the gutter until I found a wet, brown snipe the size of my little finger joint. In her silver evening dress, Merikay was kicking me in the ribs. "How could you!" she cried over and over. "How could you!"

I couldn't bear to touch the filthy snipe with my fingers, so I took the long pin fastening my carnation and carefully picked it up. It was wet. It wouldn't burn that way. So I toasted it with a match, turning the pin while Merikay kept kicking me. Hundreds of times before I had stopped smoking. For a day. Sometimes two or three days while my nose was stopped up with a cold. Once I even managed a tortured week. But as Mark Twain once said, "I'm the world's greatest expert on stopping smoking. I've stopped five hundred times. But I began five hundred and one times."

I had always kidded myself that if I *really* wanted to stop smoking I could. Each time I failed I rationalized that I hadn't *really* wanted to stop that time. But now, kneeling in the gutter, eyes glued to that cigaret stump turning slowly in the matchlight, I got honest with myself.

I admitted I was a slave, a total absolute slave to nicotine. There was nothing I could do about it.

"Oh, God," the cry came from my innermost depths, "if You are, if You're out there somewhere, have mercy on me!"

All desire left me. I dropped the stub back in the gutter where it belonged. I never smoked that stub. I never smoked again.

Often I thought afterwards if it hadn't been for Merikay's disgust, I might not have realized the depth of my need. As it was, like most of us, I didn't give God any credit. After all, how could I be sure He really existed?

But what of Merikay's increasingly strange actions? Finally one night as she hysterically complained that all sense of touch had left her hand, that she was becoming paralyzed, in desperation I called in an old friend, a medical doctor. His usual grin was gone after he treated her and put her to bed.

"Hate to tell you this," he said slowly. "But your wife is an alcoholic."

"But, Doc, she drinks very little. Just once in awhile when we're out somewhere."

"There's no cure." He sounded as though he were giving a death sentence. "She's been an alcoholic for years. Probably a secret drinker." He shook his head. "A lovely girl. It's too bad. Women alcoholics are the worst."

I fell on my knees as he closed the door. It was such a shock. "Oh, God. What am I going to do? Oh, God! Is there a God? There's got to be a God!"

# 4

# Bubble Trouble

So I found myself kneeling one afternoon in a wooden pew in Marble Collegiate Church, which advertised the "Old Time Religion and Old-fashioned Friendliness."

After an eternity of agony, crying to a God who seemed to have no ears, *if* indeed He existed, I checked the white card asking the minister to call. Some months before I had met the pastor, Dr. Norman Vincent Peale, when he was a guest on my radio broadcast. He certainly had been friendly. He really inspired confidence. Of course, I hadn't needed anything then. I was supremely self-confident. There wasn't anything I couldn't do. And if God did exist, and it wasn't all a fairy tale as my gray-bearded professors taught, why He could go His way and I'd go mine. Who needed religion?"

But now . . . as I checked the little white card, I knew I needed help. I was desperate. When I had asked LB about Merikay's condition, she had become angry. There was nothing wrong with her daughter! It must be something I had done to her. She knew from the beginning I was the wrong man anyway. How could I have surreptitiously pursued her only daughter to Europe and then—far away from family and friends—hypnotized her into getting married. Why I was nothing but an old goat, a cradle snatcher.

So I wrote her Aunt Gracious, who sent a long, loving letter explaining how Merikay had grown to girlhood without ever having her parents home for her birthday. How, because of mustard gas in World War I, Tex on doctor's orders had to take an annual midwinter ocean voyage to get away from the piercing Chicago wind. That meant she spent every birthday, February twenty-sixth, without her parents. Oh, of course, her mother had showered her with presents, arranged special treats. Merikay loved her grandparents, she loved her uncle and aunt. But nothing took the place of her absent mother and father. At first she was too young to understand. But she grew up with a bitterness deep inside that nothing ever really melted.

Finally tired of the family pretense that nothing was wrong, I flew to Washington, D.C. to see a mutual friend. Marguerite Church had attended Wellesley with LB. Now she had taken over the congressional seat of her late husband, Ralph. Gravely she substantiated the alcohol problem. LB, she said, had encouraged Merikay to start drinking at an early age, and had continually attempted to conceal the problem.

Now that I knew the problem, I was sure I could cope with it. The answer was to keep her away from bars and restaurants that served liquor. But it wasn't that simple. Even when she stayed home, I'd return from the studio to find her wobbling about. In desperation I searched the apartment from top to bottom. Still she somehow got hold of the forbidden fruit. I visited neighboring liquor stores, returned bottles where I could, begged them not to deliver any more. Some were sympathetic. Some just shrugged. How could they tell who was an alcoholic and who wasn't? They had to make a living, too. It was impossible to close down all of New York City.

In this situation we stopped going out for dinner, had our meals sent in by Casserole Kitchen. Steadfastly Merikay refused to admit her problem, even when I caught her with a newly-poured drink in hand. She took to drinking vodka. "It leaves you breathless." They should have said, "lifeless," I thought, looking one night at her helpless, crumpled body. Anger rose within me. Four Roses! They, too, promised a fragrance that turned into halitosis. Hidden by the pretty green leaves were thorns. And the cigaret that claimed to "satisfy." All it delivered was emphysema and death from heart attack and lung cancer. I suffered from the zeal of the crusader delivered from alcohol and nicotine. My heart was hard with judgment and condemnation.

How we had loved to dance, to glide across the floor to the lilting strains of Viennese waltzes, to the joy of "Wunderbar." We clasped each other close in the love song of the Tango. "Miss Twinkletoes," I had called her. But all that was gone now. She could rarely rise up on her toes any more. It was all she could do to shuffle slowly in the pink bedroom slippers I came to loathe as much as the fluffy pink robe that she wore perpetually, day and night.

Sometimes I wanted to put a bomb in every distillery, every brewery in the whole, wide world. Such utter helplessness. Then a faint ray of hope. Merikay had become so dehydrated that the doctor hospitalized her. One wintry night "Mac" Pierce, as the whole congregation called him, answered my check mark on that little white card. He trudged from the subway at Columbus Circle through knee-deep snow to her bedside. Touched by this love from a man she didn't even know, Merikay blossomed back into health.

"Just imagine," she exclaimed in awe, "it's the first time any minister ever called on me in the hospital. And he didn't even know me!"

To her it was a miracle. I never told her about the little white card. After this we began attending Marble Collegiate Church Sunday mornings. Following the always-inspiring message we'd go on down to Chinatown and wallow in Oriental food, climbing the stairs to the second floor restaurant. Then we'd visit the quaint little stores with bunches of strange Chinese vegetables and large, hanging bladders which the smiling, bowing storekeeper referred to as "fishes' brothers." It became a way of life, an oasis of hope in the midst of our agony.

Soon we officially joined the church. But we were only "mouth" Christians. There was still that restlessness, that emptiness, that never ending ache within. No one made clear to us that it is not with the mouth and the mind, but with the heart, that we come to know the Lord. Salvation is only an offer. It becomes a gift—our gift from God—only when we accept it and hug it to our hearts.

Merikay and I received much help from the encouraging sermons. But we were still weary, wandering spirits. Both of us had been raised in the Episcopal Church. But with just enough knowledge to be inoculated against His supernatural power.

So from misty mountain peaks of ecstasy we plummeted to dark depths of despair. We argued more and more. Wrestled in a tangle of panting arms and legs, as I tried to keep her from the deadly drink that all within her screamed out for, had to have for her raw nerves. Even one dismal night we hurled our precious pink china bowls at each other. Love smashed into smithereens. Yet the next day she was her own sweet, sunny self again. She left a tender "get well" card at the breakfast table.

"Last night," she had written in that dainty print-like hand, "we broke US. Let's put us together again." Pinned to the card was a sliver of pink from the broken bowl.

How could I not forgive her? How, in spite of the mess, the growing sense of helpless horror, how could I stop loving her? So often those most bound by alcohol are the fragile, beautiful, sensitive souls. Perhaps their very sensitivity makes them more vulnerable to life's bruises.

We had a code for answering the phone when outsiders were around. "Klugelmeyer's," one of us would answer gaily. Then the other would say "Klugel?" And the caller would respond, "Meyer." Sometimes I was Klugel. Sometimes she was. It really didn't matter. It was one of those silly patterns people in love slide into.

Yet again and again would come the sudden thunder. Always over her drinking. So we lashed out at each other with sharp blows and sharper words. Sank our harpoons deep as only those whose love is fully shared can do. Hurt each other to the depths where even death would seem a joy. Or anyway release from all this mortal agony.

"Oh, God," I prayed, "is there no help? Oh, God, *are* you? *Can* you . . . *Will* you?"

Answers to prayers come sometimes in strange ways. This time it was in the form of a toy French poodle. He was so little when I led him home with the tiny leash that his fat belly got hung up on the curb. And long before we'd gone those three short blocks, his puppy legs gave out and he slumped into a squat. I carried him the rest of the way.

Little did I know then that months later, still more toy than dog, he would be my constant companion on my midnight trots to the Grand Central Post Office a mile away, little toothpick legs churning so fast they looked as though he were standing still. Merikay's wide open arms swallowed him up at once. With that first lick of his tiny, pink tongue on her pert up-tilted nose, he had won her heart for always. Everywhere that Merikay was, there was Zookie. Tight against her breast as she poured the breakfast coffee. Cuddled in her lap as she sat before the mirror fixing her hair. Lying at night between us in the bed, his black nose pressed hard against her cheek.

Zookie helped. He brought light into our darkness. And flying off to Bermuda that Easter helped. But not enough. We danced to the native guitars. We swam and lazed around Elbow Beach. Went night-clubbing at the Princess Hotel in Hamilton. We both had our portraits painted. As I look at hers now, I see her again as she was that spring, flower-filled day. Like a blonde, green-eyed angel—yet haughty, green eyes clouded, with a certain hardness about her jaw. She looked about seventeen. Would she, I wondered, always look seventeen to me—no matter how long or how short our marriage? No matter what?

Yes, Zookie became the most important member of the family. He went with us everywhere. Everywhere that dogs were allowed. And some places where they weren't. Like our favorite East Side bistros. Or like on our airplane visits between New York and Chicago, tucked in the big wide sleeves of Merikay's fur coats until he looked like a muff. I remember once as the plane was taxied out, how the busy driver of a passing baggage cart almost fell off when he looked up suddenly and saw Zookie's whiskered face peering out the window.

Yes, Merikay was really an angel. Sweet and warm and generous. Would give you anything she had. And she gave me her love and her laughter— and a piece of her mind. Especially when she'd been drinking and jealousy over some woman in my past life would flare up and cause problems.

How many times I winced and felt deep lash marks every time the alcohol turned her from angel into demon. Fear ruled my life. Fear that business associates would see how helpless and how hopeless our life was behind the pretense of normality. And for my darling, how much worse for her. The guilt, the shame, the condemnation, the desperate attempts to cover up the secret drinking, hoping nobody knew . . . when everybody knew.

Sometimes it seemed as though divorce might be the only way of escape for her and me from this endless quagmire which seemed destined to swallow up our happiness . . . our lives . . . even our souls.

There were dark times when anger bubbled within me like a cauldron full of witches' brew. And I feared I might lose all control and kill her. The haunting words of the man who murdered for love beat like the waves of the sea within the walls of my mind.

"For each man kills the thing he loves . . . "

# 5

# Digging the Hole

Nestled in the back seat of our old green Cadillac, Lance was busily counting his treasures: caps from assorted soft drinks. Sometimes I thought he bought the bottles more for the caps than for thirst. Merikay, Lance and I and Christopher Story, VII, our always enthusiastic male secretary, were driving up the snow-capped summit of the Rockies enroute to the Pacific Northwest to look at what just might turn out to be a mine.

It had seemed to me the best way to help Merikay escape the temptations of New York was to get as far away as possible. So when a friend suggested mining possibilities in the Snake River country of Idaho where he had been sheriff, I decided to look into it. There was also a possible beryllium mine farther west on the Washington-Idaho border. And that was even farther away from Manhattan. There were some good tax breaks in the mining business.

In wildly beautiful Estes Park, Merikay flowered into the girl she had once been. In her teens she had spent summers riding her own horse on a working ranch. Back astride a horse again, hair flowing in golden streams behind her, she clung to her saddle like a burr, even when he unexpectedly leaped a high wire fence at full gallop.

"Whew!" cried Lance excitedly. "Just like Madison Square Garden."

He was also impressed with the expertise with which she hooked her trout and landed it. But she did not unhook her catch—that was my job. We galloped away together, only to find when we returned two hours later that Lance had practically emptied the trout pool—at more per pound than we thought worthwhile. So we bargained with the hotel and sold the excess fish at a price far below the cost at the fishing pool. As it was the three of us ate broiled fish the next few days until we wished we had never heard the word *trout*.

Another day there were sheep. Endless rivers of white sheep pouring across the road, overflowing it, eddying around our car.

"Just imagine," Merikay's bell-like laughter floated above the baas, "drowning in a river of sheep."

"Oh, boy," added Lance, eyes shining, "about a million people could go to sleep counting all those sheep."

There wasn't enough silver to be worthwhile reopening that hardrock Idaho mine, according to our consulting engineer, Norman Stines, so we pushed on past beautiful Lake Pend Oreille into the Colville National Forest. We headquartered at the only hotel in tiny Chewelah, just about an hour's drive from the larger city of Spokane.

This prospect, some far-ranging pegmatite dykes tucked away in a cul-de-sac in the mountains, was more promising. I had first heard about beryl, a nonmetallic mineral used in hundreds of parts in aircraft, through my friend, Andy. He had bored me during our mutual bachelor days for hours at a time, relating over and over how he had founded the Beryllium Company and bought up enough beryllium just before the USA got active in World War II to keep our aircraft industry going full blast.

We engaged Norman Stines to explore the prospect. But first we had to obtain a mineral lease from the Northern Pacific Railway, which kept me busy for the next few months.

Back in New York in our East River apartment, we brought Lance in from the country to live with us. With some misgivings about the quality of the education, we enrolled him at the dilapidated public school. Football season burst upon us bright and chilly. Since Gene, Merikay's star athlete brother, was quarterbacking the Dartmouth team, we went up to Columbia to root for the Big Green. We took along the Reverend Eugene McKinley Pierce, a real football fan. Every time Gene kicked or threw a record-breaking pass, Mac began jumping up and down and pounding Merikay on the back. Afterwards at home, ruefully bathing her swollen feet, she said, "I've owned these feet for thirty years. But Mac got more mileage from them during the game than I ever thought possible."

Came winter and the always explosive be-furred and perfumed, exotic-hatted arrival of LB. Immediately upon entering the apartment Merikay had just painstakingly and beautifully decorated, LB began moving furniture and pictures around. Again it was the old love-hate theme. If looks could kill, her mother would have dropped dead on the spot.

"This looks *so* much better this way," she said in her strident voice. "And I like that picture better over there . . ."

Not so kindly, but firmly I laid down the ground rules. She was welcome to visit at any time convenient to us, after due notice. But she was never to comment on Merikay's taste, or the place would be off-limits to her from then on. Love and hate, so close. Even sometimes the same. LB and Tex were generous. They took us to the theater, to expensive stylish restaurants. But it was always where LB wanted to go, and it was always what she wanted to eat. And drink.

She loved the Hawaiian Room at the Hotel Lexington, Arthur Godfrey's longtime favorite hangout. And she urged Merikay, "A drink will be good for you, darling. It will relax you."

When I protested, Tex would weakly echo my words. But LB was deaf to him, too. Then off she'd rush after dinner and dancing, leaving me to cope with an alcoholically belligerent Merikay. Swaying unsteadily, she would caustically mimic her mother and repeat all the things they both didn't like about me. In a way it seemed almost as though my mother-in-law was intent on breaking up our marriage just to prove her widely-shared hunch that I was the worst possible choice her gifted daughter could have made. Sometimes it got pretty thick. And words between LB and me came close to blows. No matter where she was, she would loudly inform anyone within earshot that I was a lazy, no-good playboy, a fortune hunter who had never done an honest day's work in his life. She was hoping her daughter would have the good sense to divorce me.

On the other hand, especially when she was not drinking, LB could be warm-hearted and lavishly generous. Especially if it had anything to do with her daughter. So we were invited on a fabulous Home Line Cruise to the Caribbean that winter. For the first time in years her mother and father were together with

Merikay on her birthday. What a beautiful party it was. Beautiful birthday cake, beautiful people, all dressed up in evening clothes, beautiful music. Years too late, LB was desperately trying to make it up to the daughter she worshipped, and for whose affection she constantly battled me over the years.

Somehow the months went on. A see-saw of joy then down again to plumb despair. The quiet horror of never knowing when my gay loved one would turn into a Mr. Hyde again. When summer came, Merikay and I flew out to the mine called "Merikay" in her honor. At least I did. But she was detained in Chicago by her suspicious gynecologist, for an exploratory operation. I left her on his promise that he would notify me at the mine right away if he found anything serious. One week later a message reached me in the mountains by jeep. It was two o'clock in the morning in Chicago when I heard my darling's trembling voice.

"Oh, Laurie," she cried, "the doctor wants to operate tomorrow. A hysterectomy. He says it's cancer."

*Cancer.* The word brought a cold chill along my spine. She told me how the surgeon, still in his bloody gown, had sat on her hospital bed, asked for a cigaret, and brusquely said, "It's cancer. We must operate tomorrow morning." Then he walked out. Some surgeons are not doctors.

Overwhelmed by fear, her first thought had been to open the window and leap out. But then she thought of Zookie, checked out of the hospital, and taxied to her parents' home at 1015 Pine Street in Winnetka. There, comforted by his cold, wet nose and tongue that licked his love all over her face and neck, Merikay had phoned everywhere for hours to reach me.

It was after two in the morning Chicago time when I reached the surgeon. I told him not to operate until I got there. Getting a flight out was hard. I had to change planes in Minneapolis, but there was no continuing space. It was the height of the Korean War and military men had priority. I had to stand by. I was the last one, number thirteen.

*Thirteen,* I thought, *it's my lucky number—the day we were married.* But would there be room for all of us? The agent didn't think so. All the others were military men home on leave.

I prayed that they could all get on the plane, and me too, without anyone having to be bumped. Twelve got on . . . the gate closed. Then it swung open again. I had just made it. This time I thanked God, whoever and wherever He was.

While in Minneapolis waiting for the connection, I phoned medical friends and experts all over the country for consultation. It seemed the operation could be modified. Arriving at O'Hare I reached the doctor from the airport while he was on the way to the operating room. I insisted that he do a less major procedure, or I would sue him for malpractice. So the hysterectomy was averted. He felt he "had got it all. Clean edges."

While Merikay recuperated in the hospital, we watched the Republican National Convention on TV as they nominated Ike. After a week I had to return to Chewelah to supervise the mining work. She promised to follow me soon. Within a week she was at the mine named Merikay; had flown out with a business associate of ours.

"Thought you'd got rid of me, did you?" she laughed, and her lips pouted so prettily I had to kiss her right then.

"Kiss me again, my darling. Nothing makes me sick," she said.

We lived and loved in a housetrailer, perched precariously on one edge of the green-firred mountains cupping our camp. No alcohol to mar our love. In blue jeans and bright lumberjack shirt, Merikay cooked for the miners and washed the dishes. She forgot all about weekly trips to Elizabeth Arden's, eight-hour creams and fancy hair-dos. I remember how, with a fresh-baked pie in one hand, she would wrangle that bucking station wagon loaded with steel and dynamite up those steep mountain roads. And the miners loved her. They even started shaving every day. Her bright presence turned the dust into dew and labor into laughter.

They even built her own private outhouse on the hillside with a peeled pine fence around it. One day she came rushing indignantly into camp. "They bombed me!" she cried. It seems the mischievous squirrels, high in the trees above had been cutting the pine cones with deadly accuracy. So the outraged miners stopped their tractors and jack hammers to throw up a little umbrella of wood to protect her.

But then back to Manhattan. And more Manhattans. And Scotch. And gin. And vodka. And tears. And heartache. And fierce quarrels. The bitter-sweet of making up. We shared again the secret heights that only lovers know.

Meanwhile Merikay defiantly maintained that she did not need help from anyone. She could stop drinking—if it ever got to be too much—any time she wanted. Didn't I think she had any will power? But she never seemed to want to stop. Not enough to try the hospital treatment. Not enough to try psychiatry. Not enough to try A.A.

"Those creeps," she'd say disgustedly. "All they do is soak up coffee, smoke the place blue, and brag about what drunks they used to be." Her green eyes sparkled defiantly. "After all, I'm not a drunk."

The great, golden wheel (or did it just look like gold?) kept spinning, round and round and round.

*Oh, God, will it never stop? Can we never get off? Is this what Hell is like?* I asked a God I wasn't sure existed.

It was hard keeping my mind on business. Somehow I managed to keep all my busy radio schedules. And work at developing the Merikay Mine. There were bright spots, too. The afternoon I came home unexpectedly and found Lance and Merikay sprawled across the livingroom floor, while his prized electric train sped noisily over bridges, through tunnels and around and around the serpentine tracks. Friends at last! In some strange way her sweetness and childlike ways would, through the years, bring her and Lance much closer than he and I had ever been. Another heart-hurt, but with joy that it was so.

As spring blossomed, we rode the Staten Island Ferry (the cheapest ride in the world at that time, just a dime), explored the Jersey wooded Ramapos, applauded the splashing sea lions at the Central Park Zoo, swam in the softly rolling breakers at Jones Beach.

Yet the strange post-midnight telephone calls increased as I became more active in the struggle to oust the pro-Communists from the Radio Writers and Directors Guilds. Every time I left for what was supposed to be a secret meeting. Again the threats. The ominous silence. The heavy breathing, more menacing than any words. I found I was being tailed. Learned the tricks. A quick last minute step into the elevator, ringing two floors in sequence. Getting off at neither one, but taking the stairs at a higher floor and running down silently. Stepping into the subway train just before its heavy doors smashed shut.

Then Lance who walked the block from school for lunch began to come running in, white-faced with fear. It seemed my enemies were stirring up the other kids to beat him up. When they started using brass knuckles made from garbage can handles, we put him into private school. But still the threatening phone calls. One afternoon I crossed the u-shaped courtyard of our apartment house to visit with a business friend across the way. There was an ominous stillness in the apartment when I returned just fifteen minutes later. There on the livingroom floor sprawled the still figure of my love. I raised her in my arms. Thank God, she was alive.

She had heard a noise in our son's back bedroom where the window overlooked the alley. Thinking it was Zookie, she had stepped into that dark room over to the partly-opened window. Suddenly a heavy blow on the head. She had turned just enough to miss the full impact. Screaming she had run to phone the police, but passed out.

The police were most unsympathetic; didn't even bother taking the obvious fingerprints on the window sill. When I tried to explain about the battle for control, they said that the pro-Communists had asked them to provide police protection against me and my trouble-makers in the coming election. It was hopeless. Peter and his pro-Commies were in, and we were out.

Meanwhile word had come from our consulting engineer. He had found a manganese mine in the Southwest. It had been abandoned for over twenty years. Everyone in town said it was "mined out, or somebody would be working there." Unable to excite any local interest, my engineer and I donned hard hats with miner's lamps and went looking among the mildewed timbers. We found enough pillars of rich manganese to be worth at least a quarter of a million dollars.

The locals laughed when we offered them a chance to participate. Crazy tenderfeet from the East. What would they know about mining? So I raised the money among a group of friends. The locals were happy to spend our money. There was many a laugh in the bars around town. But as the mine began to produce, the townspeople became greedy, and asked to be let into what now looked like a sure thing. After all it was their country, wasn't it? They had a right to profit from their own minerals.

I firmly rejected their offers. They'd had their chance.

Perhaps I was undiplomatic when I laughed in their faces. I made some enemies. What did I care? I'd had enemies before. I could handle them.

As the mine developed, personality clashes also developed among our investors. Exploration and development work had proved a good body of ore, but it was more out-go than income for many months. Bills piled up. The investors refused to release any further funds. We came to a grinding halt. And the locals rubbed their hands in glee at the thought of moving in for the kill.

My mind was made up. New York was no place for Merikay and Lance. Too much temptation. Too much danger. New Mexico was too far away for the nighttime phone calls and the muggers to follow. And Southwest Manganese, as the partnership was called, needed my immediate attention. Otherwise the whole investment, with most of my money, was about to go down the drain.

Tex, big-hearted guy that he was, agreed to loan some interim funds to give the operation a chance. After all he'd been in the mining business. "It takes money to make money," he said wisely, noting that Wall Street says it takes a minimum of a million dollars to start a mine. We'd started with less than a quarter of that.

So the three of us packed up and set out for Deming, New Mexico.

# 6

# Digging the Hole Deeper

In the sun-swept climate of Deming, high in the mountains marching up from Mexico, I learned how to get out of the hole. The hard way. The way to get out of a hole—especially if it's a mine—is to dig it deeper.

I'll never forget my welcome that night we arrived at the Round-Up Lodge. I put out my hand to shake hands with old Hi, the local constable. And he put a summons in it.

All of our partners were equally liable for the debts, which had mounted up when they had refused to release more funds. But I was on the spot. And the irate citizens of Deming had no idea of letting me get off that spot. They besieged the Round-Up with bills. Some old, some not so old. And some almost too new. As if they'd been made up to take advantage of the situation. After all, the bookkeeper was gone, the office was closed down. Who could really check up? All's fair in love and war. And this, as I soon found out, was war. Total, all-out war.

The stakes were high. A potential multimillion dollar mine. It's a hard, barren, sun-scorched area, the Southwest. And the people have a hardness, too. Perhaps it's the only way they've survived in that land of mountains and canyons where the rivers run dry except for a few months of the year; where there are bats and mountain lions and lizards and those fatally poisonous, obscene-looking yellow and red Gila monsters.

Next day at high noon—just like in a typical Western—I stood at the town's main intersection with its only red light, right in front of J. P. Mahoney's Hardware Store, which was glad to provide all the amenities of life, including a funeral with a special black carriage and matched horses.

In a loud voice I yelled, "If anyone has a just bill against the partnership, bring it to me today, and I guarantee payment in full." The crowd came from everywhere. And they came fast. Of course, they weren't happy when I explained they'd have to give me reasonable time. I couldn't pay them all right away. But they'd be paid. The new corporation my father-in-law and a few loyal friends had formed would see to that.

"Florida Manganese" we called the new company, after the Little Florida Mountains in which it was located. Often I smiled as I thought how barren and unflowerlike those mountains were, except briefly in spring when the rain resurrected the pastel cactus. And *luna* means moon in Spanish. How appropriate for moonstruck miners.

But I didn't smile often in the months that followed. I became hard and bitter, too. The whole town treated Merikay and me as though we had leprosy. All business had to be done on a strictly cash first basis. No credit. One of the only two people who would talk to us was the owner of the local department store, Bower Miller. He had once attended a stylish wedding in Winnetka and knew anybody who came from there had to have money. The other was Bethene, the masseuse, best Merikay had found anywhere. Bethene had lost her sight and sense of smell when she had tried to shoot herself some years before, despondent over her boyfriend being sent to a mental institution.

I discovered what it meant to live in a one-bank town, too. When I applied for a two-week loan to meet my $10,000 weekly payroll, the bank official smiled and charged me 14 percent interest. He had the signed documents for a one hundred ton carload of high grade manganese worth more than that. The U.S. government had already assayed it and signed the acceptance sheet. The funds usually came from Denver within five to seven days. But he smilingly called it "unsecured." I discovered, too, that the bank never gave me immediate credit on my government checks, waiting to credit my account until several days later after the checks had finally cleared.

"After all," explained the banker, whose smile resembled a barracuda's, "the government's no different from anybody else. They might be out of money, too."

Then there were the miners. One day as I was walking across the main street, one of them tried to run me down in his dusty pickup. Then he leaped out of the cab, knife in hand, red-eyed with tequila.

"No dinero," he kept crying as he swung at me viciously. "No dinero."

It seemed that the bank had turned down his paycheck. Insufficient funds, they said. I thundered into the bank with him and faced the banker.

"Just a bookkeeping error," he said suavely. "Delayed posting. We're always two days behind in crediting funds."

Three days before I had transferred thousands of dollars from the friendly bank in El Paso one hundred miles away which treated me more like a valued client than a criminal. I determined to help start another bank in Deming if it was the last thing I ever did. Some years later that dream came true.

Meanwhile life at the mine was a constant series of dangers. Huge rocks a hundred feet above me in the roof of the tunnel would suddenly tear loose and miss me by inches. Rungs on the wooden mine ladders would suddenly break under me, though my two hundred fifty pound mine boss, Joe Hales, had had no trouble. Eventually I uncovered a conspiracy to take over the mine, by slowing down production. And if that didn't work by slowing me down.

While I was away at the mine, desperately trying to plug the leaks, Merikay was left alone in our little half-a-house at 113 South Tin to face drunken miners who had been fired, or worried wives clamoring for their husbands' paychecks before they drank it up at the nearest bar. Or somebody was sick. Or the children, clinging to her skirts, were big-eyed with hunger. Often she had to face knives. And sometimes the shrill, screamed words were even worse.

It was a hard life for Merikay, transplanted from the cosmopolitan world to which she had been accustomed—formal dinner parties, operas, concerts and race tracks—to a small town in the middle of the desert with no friends, no contact with the outside world.

But she reacted with her usual gallantry. Night after night in the cold winter she shivered beside me on the picking belt, throwing out the worthless pieces of country rock to upgrade the black manganese to meet the government specifications. Sometimes I got so weary from reaching out into that never-ending, always-faster-moving stream that I'd start throwing away the precious manganese and letting the worthless red rock thunder into the ore bin far below.

"Oh, oh," she'd reach out a warning, mittened hand, "remember, the winning color in this roulette game is always black."

Even one night, encouraged by Snag-toothed Riley, she took over the Little Mancha electric train. Somehow he forgot to show her where the brake was. She came barreling down the curving 6 percent grade with twenty ore cars thundering behind her straight for the open switch that would have sent the whole trainload tumbling thirty feet to the rocky ground below. But somehow she found the brake in time. Just in time.

Her face was chalk white and she was trembling when I rushed over and helped her out. "Just like Superman," she said in a shaky voice. "Just like . . . oh, darling!" and she collapsed into my waiting arms.

Soon after reaching Deming I had gone looking for an Episcopal church. I turned in at the first one. Months later when I asked why they didn't have communion every Sunday, I discovered it was a Presbyterian church. But the minister, little Bill Dalton, preached good sermons. They always kept us awake and made us feel better. Sunday became a bright spot in the week.

But we still didn't know the Jesus he preached about. Not in a personal way. Neither of us realized that was possible. Nobody ever asked us if we'd been "born again." We wouldn't have known what they meant.

Lance spent most of that first hot summer with us. He was artistic, like his mother, Maggie, and took some prize-winning pictures of curious rock formations in the area. He pitched in and helped where he could at the mine, carrying replacement parts and steel bits for the voracious drilling machines. Sometimes the powder monkey, as the explosives expert was called, let him carry caps and dynamite sticks. Sometimes he sweated busily along with the other men, black as coal from the grimy manganese. But it all proved too dry and hot and dirty for his taste. We wanted to put him in school in Deming. But he preferred to go back to 1015 Pine Street and stay with his "grandmother," as he called LB. Besides, Zookie was there. Merikay had heard somewhere that many of the Mexicans ate dog meat, sprinkled with chili sauce. She didn't think fat-bellied Zookie would be safe in Deming.

Our mine area was infested with copperheads, coiled on the rocks in the sun, ready to strike out at any passerby. Knee-high boots were essential. But the copperheads weren't all at the mine. There was the Pine Street Liquor Store, which obligingly opened its doors just in time for my morning shift to stop by for a quick swig on the way to work. Many a miner I had to send home by safety rules when he showed up with liquor on his breath. Over the weeks I discovered that they were also servicing Merikay's habit on a twenty-four hour basis, rushing bottles in brown bags whenever I was away at the mine. Which was most of the time.

No amount of talk on my part prevented the lady owner from poisoning my wife. Merikay was getting progressively weak and wobbly, though the size of her stomach led me to think she might really be pregnant as she claimed. In a desperate effort to break the "Pine Street habit," I took Merikay on little sightseeing trips. We visited Santa Fe, high in the Sangre de Cristo mountains in northern New Mexico. The Navajo reservation in the Four Corners and the Indian gala dances at Gallup. Tried the hot mineral baths of Truth or Consequences. Took her to the Cortez Hotel in El Paso to get away from dusty Deming for the weekend. Went night-clubbing and shopping in Juarez across the border. Nothing seemed to help for long. Ostracized by the whole town, away from familiar places, she missed Zookie and she missed her mother. But LB didn't miss an opportunity to long-distance Merikay almost daily with some tale of woe, or report of cancer striking some friend. I began to dislike Alexander Graham Bell. Was there no way to cut that silver chord?

Then Snoopy Snoozy Gonzales appeared. That's what she called the straggly alley cat she rescued out of a nearby garbage can one day. He became her Zookie substitute as he followed her adoringly around the house, cuddled into bed with her during the long nights I was detained at the mine. Trying to push production, I started running all three shifts, on three to four hours sleep a night. There was no one else I could trust.

She rescued children, too. The skinny, brown kids of our mine mechanic, Pete, left motherless by a California earthquake. She taught them to sweep and to cook and to read. And to laugh again, snuggled in her warm arms of love.

"Some day soon," she'd whisper in the quiet of our bed, "we'll have our own little one." A deep sigh. "I hope he looks just like you."

Merikay had another battle to fight also. The battle of the bed sheets. No matter how many baths or showers I took, every morning the black outline of my sleeping body dirtied the sheets. Manganese works its way under the skin and oozes out slowly. Other miners told me it was impossible to get it out of the system. Actually it is poisonous. I came to recognize it in the thick eyelashes of my miners, in their slow sleepwalking motions, in their deep hoarse voices. It was one of the hazards of manganese mining. There was a brand new change room with showers at the mine, and the wives every week tried to wash the grimy clinging stuff from their husbands' mining clothes. Nothing really helped, except to stay out of the mine. That meant no beans and tortillas on the kiddies' plates.

Every day Merikay, fighting insurmountable odds, changed my sheets. She gave up white sheets right away. Tried pink, sheets, blue sheets, finally purple sheets. It was no use. Even the dark purple sheets turned black.

Besides the daily battles with my rough crew, as I spurred them to increase production, there were other crises. One day while eating lunch with Merikay at the Round-Up, I saw through the window an out-of-town sheriff with that "I've got a warrant for your arrest" look on his face. With him was Milford, my onetime associate in drilling an oil well near Chadron, Nebraska. By his scowl I could tell they were going to make good his long-time threat to "get me and put me away" because of my partner's failure to finish paying their drilling rig bill. My partner was one of those people who is fine right up until the moment of truth. But when we got within the last few feet when we'd know whether we had a well or a dry hole, he had blown up under the pressure and disappeared, papers, money and all.

Asking Merikay to excuse me for a few minutes, I ducked out the back way and started walking through the motel grounds to take a short cut to the mine. Trouble? I already had enough trouble. So my first mistake was not facing up to the inevitable. A fat man lounging in one of the doorways noted my dirty mining clothes, my haste, and the expensive brief case. Thinking I had stolen it, he yelled for me to stop. I speeded up and started running. Suddenly I heard a sound like the sharp snapping of a branch. Then another. With a shock I realized he was shooting at me. So I made my second mistake. Fear, unnamed fear caught me and dried my throat and set my adrenalin going. I ran at top speed, turned into a cotton gin and hid behind a row of bales.

The fat man had grabbed a car and we played hide and seek among the cotton bales. I set off cross country through the cactus, tearing my new leather briefcase as I got caught squeezing through a barbed wire fence. Still running I ducked into the shower room at the nearby country club. When he came looking I stood on the toilet seat. Soon as he left I sneaked out the side door. If I could just get to the trucking headquarters of my trucker a half mile down the road, I could get Joe to drive me to the mine and safety.

What I was trying to escape, I do not know. But terror had me in its clammy clutch. I panted up to Joe who suspiciously asked me what I had done and why the sheriff, who had now joined the chase, was after me. Just then the sheriff's car sirened up. I took off like a rabbit across the fields, stumbling through the tumbleweed and sharp cactus. Suddenly the ground opened beneath me. I fell eight feet into a cement pit. Tumbleweed covering the bottom cushioned my fall. My lungs were about to burst. My heart was beating like an air hammer. I made up my mind, no matter what happened, I would run no further. I covered myself with the tumbleweed.

Soon a hoarse, excited voice yelled at me, "Come out, or I'll shoot." Slowly I climbed up to the top of the pit. He already had the handcuffs out.

"Hold on," I said trying to sound tougher than I felt. "Let me see your credentials."

Out of his wallet he pulled a card, stating that he was a deputy sheriff.

"That's no good here," I said, throwing it into the pit. "That says you're authorized in Pima County, Arizona. This is Luna County, New Mexico."

Before he could recover, I pushed his pointed gun away. "Put that toy away, boy," I said, walking off as dignified as is possible with tumbleweed clinging to my clothes and hair. "You just might hurt yourself."

I learned it never pays to run away. Even if you don't know

what you're running away from. The whole town of Deming had a big laugh over this. It certainly didn't gain me any respect.

In spite of Snoopy Snoozy Gonzales, Merikay was still battling ever-deepening loneliness. And the lonelier she became, the more she turned to the bottle for comfort. Meanwhile I was hunting in desperation for an honest bookkeeper. I wanted someone, if possible, from out of town, who would not be part of the hostile closed circle around us. Someone who wouldn't gossip about our intimate financial problems. Weeks passed.

Then one day when I had made my usual midafternoon check to see how Merikay was, the doorbell rang. We hadn't used that front door in months. I usually slid out the secret back door to avoid irate miners and bill collectors. I started out the back door, when I heard a voice say, "Go to the front door." I called to Merikay in the bedroom, "What did you say?" She was in a deep alcoholic slumber. I turned. Again the same voice, the same words. And a third time as I had my hand on the kitchen doorknob.

I rolled up the drawn shade. Outside was a strange woman. One of the "Avon calling" girls. Merikay had plenty of cosmetics. Then I remembered I had been wishing for a new friend for her. Could it be?

Inviting the woman in, I found out she had recently arrived with her husband from Minnesota. Ralph Henderson, her husband, was a bookkeeper as well as a Nazarene minister starting a little mission in town. Fern and Merikay became close friends. And I got a good bookkeeper. I was even willing to overlook the fact that he was a Nazarene minister, as long as I didn't have to attend the church he was always inviting me to.

# 7

# The Devil, You Say?

In the middle of a shift one evening I suddenly thought of an urgent matter. I had to see my bookkeeper right away.

So I climbed up the several hundred feet of rickety wooden ladders, jumped into my dusty jeep, and bounced off to find Ralph. I skidded to a stop in front of the struggling little church he pastored and where he lived in a few cramped rooms at the rear. Across the doorway hung a big sign, "Revival."

This made me indignant. As an Episcopalian I considered revivals spiritual circuses. I jerked the door open. There by the pulpit stood my bookkeeper-minister. I didn't care that he was serving God. I was his boss and I needed him. So I shouted at him to come out at once.

He paid absolutely no attention. Finally I stomped inside,

my steel-plated miner's boots clanking across the floor. I wigwagged at him, coughed vigorously. He wouldn't even look at me. I sat down.

The candlelight service droned on. Finally the visiting evangelist with the dull, dry voice began his altar call. Even the words of the hymn were nauseating. Something about "come home, come home." It was disgusting. Now grown men and women were going to get up and make utter fools of themselves by going to the altar rail and moaning and groaning.

But strangely, nobody went forward. Why didn't someone, anyone, go forward? I'd heard all about these fanatics. If some poor fool didn't go forward, why they'd stay here all night. My business with Ralph couldn't wait that long.

A scientifically trained engineer, I often doubted the supernatural. If I couldn't measure it, separate it, smell or taste or feel or see or hear it, then how could I be sure it existed?

Yet, suddenly, without moving a muscle, I found myself lifted out of that pew into the middle of the aisle. I'd been concentrating that someone, anyone, would go forward, but I certainly hadn't thought of it as a prayer. And I certainly hadn't meant me.

Then I met the devil. He stood beside me, invisible to human eyes, but I could sense his presence as one is aware of someone nearby in the dark. With a shock I realized that he didn't have any horns, or a tail. No red suit, He didn't even smell of brimstone.

Until then I hadn't really believed he even existed. Of course the Bible does mention him from time to time. The snake in the Garden of Eden. Lucifer who fell from heaven as lightning. That great dragon, that old devil, alias Satan. But a real devil, living and breathing? And such a friendly fellow?

It was as though he was speaking to me through my

thoughts as they came one by one to my mind.

"It's wonderful to worship God," he murmured approvingly. "But just look at yourself. Everybody else is dressed up in white shirts and skirts. Look how dirty you are."

Manganese is blacker than coal. Dirty? I was filthy.

"Go home," the friendly voice continued, "and use some soap and water, and then come back again when you're clean. Show some respect to God."

*They've maligned him for centuries,* I thought. *Why the devil is really a good fellow after all.* That's the way the devil is, always looking at the surface dirt. But the Holy Spirit looks deep inside at the dirt in our souls.

My miner's steel-plated boots were dug into that wooden floor, like an old Missouri mule. Suddenly some supernatural power moved me forward as if I were on roller skates. Like a tiny metal filing drawn inexorably by a mighty magnet. This time the devil came around on my right side. He knew my weak point. Pride. I was the most arrogant person in the world.

"You're the most important man in town," that soft, seductive voice continued. "You have the biggest payroll. A big mine. A big mill. Hundreds of men working for you. They're even talking about running you for senator this year."

"Yes," I reminded him, "and I'm even listed in *Who's Who in the East*."

"Exactly!" he continued confidentially. "This is just a small town. Only eight thousand people. If you go to that altar rail now and make a fool of yourself, everybody in town will know by tomorrow morning."

He wasn't kidding.

"And think of your miners," that persuasive voice flowed on. "They're tough. You'll lose their respect. You won't be able to control them any more. The mine will close down and the stockholders will lose all their money, and it will all be your fault."

That's the devil for you. His greatest weapon is convincing us that he doesn't exist. If there is no devil, then there is no hell, and if no hell, then no judgment. So what do we have to worry about? We are our own god. But if he is forced to reveal himself, then he tries his second greatest weapon. "No hurry," he says soothingly, "there's plenty of time." He reminded me that I was being disloyal to my denomination even to be in this Nazarene church. Why not wait till Sunday, he tempted, and do this in your own church?

But the supernatural power of the Holy Spirit kept moving me slowly toward the altar rail, in spite of my deep-dug heels. Suddenly I saw before me every sin I had committed since infancy. They stood like an endless series of statues, staring me straight in the eye. Until that instant I had wondered how in a few brief moments a drowning man's whole life could pass before his eyes. Now I knew. In moments on the brink of eternity, time stands still.

Then an even longer series of statues stared into my eyes. I had been a normal Episcopalian. I had "done those things which I ought not to have done, and left undone those things which I ought to have done." The kind word I could have said. Sometimes I think if there is any degree, these sins of omission may well be the worst. Only God and we ourselves know what they are. For the first time in my life I saw myself as God Almighty saw me. And there was no good thing in me. All was garbage and ashes.

Then before my wide open eyes I saw a vision. Until then I had believed that people who went around talking about visions really belonged in some institution. Now before me I saw a lake of fire, with men and women struggling in the fierce flames of remorse. It was like the crater of a volcano with a seething sea of fire that burned without consuming.

Each was crying out, "Oh, if I could only go back and right the wrong I did—if I could only go back and do the thing I *should* have done."

I remembered how in the Bible the rich man in the flames had called the beggar Lazarus who had lain so long untended at his gates. The rich man had begged for only a drop of water to moisten his tongue, and the answer had come back, "Between us there is a great gulf fixed."

My heart knew then that it is in this life that we must make our decision for eternal life—whether to spend it in fellowship with God, or in that lonely pit of outer darkness, separated forever from His love.

Oh, how I repented of my own hardness of heart and smug unbelief. Then beyond the lake of fire I saw another vision, this time of the heavenly places, where all is a glory of gold and music and joy beyond description. Everything in me yearned to enter into that realm of praise.

The Holy Spirit prepares us for our times of choice. Just a few days before, I had turned on the radio to hear the news. By divine intervention, which I credited to pure coincidence, I heard the end of "The Hour of Decision" and the voice of Billy Graham. "Each soul has a time for decision—it may come only once and never again." In my heart I knew that this was my time. God would never speak to me again.

I rushed toward the altar rail. But the devil was not going to give up that easily. "This is the harvest night of the revival," he reminded me. "No one has come to the altar yet. Look at all those clean white shirts and skirts. If you kneel first, do you think any of them will want to kneel next to a dirty old bum like you? Why, you'll spoil the altar call and souls will go to hell, just because you're selfish."

I asked the Lord to forgive me if I came between anyone else and salvation, if nobody else came up that night. But I knew it was my night, that God would never speak to me again. So I began to kneel. As I did, the devil tried one last dart. He knew my weak point—pride.

"Remember," he whispered warningly, "you have a big rip in the seat of your pants, and you're wearing red underwear. How do you think that will look when you kneel?"

If I had not already been kneeling, that would have stopped me cold. That's how tissue-paper close I came to missing salvation. But I knelt. Into my mind came that lovely picture of Christ standing with a lantern in one hand, the other hand raised as He taps lightly on the door of our heart. Soft and sweet His voice was. Yet it filled the whole church. Like the sound of many waters. Like silver trumpets in the dawn. "Behold, I stand at the door and knock. If anyone hears My voice and opens the door, I will come in to him, and will dine with him, and he with Me."

Right into my ear the devil whispered, "You've done everything. You've been baptized. You've even been confirmed. Saying those few simple words won't make any difference."

But I decided to say them anyway. Until that moment I had never realized that salvation is a free gift. But a gift requires both a receiver and a giver—or it is only an offer.

I'd been a choir boy, an acolyte, even a lay reader. I'd done everything I thought that had to be done to become a Christian. But I had never realized that I had to make a personal invitation to Jesus to come into my heart. Again came that soft sweet voice, "If you will confess with your mouth the Lord Jesus, and . . . "

So I said those few simple words, feeling foolish as I did. But with a great yearning in my heart that something supernatural would happen.

"Words, words, words," the devil taunted. "What difference will they make?"

All my life I had suffered from two haunting fears, the fear of the dark and the fear of tight places. Yet every day I had gone down into the blackness of the mine, buried alive. Often stepping from one slippery ledge to another, I would freeze with fear, unable to move for endless seconds. Fear is an old enemy. I know every shape and size and color and smell of fear.

Yet that instant when I asked the Lord Jesus to come into my heart, He came in. Like a great photo flash lighting up all my dark places. And these excessive fears departed never to return again. I knew then what the Apostle Paul meant when he said, "If any man be in Christ, he is a new creation, old things have passed away and all things are new." From that night until now I have never had an instant fear of anything or anyone on the earth, below the earth or above the earth.

That night twelve youngsters came forward. The Rev. Potter, evangelist, tried to make me feel at ease. "If you hadn't come forward," he said warmly, "I don't think those others would have either. But they felt if an old bum like you could do it, so could they."

The eyes of my bookkeeper-pastor opened wide. "Brother Potter," he cried, "that's no bum. That's my boss."

The evangelist recovered quickly. "It's a wonderful thing," he said, pumping my hand vigorously, "to see a man who loves the Lord so much that he rushes here straight from work without even stopping to wash up."

As I opened my lips to accept that compliment, the Holy Spirit reminded me that "No man comes to me, except the Father which hath sent me draw him."

"Brother Potter," I gulped. "I didn't come here tonight. The

81

Holy Spirit is the one who brought me here."

That great urgent piece of business I had had to see my bookkeeper about that night? It was forgotten. The real business had been my salvation. In His wisdom God the Holy Spirit had appealed to me through my mine, which had slowly over the years become my god. And He had used the faithful prayers of that little group who had been praying unceasingly for me for six long months.

What else happened that night I do not remember. It was about a quarter past nine the last time I had looked at my watch as the altar call started. The service must have finished by ten o'clock. It is impossible to walk the empty streets of Deming, New Mexico, unseen late at night. But nobody saw me. I was caught up in a beautiful golden glow. I don't know what happened or where I went. It was two in the morning when I went to bed, my heart singing with my new-found love of God. Next thing I knew it was morning. Dawn was breaking. Time to start the morning shift at the mine. My heart was full of joy and a new song was on my lips.

Again the devil reminded me that I had never returned to the mine last night to complete the shift. Nor had I supervised the graveyard shift that began at midnight. The balloon of my joy began to spring a leak. What a king-size fool I had made out of myself the night before at that little Nazarene mission!

My miners were a tough, unruly lot. The news would have gone all over the little town. They'd be waiting for me. The same rough, hard-bitten crew with which I had tussled and fought to keep their respect. Now they'd just laugh at me. In the past, drink-crazed miners had run at me with broken bottles and knives. Why, if I went out to the mine this morning, those roughnecks would tear me apart. They'd tie me up like a pretzel and drop me down the mine shaft, and that would be the end of me. Rather an inglorious way to go.

There was no fear left in me. That had evaporated the night before when Christ came into my heart. But the devil kept after me until I was so discouraged that I decided not to bother to go to the mine. I would accept the inevitable and turn in my resignation to the directors. I began to pack to return to Chicago.

Then the Holy Spirit reminded me that it was my duty to go to the mine. The miners had known me as one kind of person. Now I must go show them what Christ could do in transforming a man. I fixed another cup of coffee. Black.

My hard hat shoved back on my head, I jumped into the jeep. One of the few joys of that mine was that while going to work in the morning I would drive straight east into the rising sun. The dawn that morning was lavish with the violence of a child's crayons. I thought, that's the last dawn I shall ever see.

The morning crew were drawn up in a circle like a football huddle. I rang the starting bell. Nobody moved. I rang it again. And a third time. "Anybody going to work?" I called out in Spanish.

My mine boss was an Apache Indian, over six feet tall. Big enough to fill a doorway, he could carry a grown man in either arm. That morning he looked over eight feet high. He motioned to me, "Ven aqui." That was an insolent way to talk to the Big Boss. "I'm a Christian now," I reminded myself, and walked over to him.

"Senor," he continued, "You not too bad. Sometime you make us work underground on Sunday. This year Good Friday you make us work. But now we hear about last night. Now you Christian like us. We work for you all the time."

That morning I made two of the best friends of my life, Manuel and Miguel. To my surprise I discovered that Manuel was different, too. Before that day I would have sworn on all the Bibles in the world that he was the biggest drunkard, gambler and woman chaser in the state. But I found that he was a good family man, neither smoked nor drank. He was even a deacon in the local Baptist church. I **had** been seeing him through my own sin-colored glasses. But now the darkness was gone.

For the first time in my life I saw my past as it really was. Until then I had been so proud of success. Wasn't it I who had discovered the first uranium in the Pacific Northwest? Hadn't I acted as vice-president of the labor management committee of Bendix Radio, supervising five plants with 12,500 employees? Making radars for all our planes? Hadn't I . . .

Yes, and hadn't I all this time been wayward and rebellious? Hadn't I turned times without number from His love, sure that in my pathetic little ego I knew what was best for me and the world? I had thought I lacked nothing, yet I was "wretched and miserable, and poor and blind and naked." Yes, I had had enemies everywhere . . . no friends . . . my wife a slave to alcohol . . . choked with fear. But now I had come out of the darkness into the sunlight . . . born again into a glorious new life through the love of God.

Now I knew the truth spoken by that great saint centuries ago, "Our soul is restless till it rests in Thee."

# 8

# Jailbird

I tried to share my new-found joy with Merikay. When I told her how I'd gone to the altar and knelt and asked Jesus to come into my heart, she cried in a shocked tone, "Oh, no! Not in those ragged old pants with the hole? And with that dirty red underwear showing? Oh, how could you!"

How hard it is, how impossible to share things of the spirit, even with the one we love most, when that dear one is not yet spiritually awakened.

There were other problems, too. It wasn't all sunshine and roses after I came to know Jesus as my personal Savior. Late one night a few days afterwards I went alone into the depths of my manganese mine. It was an abandoned section. I wanted to be sure it was safe for the men before sending them there.

My little miner's handpick had stuck in a crack. When I

tugged, there was a sickening roar. I lay imprisoned in a coffin of stone. I realized numbly that no one knew where I was. It might be weeks, or months before anyone found me. Meanwhile, no water, no light, no food.

Before my recent experience at the altar rail, fear might have frozen me. But now the peace of God filled every fiber of my being. Like a wondrous golden light I sensed the presence of the Lord. "Lo, I am with you always," He had said, "even to the end of the world."

How many hours later I do not know, one of my miners, alerted to my danger in a "dream," came and dug me out.

Then a few days after this evidence of God's loving care, a bigger test came. For months I'd had a running battle with the local Mexican sheriff. He raked in the money by fining my miners when they crossed the border after enjoying a beer or two with their families. He would put them through absurd tests like balancing on one foot, fine them $150 for driving while intoxicated, and clap them into the calabozo until their friends scraped together the last, greasy dollar bill. And of course they lost their driver's licenses for six months. That meant they lost their jobs, as they could no longer drive the twenty-six mile round trip over the rough mountain roads to the mine.

I had given Big Joe, the sheriff, warning. When he refused to stop this racket I got the best lawyers and fought the phoney arrests and got my men out of jail. So Big Joe hated me, $500 a week worth, which is what his racket had netted him.

About ten o'clock one night I was driving down the highway toward home. Suddenly the sheriff's car swerved in front of me. I was strong-armed into the patrol car, and tossed into a smelly cell in the calabozo. The heavy steel door clanged shut.

Alone in that smelly, thick darkness I smashed the tin cup, screamed myself hoarse. I remembered how the sheriff had laughed when he told me that some night he was going to put the local knife expert in the cell and let him carve me into little pieces. Only it didn't sound at all like laughter.

Nobody knew where I was except God. I cried out for some supernatural evidence that He cared. There in that thick darkness suddenly appeared a little glow like a firefly. I picked it up and the light came with it. It was a tract, "Dios Habla," from the book of John. "Ye shall know the truth and the truth shall make you free."

I thought of Daniel in the lions' den. The Hebrew children in the fiery furnace heated seven times hot. I thought of Peter in jail. He'd been chained to a guard, and the guard had a sword. Of course a lot of people had been praying for him.

I lay down and slept like a baby on the floor. About two in the morning, some miles away, the Holy Spirit wakened a business acquaintance. Jonesy and I had made an iffy sort of date. Any time in the next six months that he drove through Deming on his way to California, he would stop and we'd talk. He decided to drive straight through to Deming.

Not finding me at the mine or mill or our little house, Jonesy decided to drive on to Los Angeles. For months there had been a big hole in the main highway. Just that morning the road crew from Santa Fe went to work. So Jonesy had to take a detour that brought him past the calabozo.

As he passed the jail, the setting sun struck the bumper of my car which the sheriff had hidden in an old shed, covered with tumbleweeds. Jonesy thought I was inside playing dominoes with the sheriff. The sheriff was away, but the jailer told Jonesy some trumped up story of some supposed crime and how I'd resisted arrest.

Jonesy had never thought very highly of me. We'd been neighboring miners, rough competitors. He'd seen my explosive temper in action, how berserk I became when defied.

How the men turned white under the searing lash of my tongue, and trembled when I grabbed the nearest pick or shovel or piece of drill steel.

So Jonesy decided to go on to California. But all the way to Lordsburg, some sixty miles, he kept wondering if anybody knew of my plight. He drove all the way back, stopped at the office of the only attorney who was friendly to me.

Raimundo laughed, "Hammond's too smart to get caught."

But the next morning there he was peering through the bars at me.

"I always wondered how you'd look behind bars." He grinned at me. "You look so natural."

"It all depends on which side of the bars you are, Ray. You look pretty natural yourself."

"Still the wise guy," he growled. "I think I'll just leave you rot."

Out he walked.

"Forgive me, Lord," I prayed. "You sent an angel, even if he didn't look like one. Give me another chance. Send someone else. Send anyone."

The jailer had a sister who had a husband who had a brother who attended this same little Nazarene church and worked at the mine. Through the grapevine word reached Ralph Henderson, who seldom got more than ten bucks in his Sunday collection plate. Somehow from some of the miners I had befriended in time of illness he gathered up nickels and dimes and quarters and greasy dollar bills.

Again the sheriff was away when the Reverend Ralph arrived with his clinking pile, enough for the $200 bail. So I was free again. And free to plot revenge.

But as I repeated the Lord's prayer in church each Sunday, the words began to take on deeper meaning. "Forgive us our trespasses, as (in the same way, to the same extent) we forgive those who have trespassed against us."

Right after my heart-changing experience in the revival, I had joined the church, begun to gather up the skinny, brown children of my miners and bring them to Sunday School. Through Ralph's joyful guidance I realized we have to pray for our enemies. I began to pray for God to give me love for Big Joe. It was hard work at first. But I kept on doggedly until finally one day at the altar rail on my knees, I realized I loved him. I'd finally managed to forgive him for those dark hours of torture in solitary confinement. Now to tell him.

When I walked into his office, Big Joe reached for the gun in his hip holster.

"Put it away, Joe," I called out. "I come as a friend. I want to ask you to forgive me."

His bushy eyebrows shot up in surprise. "Me? Forgive you? After tossing you in the calabozo?"

"You see, Big Joe," I explained. "Jesus said if you hate your brother, you're a murderer. I killed you a thousand times in my thoughts." I threw my arms around him in a Mexican style abrazzo. "I love you."

Big Joe gulped. There were tears in his eyes. "Tell me," his voice was shaky. "Tell me about this Jesus." By that night God's family had increased by one big Mexican sheriff.


I had been unsuccessfully trying to tell my beloved Merikay about Jesus. She went most Sundays to the Nazarene church with me. But my tastes were changing. I had been a regular movie-goer. There wasn't much else to do in Deming. Merikay and I saw all the new films and even all the Spanish pictures. We went every weekend to El Paso or Las Cruces or Albuquerque. Anywhere there was dancing and music and laughter, and where we could escape for a few hours from Deming and its endless sandstorms. But all these things had lost much of their allure for me.

There were more battles between us. It seemed that Jesus, instead of bringing us together, was pushing us apart. There were more tears. More drinking. More condemnation on my part. Gone were the savage rages when, in a desperate attempt to stop her senseless drinking, I'd shaken her until her teeth chattered. But the critical thoughts . . . I tried to act like a Christian should, full of love and joy and peace. And forgiveness. But I had a continuing battle to forgive her. It all seemed so crazy to keep on drinking day after day when the doctors had warned her it would kill her. Or she'd end up being a wetbrain, out of touch with reality. My golden-haired green-eyed Merikay, whom I loved above anything in this world.

Day by day before my eyes she became thin and gaunt and hollow-eyed. Her legs swelled. She took to bed, turning and tossing through nameless terrors in the night. The doctor brought in a nurse to care for her. I had a busy mine to run, and nobody to help me. I tried and tried to share Jesus with her, help her find the peace that now sustained me through my trials.

Then one day I came home sweaty and tired to find our family doctor leaving the house with the practical nurse who had been taking care of Merikay. Long ago he had explained that the type of cancer she had had spreads like wildfire. For the last several years she had been examined every month. Then for a few days she'd relax. But then the tension would begin building up to the point of explosion. Would the next report be negative? Or . . . every month the same torture over and over again. It was enough to drive a strong person to drink. And now . . . .

"Your wife can't last much longer," said the doctor gruffly. "Better telephone Chicago." He put his arm around my shoulder. "Tell the undertaker you're bringing a corpse."

Tears made it hard for me to see the doctor's face. Even when you suspect the truth deep inside, you hate to hear it put into words. All these weary months I had been hoping against hope. I had tried to close my mind against what by every appearance seemed inevitable. Day by day, month by month, year by year I had watched her sink lower and lower.

So here it was, I thought. It had finally happened. The killer cells had spread throughout her body. Fear, discouragement, despair had wrapped their slimy tentacles around her. Edema was in the last stages. My wife was five feet, seven inches, usually weighed 125 pounds. Now she weighed only eighty-eight pounds. Her feet were swollen like grapefruits, her legs enlarged as if with elephantiasis. I cried inside each time I looked at her. She was as dry and wrinkled as a mummy.

In my anguish the Scripture verse came back, "Come to Me, all who are weary and heavy laden, and I will give you rest." With a prayer on my lips I managed to get my wife out of her bed and into our car. Somehow I drove the one hundred miles from Deming to El Paso. I could only seem to pray for each leg of the trip at a time.

"Lord," I cried with all my soul, "don't let her die until I get her to El Paso. Lord, please don't let her die until I can get her to a hospital." I tried every hospital in El Paso. Each time I rushed in, wild-eyed, carrying her in my arms, to the reception desk instead of emergency. They all refused, calling her DOA (dead on arrival). They were not being unkind. After all, there was really nothing they could do to help her.

My eyes were on man all the time, what man could do for her. Yet Dr. Noll had made it clear that man could do no more. When the last hospital closed its doors, my soul cried out to God in anguish. I dropped on my knees on the sidewalk.

A few weeks before, our Christian neighbor had called us

over one Sunday afternoon to watch the evangelist, Oral Roberts, on television. It had all seemed so real. As he prayed and laid his hands on the people's heads, they actually looked as though they were healed. But I had been brought up to believe the day of miracles was past. I knew enough about television and the movies to realize they could edit a program and make these "healings" appear to happen.

But now as I knelt on the sidewalk, crying out to God for help, I heard Him answer in an audible voice, "I will heal your wife. But it will be through the prayers of my servant, Oral Roberts—because I do heal my children through this servant."

I repented of my doubts. I besought God to lay a burden on Oral Roberts's heart, right then, that very minute, to pray for my wife. Somehow, miraculously, I carried my wife aboard the airplane without a doctor's certificate. The Lord seemed to blind the eyes of the passenger agents.

When I carried Merikay into her parents' home in Winnetka, Dr. Jim who had known her since "before she was born" burst into tears.

Tex grabbed him and shook him like a terrier shakes a rat. "You've got to do something."

They called in the chief internist of a large hospital, a fine diagnostician who lived a few houses away. For several minutes he looked at my wife. Then he called me outside. He asked if I wanted to know the truth.

"Always."

"There is absolutely no hope."

He named five complaints, any one of which could kill her.

"Couldn't God still heal her?" I asked desperately.

He just smiled sadly. "She is beyond medical help. There is no point in even taking her to the hospital."

In *Guideposts* magazine I found the names of several

prayer groups—Protestant, Roman Catholic, Jewish. Need makes us all ecumenical. I wrote each one asking them to pray. I even wrote Roberts to make sure he got the message. Later I found there were several prayer groups nearby ready to believe God Almighty can do anything He ever did before.

Little by little, day by day, God graciously healed my wife. As an incentive I had promised Merikay that if she was well enough, I'd take her on a long-desired trip to Europe, never really believing she'd be strong enough. Almost overnight her liver function test had gone from a fatal low to almost 98.5 percent. So unbelievable was it that test after test was made to be sure the laboratory had the right sample, or had not made a mistake. It is during such moments of tribulation that God teaches us. He taught me how to pray. It was the first miracle of healing I had ever seen. And it happened right in front of my eyes—to the person I loved most in all the world.

One day she asked me if I had obtained her passport and ticket yet. That very day I drove to Chicago's Loop and arranged everything in faith.

Bravely Merikay toured southern Spain with me and our loyal chauffeur-guide, Julio. He showed her the utmost compassion and respect, even when her drinking problem snarled up our schedule with late stops and early starts. She reveled in the liquid beauty of Granada and the Alhambra, exquisite jewels wrought in lacy stone by the Moors long ago. She loaded up with fine laces and gleaming Toledo steel scissors.

After a joyous, busy round of revisiting the places where we had wooed and loved six years before—the same hotel off the Place de L'Etoile . . . the little boats skimming the River Seine . . . Maxim's . . . We were packing to return home. Suddenly pain with the force of a pile driver struck me in the pit of the stomach. I fell to my knees. The Paris edition of *The Herald Tribune,* which I had been reading, fluttered to the floor. I didn't know any doctor. Not even any hospital. Paris had always been a fun city to me. But there, right in front of my nose, in answer to anguished prayer, I saw a tiny one-inch ad—the American Hospital in Paris. Merikay started to phone for the house doctor. Doubled over with pain, I prayed he wouldn't answer. In my need I wanted an American with whom I could communicate easily.

I crawled on my hands and knees across the worn, red carpet and down the stairs, while Merikay was still frantically trying to make the operator understand. Then across the marble lobby floor, unable even to speak. The blase hotel clerk probably thought I was just another drunken tourist. The heavy revolving door loomed before me. How could I ever push it, when I could barely crawl? The nearest taxi stand was nearly a mile away.

"Lord, move that mountain!" I cried.

Just then a taxi swooped up, discharging its passenger who pushed the revolving door, thus sweeping me out onto the sidewalk. I crawled through the still open taxi door onto the floor. I was barely able to groan, "Hospital American." As we zoomed off, I prayed that there would be an American surgeon. I didn't trust French techniques.

God answered that prayer, too. The chief surgeon was an American who had been there many years. The male orderly plopped me into bed and stuck tubes down my nose and throat to relieve the pain. Early the next morning the chief surgeon decided an emergency operation was my only chance. Meanwhile Merikay, not knowing where I had gone, finally located me at the American Hospital, and promptly had herself hospitalized to keep an eye on me.

"After all," as she later explained, "that hotel was freezing. Hadn't turned the heat on yet. I was shivering in the bathroom with a hot shower going full blast. And," her eyes glowed brightly, "they give you a choice of red or white wine with all meals. This is some kind of a hospital. Of course I moved in. It'd even be worth getting sick for this luxury."

So three floors below, across the courtyard, Merikay nervously watched the electricity suddenly go off during the eight hour operation, only to wink back on moments later as standby equipment went into action. It seems that the intestinal obstruction had been caused by a scar from an old ulcer that had perforated unknown to anyone years before—one of the relics of my nervous days of producing radio and TV shows.

Later as I was wheeled out of the operating room, flat on my back, I realized suddenly that I was clutching my little pocket New Testament. But it was closed tight. The Holy Spirit convicted me.

Earlier that summer I had seen my wife, given up by the doctors, yet healed by the power of God. But I hadn't even prayed to God to heal me. I had prayed for Him to show me the right hospital, the right doctor, to provide the needed taxi. But I hadn't given Him a chance to heal me.

The strong sedatives had blurred my thinking until I had not known what was going on around me. My signature authorizing the operation looked like a wildly scrawled horseshoe. They had insisted that my wife sign, too. So flat on my back on the stretcher I made a compact with God. I promised if I were ever seriously ill again, I would rely on Him and not on man for healing.

I was to learn many months later that we should never make a compact with Almighty God unless we fully intend to keep it.

Meanwhile in an elegant Elizabeth Arden butterfly housecoat, covered by one of the hospital's drab Army issue robes, Merikay buzzed about from room to room spreading her bubbling laughter. She became assistant librarian and arranged Westerns so well that the elder Joseph P. Kennedy, recovering from an appendectomy, sent her his compliments. From time to time she would sortie out of the hospital with one of the young nurses to go shopping along the Place de la Concorde or visit the elegant Ritz. But as soon as I could tell a young nurse from an old one, she yanked me out of the hospital. "Buzz, you're okay now."

Always the first to help, LB had cabled over substantial funds to cover our unexpected hospital stay. My recovery was eased by Merikay's merry company. "I'm so glad you're still alive that I'm not even going to argue with you any more about anything."

But I could tell she was still drinking secretly—bursts of almost artificial gaiety, then depths of despondency. She was beginning to use sleeping pills, too. A bad combination. All I could do was to pray. And to hope as I became stronger, that her anxieties would diminish. I determined never to argue with her about her drinking again. But it was a decision I violated more often than I kept. If only she would turn to the God who had so marvelously healed her. If only she would give Him the credit, instead of taking all the credit herself, saying, "I'm too tough to die. I made up my mind to get well. And I did."

# 9

# Twenty-four Hours to Live

Merikay and I recovered that fall in our Eastside New York apartment. Stretched out on the chaise lounge, I concentrated on solving a crossword puzzle called "Blackout Pete." Every morning Allen Marks would trudge from his nearby stationery store with a backbreaking bundle of newspapers. I figured if I worked enough different answers and enough entries, I was bound to win the thousands of dollars in prizes offered daily.

Laboriously I pasted my answers on postcards. Then late at night to make the last pick-up, silver-grey Zookie and I would set out, his tiny legs pumping like pistons, for the post office. Newspapers piled up everywhere. It became a disease. Whenever a friend would drop by, or telephone, I would ask his help. Soon they all stopped coming by or even telephoning. Merikay had her problem. I had mine. I must have spent hundreds of dollars and wasted hundreds of hours. After some weeks of this madness, I came to my senses. It was gambling.

Which was worse—drinking or gambling? I called on God to deliver me. And He did, just as instantly and completely as He had freed me from nicotine and alcohol.

Just as I knew He would for Merikay . . . if she would admit her problem and call upon Jesus who still sets the captives free. She was so sweet and loving to me, until the liquor began to speak. Then life would swiftly change from heaven to hell.

Again I suggested hospitalization, psychiatry, AA. She staunchly maintained that she didn't have a problem. In that clever way of alcoholics, she switched everything around. I was the one who had the problem. I was the one who needed psychiatric care. Well, during my "Blackout Pete" craze she might have had a point. She agreed to go to a psychiatrist if I would. But when I made all the arrangements, she changed her mind.

We did start going back to Marble Collegiate Church, listening to Dr. Peale, and gypsying around Chinatown afterwards. Lance was still at school in Winnetka, living with LB and Tex. They were most gracious and generous during this period of my enforced idleness. But I was itching to get back to the mine. So many problems there, with powerful outside forces moving in to take over all I had worked and saved for.

Just before Christmas, my strength regained, Merikay and I flew back to Winnetka where LB, in her usual lavish, warmhearted way, had rented a beautiful furnished house for us just off the grounds of the Indian Hill Country Club. And only two miles from 1015. They became the shortest two miles in the world as LB swooped over daily in her yellow Cadillac to take Merikay to Elizabeth Arden's (where I later learned that not only sandwiches but drinks were sent in during the beauty treatments), to lunch at the Whitehall or International Club, or the races at Arlington Park. Or anywhere they could be together.

LB liked her liquor. She liked it better if she had somebody to share her drinking. And that somebody was usually Merikay though the doctor had warned that her next drink might be her last. Even a teaspoonful was enough to set her off on another bout with the bottle, not eating, not dressing, not caring, until she passed out in a coma. And she often did. Then there was the frenzied rush to the hospital, the agony of drying out. She came back home again days or weeks later, weak and wobbly and trying so hard to make up for all the heartache, but never admitting her problem.

She could always find some reason to blame me. I was too weak from my operation to go with her. That was why she had to go with her mother. I spent too much time talking on the telephone. Or writing business letters. I had changed. I wasn't the same gay beau with whom she'd danced away so many enchanted hours. I wasn't fun any longer.

She was right about that. My tastes had changed. I didn't care about going to plays or dances or the racetrack or parties. I was a "new creation." But one that convicted her by my very presence.

Sometimes she threatened to divorce me. Divorce would have been such an easy way out, I often thought as I reached the end of my patience. "Count it all joy," the Bible says. I hadn't learned the secret of praising God in everything. Not yet. Didn't even know that was in the Bible. Yet I was a Christian. "Whom God has joined together . . ." No matter what happened, I'd never be able to divorce her. Even if our love, once so radiant, should turn to ashes. Yet how could I endure the endless heartbreak of watching my love, my

Merikay, like a beautiful painting, dissolve before my eyes into a bleary-eyed, swollen-faced, wobbling caricature?

I thought of the picture of Dorian Gray as, in the endless night hours, Merikay tossed and moaned and mumbled beside me in our bed . . . . I wept for the love that once was ours.

Lance, now living with us in that big house, began to avoid Merikay. She embarrassed him when he brought his school friends home to see his model airplane collection. Only faithful Zookie never forsook her, but huddled close even when she'd sometimes kick at him in a drunken tantrum.

Yet, strangely, Elsie and Gerda, whom LB hired to cook and clean the house, were both born-again, Spirit-filled Christians. In the kitchen while they were cooking, or under the purring noise of the vacuum cleaner, I could pray with them. And I joined their monthly Winnetka Prayer Band, which shifted from house to house. These cooks, gardeners, housemen, and secretaries knew how to pray. Without their constant daily prayer support, I don't think I could have continued that crazy, mixed-up existence. Every time the fragile flower of hope raised its head, another insane spree smashed it.


During this time I became aware that the power struggle back at the mine was reaching a climax. I made several quick trips to try to stop this takeover by Eastern financial interests. On one of them I stole into the mine with another engineer in the early morning hours during the graveyard shift. The Easterners had declared the mine off-limits to me, even though I was executive vice-president, general manager and a member of the board of directors. The engineer and I discovered that the main tunnel was being drilled into a new and unreported vein of ore. Our cubication showed that nearly one million dollars worth had been taken out, sold, and not reported on the company's earnings!

Once they knew that I knew, the Easterners began a cruel campaign to discredit me with the other directors, the stockholders, and my friends and family. Dick, the leader, sitting high in his Park Avenue eyrie one fall afternoon, had disclosed to me his plans for taking over the company and freezing out all the original stockholders. First he would start loaning the company huge unnecessary sums in return for further dilution of the original shareholders' stock. When he had increased his stock holding from his original 50 percent to nearly 80 percent, he could then do what he wanted with the company. So he'd bankrupt it by overspending for exploration and development. Then he'd buy it up through one of his other profitable mining companies and offset the tax loss against his other profits. It was neat, he said. And if I went along with him, I'd continue managing the mine (his way of course) and share in the tremendous profits he foresaw.

Indignant, I refused to betray my friends and fellow stockholders who had risked so much. I intended to report this conversation and his scheme to the board of directors. He took a long swig from his bourbon on the rocks and sneered. Nobody would believe me. He was an important figure in a world-wide banking-mining combination worth billions. How did I think they accumulated such fantastic wealth? By outsmarting people stupid enough to trust them. They'd acquired seven world famous mines this way. And they'd soon add Florida Manganese (what a stupid name, they'd have to change that when they put the shares on the Stock Exchange, no romance) to their string.

Dick and his friends went to work on my father-in-law. I watched helplessly as Tex slowly lost his respect for me. The more I sought to expose the truth, the more the other stockholders thought I was crazy. Probably a result of that operation in Paris, Dick suggested. Who knows? But the poor fellow is ranting and raving like a maniac. Or is he a secret drinker like his wife? Maybe he's on dope.

The pressure became almost unbearable. Merikay and I had joined Christ Episcopal Church, where she had been baptized and married to Whit Duncan. The minister preached good sermons. Merikay would pull herself together, and we'd get there, sooner or later, most Sundays for the eleven o'clock service. Lance usually went with a pal to the Congregational Church a mile away.

One night a swift, painful illness seized me. Throughout two long days of indescribable suffering I fought to keep my promise to God that I would rely on Him for healing. I prayed. I rebuked Satan. Finally a worried Merikay insisted I go to the hospital. She pointed out that I could have faith in the hospital, and with more comfort.

But hospitals have a way of taking away your clothes, your personality, even your will power. I was concerned that I might yield to professional pressure and break my promise. On the way in the taxi I begged God to give me the strength to keep my word. He gave me a Scripture verse I didn't know, "God is faithful, who will not allow you to be tempted beyond what you are able; but with the temptation will provide the way of escape also, that you may be able to endure it" (I Corinthians 10:13).

At Wesley Memorial Hospital, the chief surgeon examined me carefully. My stomach was bloated like a blow fish. Peritonitis had set in. One intestinal obstruction is enough to kill a person within a day or two. I had four. Not even a hair could pass through. If only I had come in a day earlier. But now it was too late to operate.

How I thanked God. The decision to be operated upon had been taken away from me.

I believe this great promise in Corinthians is why the early martyrs were able to face the flaming stakes, the bloody fury of lions, with a hymn upon their lips. At one with God, exalted far above mere human pain, they never felt the scorching flames or tearing teeth. I shouted, "Hallelujah." The doctor decided to check my mental condition.

By all rules of medical science I should have died within twenty-four hours. Yet I clung to life from one endless, pain-wracked second to the next—for nearly thirty days and nights. During that time I refused all sedatives. I believed God would not permit me to suffer beyond endurance. My mind must be kept clear so I could keep on praying and believing in His divine healing.

With pain-sharpened vision I looked back on my life. It was strewn with regrets. The wreckage of good resolutions. The jagged rocks of selfishness, ingratitude and lack of charity toward my fellow men. The arrogance, the pride, even after I had become a Christian. I begged God to give me another chance.

I relived that vision of the lost souls in the lake of fire, heard their anguished cries. If they could only go back and right the wrongs. If they could only do that which they had failed to do. If only . . . if only . . . if only . . .

Some weeks before, I had sent away for a book by Oral Roberts, *If You Need Healing, Do These Things.* I had completely forgotten about it. But through the providence of God, that little book arrived just the day before I went to the hospital. Through this book God gave me the grace to endure this trial. As I read its vibrant stories of the miracles of healing still performed by Christ today, my faith was renewed.

I began to see that I had been praying wrong prayers most of my life. I used to ask God to answer my prayers whenever He was ready. But God's power is like the electric current in a house. The rooms are dark. Yet the power is always there. When we reach out and touch the switch, the power comes on.

For the first time I understood what Roberts calls "the point of contact." When Jesus spoke the word, the centurion believed, and his sick servant was instantly healed. The spoken word was the point of contact. When the woman suffering from an issue of blood for many years reached out and touched His robe, that was her point of contact with the Divine Healer.

I saw too that my first prayer had been selfish. I just wanted to be healed. But God did not answer that prayer.

Then as the suffering became more intense, I prayed that He would take me home to be with Him. He didn't answer that prayer either.

Finally I came to pray that prayer for which God had been waiting. The prayer of surrender. "Not my will, oh Lord, but Thy will be done!"

Then I was ready for healing. As the miracles of the New Testament came alive for me in the light of that book, I began to feel better. On Easter Sunday I felt so good I began to congratulate myself on being such a good Christian, thinking, me and God, we licked this thing. The doctors ordered my first food in nearly a month. But that night chaos broke loose. The tearing pains came back far worse than ever. Through my agony I cried, "Lord, have mercy, save me!"

Never have I been so humbled. In a flash I saw how much pride I still had.

As I cried out in my soul, "Lord help me," the Gideon Bible lying across my knees opened as if with invisible hands. Like a spotlight the Holy Spirit centered my attention on just one verse. It was Psalm 46, verse 10: "Be still, and know that I am God." Stillness, the beginning of the knowledge of God. Then as if turned by the breeze from an electric fan, the pages fluttered again, to Matthew 28:20, "Lo I am with you alway, even unto the end of the world."

How close the end of my world seemed. Then the pages fluttered again to Hebrews 13:8, "Jesus Christ is the same, yesterday, and today, and forever." God was giving me just the right words to assure me of His presence, His love.

But how could I find His healing power? I cried soundlessly in my soul, "What do I need to do to be healed?"

In answer to my prayer the pages of the Gideon Bible fluttered to James 5: 14, 15. "Is anyone among you sick? Let him call for the elders of the church; and let them pray over him, anointing him with oil in the name of the Lord; and the prayer of faith shall save the sick, and the Lord shall raise him up."

Then came one of those conditions. All God's blessings have prior conditions. *"If he has committed sins, they shall be forgiven him."* I knew that meant repentance, coming to God with clean hands spiritually.

With a tremendous effort I knocked the bedside phone off its cradle. Miraculously, Merikay came on the line thirty miles away. With no thought in mind, I opened my mouth and out came the single word, "Oil." I thought that with my little faith, plus the minister's bigger faith, plus this holy oil and laying on of hands—whatever that was—I could believe enough to receive my healing from God.

My wife thought I was delirious and dreaming about drilling oil wells. She rushed to the hospital to see me one last time before I died. Merikay had been under daily mounting pressure. She had visited me as much as her frail strength permitted, somewhat wobbly, her breath revealing she'd been seeking courage from the bottle. But I loved her for the effort, knowing what a battle she had with fear. In spite of the fact that

LB "couldn't stand that hospital stink," she had come once with Tex, who kept clearing his throat awkwardly, anxious to get back outside to his Havana cigar.

But Merikay was, like me, spiritually illiterate about divine healing. So in His infinite wisdom God used Gerda Anderson, our housekeeper, who understood at once what I meant. They began searching for our priest who, it turned out, was out of the city.

A day dragged by. No minister. No comforting word from anybody. I was a church member. I figured he could certainly get there within a couple of hours. But I decided that any time he came, within the next two days, I would release my faith and accept my healing from God as soon as he laid his hands upon me. My deadline was noon, just forty-eight hours away.

Up until this time someone had been in and out of my room every five minutes—a nurse, doctor or intern. It seemed that every doctor associated with that hospital had been in to see me. I was a freak. I should be dead.

But now the door remained closed. Nobody came in or out. Later I was told a sign had been placed across the door: DEAD—DO NOT DISTURB. Nobody knows who put it up. Nobody knows who took it down.

It was my most severe time of testing. How I longed for a human touch, just the sight of a friend. Merikay had been obedient in calling the minister, but the strain had been too much and she had collapsed. She couldn't drive into the Loop, and LB wouldn't.

But I could not even cry out for help. I was too weak. No one needs to tell you when you are dying. Hour after hour I lay on that sharp knife-edge between life and death. Many times I seemed to drift softly through that invisible veil between the Here and the Hereafter. I was almost through the mist and into the golden glory of the Presence of God where all is brightness beyond imagination, with music no human ear has ever heard, and joy unspeakable. It was like being bathed in an endless sea of love, even as a sponge is in the sea and yet remains its individual self.

That night I had the second vision of my life. I was in heaven and there was a brightness beyond a thousand suns, so bright the human eye couldn't stand it. There was a glory of gold and music that cannot be described. The people had faces shaped like hearts. I recognized friends who had gone on before. Regardless of their age, they all possessed a radiant glow, a youthfulness. And they were so happy. They seemed to move with the speed of light from one edge of infinity to the other.

Another thing impressed me. I had always thought of heaven as being way out beyond the stars. Yet here the other world was close. Those who had gone before into this larger life were so close I could almost reach out and touch them. It was just another dimension. Just as today we sit in a chair, tomorrow someone else. Another dimension, a spiritual dimension. I wondered why the faces were shaped like hearts. Softly came the answer, "Haven't I promised to give all my children new hearts?"

There was a thin mist between this world and the next. Many times I would seem to be sliding through that curtain. I was sliding feet first. Somehow I knew if my head went through, I would be on the other side. I would slide up to the nose, sometimes up to the eyes, but never completely through the curtain.

I yearned to go through. Dying is easy. It is living that is hard. Yet each time I almost slipped through this misty veil, it seemed I was brought back again into the reality of ferocious pain.

Somehow the dark hours of the night passed. At about midnight a strange peace came over me. Later the nurse showed me the telegram that came that night in answer to my wire to my Nazarene friends in Deming for prayer.

WE ARE BELIEVING WITH YOU THAT GOD WILL HEAL YOU WITHOUT AN OPERATION. GOD IS ABLE.

The telegram was signed by my bookkeeper, Ralph Henderson.

Dawn finally came. As the morning bloomed there was still no word from my minister or Merikay. Discouragement pressed me down. Noon was my deadline, the end of the forty-eight hours. I lay staring at the slowly moving clock hands. At last it was about ten minutes to twelve. My faith faltered. Surely God had forgotten me.

Suddenly the door opened. In came a minister. My heart sank. Instead of the priest in whom I had confidence, it was his young assistant. Without even removing his hat or overcoat, the deacon said timidly, "I don't suppose you want me without the holy oil. I've searched all over the diocese of Chicago, but the bishop is away and all the holy oil is locked up. Besides," he continued, "I've never performed the laying on of hands before. I'm not even sure if there's a prayer in the prayer book, or where it is." Anger swelled up within me. Wait till that bishop asked me for a donation! What on earth did they teach them in that seminary anyway?

"I'm not sure it will work, especially without the holy oil. And besides, you're dying," he continued. "So don't get your hopes up. But anyway, if you insist, it can serve as last rites and you can die happy."

My heart hit bottom. The wrong man. No oil. No faith. I don't know how Colonel Glenn felt in outer space, but I felt like an infinitesimal pebble lost in empty silence. I became indignant with God. I had claimed His promise, sent for an elder, and got a junior!

Slowly I realized I had been telling God just how to go about

His business—whom to send, all the conditions I had demanded for believing and being healed. But God had taken these crutches away one by one. The Holy Spirit showed me that it didn't matter about the holy oil, or who the priest was, or whether he had any faith. It was my faith He was interested in. And God gently reminded me that He always sends the right man. The loving kindness of God overwhelmed me. All these weary days and nights I had been scraping together a little pile of faith. Now I realized that it had evaporated.

"Lord, forgive me," I confessed. "I just don't have *any* faith."

It was then the Holy Spirit brought to my mind that rock bottom prayer, the prayer I believe to be the greatest in all the Bible, "Lord, I believe . . . help thou my unbelief."

The Holy Spirit seemed then to say, "If you have faith as a grain of mustard seed and can believe, with no doubts, nothing shall be impossible for you."

I asked the young curate to proceed. He fumbled with the prayer book, and reached out one hand toward my head. I closed my eyes. If Jesus Himself were standing there, I'd be instantly, miraculously healed. The sick had lined the streets, with all manner of diseases, and He had healed every one.

When I felt the touch of his hand on my head, I believed with all my soul, from the innermost depths of me, and concentrated my faith like the flame of a Bunsen burner.

At that moment I felt an electric shock as though I had stuck a finger into a light socket. I lay quietly in awe. The glory of God burst above me, brighter than a thousand suns, gold unlike any gold on earth, shimmering and alive like golden raindrops. Warm, electric, living love.

This glory swept down through me, as though through a funnel, washing the pains from my body. Instantly I began to feel clean from head to toe, in every cell of my body. It was like the clean smell of ozone after the storm. I felt light, weightless.

The young minister was on his knees. The same glorious power of God had knocked his hat off his head, his glasses off his nose. My stomach, bloated like a blow fish, began to shrink before my eyes. All the accumulated poisons of the past weeks began to rise from my body like the morning mist from the ground. The pain was gone. I was being healed!

The young priest picked up his glasses and peered at me. "Do you feel better?" he asked anxiously. "You look better."

I tore the rubber tubes out of my nose and throat and waved them like spaghetti. "Hallelujah!" I shouted. "God has operated on me. I'm healed."

The young minister began shouting loudly, "Praise the Lord!"

I'd never heard an Episcopal clergyman shout that loudly before. Next door was a Jewish patient, a traveling salesman, who used to stick his head into my room every day and try to cheer me up with corny Joe Miller jokes that you couldn't laugh at even if you were healthy. But I appreciated his compassion.

He jerked the door open. "What's wrong? Are they hurting you?"

"God has operated on me," I told him. "It's a miracle."

The Jew ran all over that floor crying out to everybody to come to my room and see a miracle. Just like the parting of the Red Sea. Just like in the days of Moses.

My room was small. But it seemed as though every patient on the floor came—swinging on crutches, leaning on canes. One man came in a wheelchair. How we praised the Lord! The sides of that little, jam-packed room seemed to go in and out like an accordion. Everyone was happy.

In the midst of the celebration came a certain intern whose

oft-announced ambition had been to see me operated on as a medical curiosity.

"All right, Mr. Hammond," he barked. "You're going to die anyway, so the doctors have decided to cut you open and see what you died from."

I waved the tubes at him. "God has already operated on me."

"What did you say?"

"God has already operated on me. I don't need you now."

Shaking his head, the intern called the nurse over and reprimanded her for giving me too much dope. I pulled open my bedside chest and showed him all the unused sedatives inside. He shook his head in unbelief, left, and returned in a few minutes with the resident doctor. The older doctor looked at my chart. The explanation was simple. I was just light-headed from hunger. After all, I hadn't had anything to eat for almost a month.

Both he and the intern started to pull me out of bed onto the cart. Though I was weak from the long illness and the loss of around forty-eight pounds, I grabbed the bedpost and hung on. The young minister pulled me back, as I cried, "Hang on, we had a miracle. Don't let them take it away."

One of the other patients grabbed hold of the minister, and we had a tug of war right there, with me in the middle. Finally the chief doctor began to reason with me.

"You are an intelligent man, an engineer, a college graduate. Don't you realize we are only trying to save your life? Surely you don't believe in this superstition, do you?"

"I was healed," I repeated. "God has healed me." I called on the minister as a witness. Still the doctors scoffed. I didn't know what to say. My mind was a complete blank. But I claimed God's promise, "for I will give you utterance and wisdom which none of your opponents will be able to resist or refute" (Luke 21:15). I knew God would give wisdom.

In faith I opened my mouth. Out came words that had not passed through my mind. "It isn't superstition. It's supernatural."

The doctors conferred together. They would believe a miracle had happened if I would explain what a miracle is, and how God performs it.

So again I opened my mouth in faith, believing God would give me the answer. I heard the words coming out, "You believe in the miracle of birth. Explain that to me and I will explain the miracle of divine healing."

Without a word the doctors left the room. Then the Holy Spirit instructed me to call the doctors back and let them examine me to convince themselves.

For two and one-half hours they poked and prodded, X-rayed me from head to toe, almost took more blood out of me than I had. They couldn't explain it. I was 75 percent cured. But they were also positive I would have a relapse. Nobody ever recovered from this condition without an operation. So they wanted to operate.

Over my protests they put me at the top of the list for an emergency operation first thing in the morning. When they came for me, I was tempted to let them operate. After all, they'd find that God had been there ahead of them. But there'd always be a question. Did God do it? Or man? I wanted God to get all the glory. So I insisted I was healed, but allowed them to examine me again. They decided I was 5 percent better than yesterday.

The next morning they found me 5 percent better than the day before. And the same thing the next morning and the next. On the fifth morning they decided I was 100 percent healed and they would release me. I asked if they were going to list this as a supernatural healing. They replied that this was not the proper medical nomenclature. They would list it as "healing from causes unknown."

But every intern, every doctor and every nurse in that hospital had known of my fatal condition. And every one of them, at least once in their lives, got to see a real miracle.

Before I left the hospital my surgeon, who had faithfully visited me morning and afternoon all those weary days, told me how impressed he was with this demonstration of faith. He never operated, so he told me, without first praying for God's guidance and help. Every morning his first prayer was that God would heal all his patients without recourse to surgery.

"Won't you pray yourself out of business, doctor?" I asked.

He shook his head. "No danger of that. If my waiting room were emptied this minute, it would be filled again within fifteen minutes. There's so little faith in the world. If only men would believe." The surgeon considered this divine healing such an inspiration that he didn't even send me a bill.

Five days after I left the hospital, I sneaked past my much-relieved but still-concerned Merikay, and took the train to St. Louis. I arrived at evangelist Oral Roberts's big canvas tent on the only night they were televising. There I witnessed for the first time what great things Jesus had done for me, how I had come to know Him in His capacity as the Great Physician.

Within six months my own doctor, who had been a confirmed agnostic, accepted the Lord as his personal Savior. He could find no other explanation for my miraculous healing.

Later in talking with the parents of the young minister one day after church, I found out why God had sent that particular man. Some years before, he had suffered severe brain damage in an automobile accident in Milwaukee. For nearly ten days he lay in a deep coma, beyond all medical help. Finally, convinced he was dying, his pastor anointed him with holy oil and performed last rites. To everyone's surprise, forty-eight

hours later the young man rose from his deathbed, completely healed, and walked out of the hospital. Subsequent
X-rays showed not a single crack in his skull. But he had
never told anyone about this miracle. Now his whole ministry changed. He began to hold his own healing services in
church.

God had taken my need, a minus, and the young minister's
need, another minus, and had brought them together to make a
plus.

And a plus is a *cross*.

# 10

# Out of the Pit

Soon after my miraculous healing, Merikay, Lance and I moved into a new ranch house in Glencoe, a Chicago suburb. A ranch house because of Merikay's increasing difficulty in walking caused by her drinking problem.

While I lay dying in the hospital, Merikay had had enough faith to put down earnest money on the house, but not to go ahead with the final closing. "I wanted to be sure you'd be around to mow the lawn and take out the garbage," she explained. "Zookie is just great, but every girl needs a man about the house." She melted into my arms, green eyes clouded. "Promise you won't leave this world before I do. Let's go together."

Life was smoother, more relaxed than in New York or distant Deming. Temporarily stalemated by the Deming situation, I made regular trips south of the border and began a new business importing manganese. This I sold to a large Chicago user. Also I imported barite for the oil well drilling industry in Houston. I knew my wife would be happier in the North Shore area, but I thought that one day when she was freed from her habit and healthy again, we'd go back to the West. I loved the burning sun, towering mountains, and "the vista," as Merikay called it.

We'd moved, all right. But not far enough. Now we were exactly two miles, door to door, from 1015 Pine Street. Close enough for the irrepressible LB to drop by at any hour of the day or night. She always had a good excuse. Her cook, "Marie, the Little French Princess," as we called her after a popular soap opera, sang vigorously but flat in several languages, but was tops as a cook. So she brought or sent luscious, hot dinners to us nearly every night. Lance and I deeply appreciated that, since Merikay seldom had the strength or knowledge to cook. However, she did make the finest scrambled eggs I ever ate. But you can't eat scrambled eggs morning, noon and night.

Ever since that night in Deming when the Holy Spirit had brought me out of the pit, and more especially since I had met Jesus as the Great Physician, I had a deepening desire for Christian fellowship. But nobody at church seemed to love Jesus as I did. Was I, I wondered, the only engineer, the only college graduate, who felt this way? I prayed for fellowship. Of course the little Winnetka Prayer Band was okay once a month. They'd prayed faithfully while I was in the hospital, and in appreciation I joined them. But there are thirty other days in the normal month. With Merikay's worsening condition, I needed something more, had to have something more.

Then one morning our housekeeper, Gerda, told me about an organization of Christian businessmen who witnessed boldly all across the nation about the reality and power of Christ. As she spoke, my heart was strangely warmed. At her insistence I wrote them and was answered by a Demos Shakarian. To me, his name looked like Demon Shakarian. It was a joke. I crumpled the letter and threw it into the wastepaper basket. God had answered my prayers on a silver tray, but I didn't see it because it wasn't in exactly the way, time and place I wanted.

The Almighty is so merciful. A few weeks later in July I was out in our garden enjoying the early morning scent of roses. The doorbell rang and there was Gerda, all dressed up with white gloves and everything. I was surprised because she was supposed to be on vacation. She explained that she always planned her vacation so she could attend the annual convention of the Full Gospel Business Men's Fellowship International. She had come to take me to breakfast at the Sherman Hotel in downtown Chicago. I had promised to attend. But nothing was further from my desire. It was a beautiful summer morning. No sweltering hot Chicago for me! Almost tearfully she reminded me of my long forgotten promise.

*If I refuse to go, maybe she won't work for us any more and then I'll have to stay home all the time and take care of Merikay,* I thought. So I drove to town, planning my escape. I would have a quick cup of coffee, then slip out on the pretext of having some business at my office.

When Gerda told me this group often spent all morning, sometimes the whole day, praising God, the thought turned me off. An hour or two at church once or twice a week was about my speed. But *all day!*

Then I saw how happy these businessmen were to see each other, throwing their arms about each other in a Mexican-type hug. I had never seen such expression of affection among men. I remembered reading how Jesus said, "By this all men will

117

know that you are My disciples, if you have love for one another."

The first cup of coffee turned into a second and a third. Evangelist Tommy Hicks gave an altar call for consecration, for those men to come forward who were willing to do anything, to go anywhere for Christ. I knelt with the two dozen others, mentally qualifying my commitment to go anywhere and to do anything with the stipulation that it be in Cook County and at any time that didn't conflict with something more important.

Then in midmorning, with the sunshine pouring into that ballroom packed with men and women from all parts of the United States, I heard for the first time in my life God Almighty speak through a human voice in an unknown language. I did not realize that this Biblical phenomenon could happen today. Then in beautiful, flowing King James English (God knew I was an Episcopalian.) came the interpretation from someone at the other end of the ballroom.

Hunger for more of God engulfed my being. I asked Henry Carlson, president of the Chicago chapter, how I too could have more of God. Henry belonged to the Pentecostal Philadelphia Church. I had never even heard of Pentecostals before.

"You have to tarry," he replied, giving me the accepted Pentecostal procedure. "Some people tarry an hour, or a day, or a year. One man I know tarried twenty-five years before he received the baptism in the Holy Spirit."

This answer cooled me off quickly. I didn't have twenty-five years to wait. I yearned with all my being for a closer walk with God. In my domestic and business situations I *had* to have more of God. I didn't especially want a supernatural prayer language. It seemed almost too mystical. Yet I was willing to do even this to get closer to God.

So on my knees on our cold tile bathroom floor for an hour every day, I asked God for this baptism in the Holy Spirit. After three long months all I had was stiff knees.

I asked Brother Carlson if he was sure this experience was for Episcopalians. He suggested I attend the following year's convention in Philadelphia where it might be easier to receive this blessing. I wasn't going to waste God's time or mine. I determined I would attend the convention and make that my point of contact. Also I surrendered. If this was part of the package, I was willing to have a prayer language even if I didn't see any point in it.

To make triply sure, I set aside the week before the convention, the week of the convention, and the week after the convention.

As the months passed, trying desperately to take care of Merikay, my business suffered from neglect. Every time I left on a business trip, she seemed to start drinking again.

I protected her all I could, went everywhere with her except the restroom. Pointedly told everybody that we didn't drink. Tried to intercept the smuggled drinks at her mother's.

"Oh," she'd lie breezily, "it's just tomato juice."

Yes, but tomato juice with vodka. One sip told me it was loaded. I took it to the sink and dumped it out. When her mother continued spiking our drinks, I would go to the butler's pantry where the liquor was. If it wasn't locked up, as I had asked, I'd take each bottle and dump its gurgling contents down the kitchen sink.

Red-faced with anger, LB would lunge for me. "Stop! You're pouring money down the sink."

"And you're pouring death into my Merikay."

"She's my daughter. I ought to know what's good for her."

"She's my wife. And I *do* know what's good for her."

So I'd take Merikay, scratching and screaming, home.

There were happy interludes, too. Like the time we went mineral searching in the Four Corners area, with two New York-type friends, Desmond Morris and Arturo Ramos. On the Navajo Reservation we yodeled in the mountain canyons for Indians. How ironic that, after the white man kept pushing the Indians back from their fertile plains into the desert, geysers of rich oil came up in the desert and a dark mineral named uranium came to light. So God protects the innocent.

Merikay was her old, gay self, even changed the words to popular tunes. "Vamos con Dios," the Western music sighed. Merikay wrinkled her nose. "Vamos con *Ramos*," she sang. "That's what we're doing." To the tune of "Hidalgo's Hideaway" she improvised "Desmondo's Hideaway."

Spring came. I flew back from Albuquerque, where I was busy on a new mining deal, to find Merikay's eyes as beautifully green as ever, but sightless. Nerve damage from too much alcohol, the doctor said. The optic nerves were destroyed. Merikay would never see again. I refused to accept that verdict. In fact the doctor told me she'd only last a day or two because every organ from her stomach down was paralyzed.

"Put it in writing," I told him.

"Why?"

"Because I'm going to pray right now and ask Jesus to heal her . . . "

The self-admitted greatest eye specialist in the Chicago area looked at our doctor and made a little revolving sign next to his head with his fingers. But he scribbled out his diagnosis as I insisted and tossed it to me contemptuously.

So I got down on my knees beside her bed. I knew I had to pray out loud. It was probably the hardest prayer I had ever prayed. "Lord," I cried from the depths of my anguish, "You raised me from a deathbed in this very same hospital. What You did for me, You can do for Merikay. I'm asking You," I took a deep breath, "and I'm *thanking* You now for restoring her sight." Another deeper breath. "Either with or without the optic nerves."

"Faith is a wonderful thing," our own doctor said as the Jewish specialist left. Our doctor was the same one who'd come to know Jesus through my miraculous healing the year before. "It'll help you when you lose your wife. But her eyesight isn't so important. In a day or two she'll be dead of paralysis."

I asked God for some confirmation of His healing. As I rose from the bedside of my love, words came out of my mouth that had not passed through my mind, "On the morning of the tenth day," I heard myself saying with shock, "that girl will walk through this doorway."

Meanwhile I phoned every prayer group I could think of, including the Prayer Tower at Oral Roberts University. And I wrote Dr. Norman Vincent Peale, asking him to hold Merikay up in corporate prayer that Sunday.

It was late Sunday afternoon when Merikay gave a little gasp, "I can see light . . . I can see light!" Then she pointed to where the sun was setting in a blaze of red glory. "Over there." She almost screamed it out. "Right over there. Oh, Laurie, the sun is going down!"

Within twenty-four hours her sight had returned.

However, Merikay steadfastly refused to recognize that there was a God or that He had miraculously healed her and restored her optic nerves. Again I warned her that if she didn't acknowledge His healing power, something worse would come upon her, as the Bible warns.

In early summer she became disoriented, hardly knew where she was. Or even who she was. More secret drinking. Every time I discovered one source of supply and stopped that, she'd find a new one. Even got one department store to

121

bring her a case of liquor along with other merchandise. I watched every delivery, eavesdropped on her phone calls. Still bottles turned up among the piled up bathtowels in the closet, under her bed, under her pillow, under everything. I nearly went out of my mind. Yet I couldn't stay home twenty-four hours a day. I had to earn a living. Try as I would, I couldn't go without sleep night after night.

Through our compassionate Christian doctor, we made arrangements to hospitalize Merikay at the Milwaukee Sanitarium seventy miles away. I tried to convince her to go, for her sake, for my sake, for our sake. Finally through her love and trust in her lifelong friend, Wally Gibbs, who ran the local gas station, Merikay allowed him to drive us there. All the way she nestled in my arms, only to suddenly flare up from liquor-induced drowsiness and accuse me of trying to "put her away for life."

The sanitarium was the locked-door type. Merikay resented it furiously. She railed at me every weekend when I would drive the one hundred fifty mile round trip through molasses-slow traffic. They dried her out over the weeks, built her up through good nutrition. I refused to allow them to use electric shock or chemical treatment. Merikay confided in me that the women in her building became so nervous that they screamed as the time for the shock treatments came nearer. Afterwards their whole personalities seemed to change. They sat around drab and listless, their minds wiped clean, hardly knowing who they were. Slowly memory had to be rebuilt. Merikay shuddered when she talked about them.

As a Christian, personally experienced in divine healing, I wanted to depend on Jesus to deliver her again. But the authorities were agnostics. Didn't even have a chapel. Refused even to allow ministers to visit their secluded patients. Finally, I insisted on having Merikay released long enough on Sundays to attend Trinity Episcopal Church in nearby Wauwatosa. At once another patient on her floor—a Roman Catholic to whom it was a mortal sin not to go to mass on Sunday—asked to go with us. Soon I had a little group who had permission to go to church with us each Sunday.

Merikay maintained that the only reason she went was to escape that locked building and "all those creeps." But she refused point-blank to cooperate with the psychiatrists, which suited me. I remembered the words of Bishop Austin Pardue when his psychiatrist neighbor was proudly giving psychiatry the credit for dredging up the past, so that patients knew just why they were the way they were.

"Yes," said the bishop smiling. "You dredge up all that scum, but it floats on the surface of their minds and you can't do anything about that. There was a Man named Jesus nearly two thousand years ago! He did the same thing. But he healed them completely. He forgave their sins."

One day Merikay had flared up when I talked to her about a personal relationship with Jesus. Every time I mentioned the name of Jesus or Oral Roberts she'd become angry.

"Don't you dare ever mention those names around me again!" she cried. "Especially that creepy character, Oral Roberts. Oral," she spat it out. "Sounds like some kind of toothpaste."

So I claimed that great promise in Acts 16:31. "Believe in the Lord Jesus, and you shall be saved, *you and your household.*" Merikay was the most important part of my household. I claimed her salvation. I appropriated this promise. Then trusting God with all my aching heart, I committed her to Him. Of course I desired her healing, wanted the bright golden girl back that I'd married nearly eight years before, the girl of the "extra bong." But would she ever be the same again? The doctors thought that the drinking had caused irreversible damage to her mind. But whether she was healed physically or not, whether she ever came out of that sanitarium, I desired her salvation above everything.

"If I never see her again," I cried out to the Lord, "if she has to live out her life shut away from the world, shut away from me, I'm willing to walk through that Valley of the Shadow. But please, dear Lord, please let her come to know you before she leaves this life."

Although I had planned to attend that Full Gospel Business Men's Convention in Philadelphia, and had set aside the week before, the convention week and the week following, I discovered that all hell seemed set against me.

Business crises lost me the first week. Then new problems getting Merikay into the Milwaukee Sanitarium cost me most of the second week. I missed an airplane connection in Pittsburgh. So I arrived at the Bellevue-Stratford Hotel on the last night. But I was there—and desperate to know Jesus as those people did.

The closing banquet was under way. Fifteen hundred people jammed inside the great ballroom. No seat anywhere. I cracked the door open, like a penniless urchin looking at candy he couldn't buy.

"Thank you, Lord," I said softly under my breath, "for letting me get here in time." But it didn't sound right. My tongue had slipped. I tried again. "Praise God." Again my tongue slipped. I was more fatigued than I'd thought. With an effort to gain control of myself, I said very deliberately, "Thank you, Jesus." Only it didn't come out that way at all. I thought, *Praise the Lord.* Again I heard a string of strange monosyllables. I turned to see who was making these strange noises. I even looked behind me. There was no one near me. Sounds that hadn't passed through my mind began pouring out of my mouth. "La-ba-ma."

*This is impossible*, I thought. *I'm perfectly conscious.* I determined to speak in English. Nobody or nothing was going to take control of my speech mechanism. *Praise God*, I thought. Out of my lips came, "La la." *Thank you, Jesus*, I thought. "A ma," came out. *Hallelujah*, I thought. That's the same anywhere in the world in any language. Out came, "Ma la-a la."

I simply could not speak English or French or Spanish or Latin or any other language I knew. The soft mellifluous sounds rose up like a fountain from deep within me. I remembered what Jesus had said, "From his innermost being shall flow rivers of living water."

A cork had been pulled, releasing my deepest unspeakable yearnings to be one with God. Joy flooded my whole being. Love saturated my every fibre. The peace of God that passes all understanding filled me to overflowing. Warm oil descended upon me like a mantle, saturating every cell within me.

As this lovely river of rippling sounds flowed upwards from my innermost being and gushed out of my lips, I knew that God Almighty had answered my heart's desire for the baptism in the Holy Spirit. But I had been seeking God, the giver of every good and perfect gift—not a prayer language. For about twenty minutes this supernatural glory enveloped me, within and without.

I strode quickly to where Oral Roberts was standing beside Demos Shakarian, the man with the funny name.

"Brother Demos," I gasped with Episcopalian dignity, "I've just been baptized with the Holy Spirit."

He looked at me unbelievingly. "You have? I didn't hear any noise."

From Oral Roberts came a word of wisdom. He pointed to the floor where a number of desperate souls were seeking the baptism by thumping each other on the back and shouting,

"Glory, glory! Glory to God! Hallelujah!"

"Brother Demos," he admonished, "it grieves my spirit to see all this striving and straining and clamoring. The Holy Spirit is represented by a dove. And a dove is a quiet, shy bird. I wonder sometimes if we don't frighten Him away with all this confusion. I believe our brother has received. The glory of God is all over him."

Until that night I had only loved about five people in the world. And I was Number One and Number Five. But from that moment I have loved everybody I meet. God is love and if we let His love flow through us, we can't help loving everyone. Before this my witnessing had been limited to dropping a tract surreptitiously on an empty bus seat, and getting off at the next stop. But from that night I have been able to help many come to know Jesus in a personal way.

This experience did not make me as good as anyone else—and certainly no better—but it did make me a far better witness than I had ever been before. From a zero I became something.

But I forgot to ask God for the gift of wisdom. I rushed to the phone in my hotel room and put in an emergency call to the sanitarium to share the good news with Merikay.

"Snuz," I exploded with joy, "I've just been baptized with the Holy Spirit."

"But you were baptized as a child in church."

"But this is different."

"How different?"

How impossible to share with my darling, who had not yet been born again.

"And I spoke a language I don't know."

A deep silence. "A language you don't know." Another pause. "What does it sound like?"

So I made my second mistake. I prayed in my language.

"A language?" Merikay scoffed. "Where's the grammar? Where's the syntax?"

Silently I beseeched the Lord. "Where's the grammar? Where's the syntax?"

"Why you know real languages," my wife continued indignantly. "Why that 'La-maa' stuff is only baby talk." She shot me down. "You know better than that. You'd better hurry back and trade places with me. You're the one who belongs in this crazy house, not me!"

But as the days went by, I discovered that I had new strength, new power to live for Jesus.

As Merikay pressed me harder and harder to "get me out of this hell-hole," I thought of getting her a television set, but delayed. Her treatments were expensive, although her parents were generously bearing most of the cost. I argued with myself that there was a beautiful big TV set downstairs in the public living room. Why should I spend money on a set just for her room?

Over the next few weeks I came to realize that the Holy Spirit was talking to me about getting Merikay a TV set. I gave in and bought the cheapest one I could find. Merikay was delighted. "Now I can look at that gorgeous 'Variety Show' without having to trek all the way downstairs and sit with those slobbering, mindless creeps."

She had a big corner room on the second floor with a view of the surrounding woods. There were hippitty-hopping rabbits and strutting Chinese pheasants—so many feathered minstrels to watch.

Sunday afternoons, after we returned from church and ate together, I would start driving my seventy-five traffic-choked miles back to Glencoe. Merikay warm-heartedly invited the other women on her floor to join her in enjoying the new TV set. They'd gossip, smoke the air blue, and sew. And they always watched "Variety Show."

Unknown to me, right afterwards Oral Roberts came on. Of course they turned him off quickly. Then one afternoon a catatonic type, who always had sat there staring blankly, protested. So they left Oral Roberts on, even though his words were drowned in a sea of chatter.

One Sunday a few months later, while having breakfast together, Merikay suddenly turned to me. "What about your friend, Oral Roberts?"

I flinched inwardly, anticipating an outpouring of verbal lava.

"What about him?" I parried, with what I hoped was an innocent look.

"Didn't you tell me he's having a crusade in Rockford this summer?"

"Yes."

"Isn't it in August?"

"Yes." I became even more guarded.

"Isn't it this week?"

"Yes."

She turned toward me, her green eyes sparking dangerously. "Aren't you going to take me? Or were you just lying to me as usual?"

I rushed to the administrative office, told them I wanted them to give her a pass for the weekend. When I told them why, they stared at me as if I'd lost my mind.

"An Oral Roberts crusade!" they exclaimed. "In a canvas tent? In a crowd of fifteen thousand? Absolutely not—she'd die of shock."

"She won't die of shock," I insisted. "God will heal her."

More arguments, more refusals. If I took her on that crazy trip, I'd be signing her death warrant. No way! I insisted.

If I took her out, they said, I could never bring her back again.

"I'll bring her back," I promised, "to show what God can do!"

It was a long drive to Rockford. Part of the way it rained. Most of the way Merikay kept taking precious time out for comfort stops. She picked her way through dinner at the Faust Hotel as if she had all night. Every time I urged haste she countered with an indignant, "Do you want me to get indigestion? This is the first decent meal I've had outside that crazy house. Let me enjoy it."

Months afterward she told me that the only reason she had agreed to go was to escape the sanitarium. It was getting later and later. The big tent, I knew from past experience, filled up hours before the service. We were already late when we finally found a parking space a good half mile from the tent. It had rained that day. The night was black and the parking area full of stones. We slowly stumbled along. Merikay was so weak I half carried her.

The canvas cathedral was overflowing. A ring of people three thousand thick stood outside.

"Dear Lord," I prayed silently, "make a way for us. Just like You opened up the Red Sea for your children. She'll never be able to hear. There are no loudspeakers outside. Help us get inside the tent."

Silently, without a word, people stepped aside, making an aisle straight to the tent. Now we were inside. I was propping Merikay up.

"Lord," I prayed again, "she'll never be able to stand through this service. Can't she have a seat—somewhere?"

Instantly, as if a button had been pushed, a baby on the middle aisle began to cry. His mother glanced at me, picked the little boy up, and came right over to us.

129

"Your wife seems tired," she said gently. "Would you like to sit in our seats while I take my baby to the restroom? I'll be right back, but at least you'll be comfortable for a few minutes."

They never came back. They must have been angels. So there we were on the middle aisle, halfway back, in the center of the great tent. "Thank you, Lord. Now please give Roberts a message on faith that will stir Merikay's heart. Whatever happens, whether she's healed or not, I want her to know You."

So Roberts preached about an old woman named Sara who became a mother for the first time at the age of ninety. The minister began his altar call.

"Lord," I prayed desperately, "move on her heart with Your Holy Spirit."

A second time he gave the invitation. And a third. Merikay gave me that familiar sharp elbow in the ribs. "Aren't you going forward?"

*I already did that once before*, I thought indignantly. *Well, what difference does it make whether it's in front of fifty people or fifteen thousand people?*

I started down the tanbark aisle. Suddenly Merikay reached out impulsively and grasped my coat. "Aren't you going to wait for me?"

My heart nearly burst with gratitude to God. He'd done it! He'd done the impossible! Tenderly I half-carried her towards the platform. I looked around at the people in overalls and faded housedresses. Had the Lord forgotten that we were proper Episcopalians? "Lord," I prayed, "I know these are Your people. But couldn't You have an Episcopalian—or anyway someone who *looks* like an Episcopalian down there at the altar?"

When we got there we found an old black man with a broken

leg and a crutch .... and a fat, sweaty woman in a housedress so faded it was almost transparent. It had rained hard that afternoon. There was a little puddle in the mud. In her mink jacket, Merikay and I, arms tight around each other, knelt together.

Like lightning the power of God shot down upon Merikay, making her completely whole in body, mind and soul. The results were almost unbelievable. My heart nearly burst with joy.

After a long weekend I took her back to the sanitarium. The doctor rushed out. "Don't bring her back here!" he cried. "I warned you what would happen to her!"

"And I told you what would happen to her," I said smiling. "Just see how Jesus healed her!"

They shook their heads in unbelief. They wouldn't commit themselves until they had had a chance to observe her and make tests. I refused to leave her in the hospital. People, I had noticed, often lost divine healing in the midst of unbelievers.

Life was so much sweeter now that Merikay was back home again. We had a great time together, the three of us. Then all too soon, summer school was over, and Lance had his diploma. He was eighteen. The ambition of his life was about to be realized. He was off to join that elite group, the United States Marines. Merikay cried a little, and his eyes were moist, and I wiped away a furtive tear. Then like a sudden gust of wind he was gone. And a large part of both our hearts went with him.

Soon after my miraculous healing in the spring of 1957, I had read an article in *The Reader's Digest* about the Order of St. Luke, an international, inter-racial organization dedicated to the restoration of divine healing in churches today.

"Why couldn't I have known about this before my experience?" I asked God.

And He seemed to reply, "Because you're the kind that

has to learn something by personal experience."

Although much stronger since the Oral Roberts crusade, Merikay was still not giving God the credit for her conversion and healing. Nor was she witnessing. I urged her to tell others so she wouldn't lose her healing. At least she was no longer drinking, and she had accepted Jesus as her Savior. I urged her to come with me and attend an Order of St. Luke conference in Philadelphia. It proved to be a wonderful experience for us.

But Merikay's healing progress seemed to have stopped. She was still weak, wobbly and gaunt. One day at the altar rail I had been crying out to God.

It seemed that every time I prayed for Merikay's complete healing, she seemed to get worse. "Why, Lord, why? Could there possibly be something in me you're dealing with?" I asked one day. I'd learned that God often speaks to us about something unpleasing to Him in our life, through the suffering of our loved ones. It's a real attention-getter!

Well, now He had my attention. I heard a voice say, "Look in the mirror." At first I thought it was my friend, Dr. Bill Reed, who'd been praying at the altar rail. But the church was empty.

Right there in front of my eyes a scroll unfolded with a dozen words, one beneath another. The first was *martyr*. What a martyr I'd been all these months! Trying to take care of our son, manage my business, and help Merikay. And what *self pity!* Next was *judgmentalism*. Oh, I hadn't hit her as often as I'd felt like it. And I was proud that I'd not said the hurtful things churning in my heart. But, oh, the thoughts. On my knees the Lord showed me that thoughts are worse than words or acts. On they go, unable ever to be recaptured. All we can do is send some good thoughts after the bad ones. But the damage is already done. He showed me that Merikay had sensed every dark thought I'd had about her. It took me weeks to pray these all out of my life. When I did, the full healing that was there all the time manifested itself, like a bud opening up into a flower. It was a shock—and a relief—to realize that *I* had been the block to her full healing.

# 11

# Together . . . but Apart

They say a man would rather be considered a murderer or a thief than be laughed at. That's me all over. It seemed as though my Merikay's sharp tongue skinned me alive, day after day. It had been bad enough when I had known Jesus as my Savior, and she had not. But now that I had come to know Him as the Great Baptizer, and she had not, it was far worse.

Things got so bad I took to praying in my prayer language in the bathroom with the shower turned on full blast. Even then with an uncanny sixth sense she'd jerk the door open and catch me, open-mouthed, causing a spiritual hemorrhage. I knew this experience was of God. Yet doubts began to creep in. And those fiery darts of the devil punctured the balloon of my joy. It began to leak through countless pinholes.

I asked God to let me meet just one other person—man,

woman or child—who spoke this same unknown language. Just anybody, anywhere. But *soon*, Lord, let it be *soon!* The months dragged by.

The oil well drilling business suddenly fell off about 50 percent. That practically put me out of the barite importing business. And Merikay's rebellious refusal to give God any credit for her release from the sanitarium grieved me deeply. The Holy Spirit kept urging me to tell her that something *still* worse would come upon her if she didn't witness to God's power. She just scoffed at me as a "religious fanatic."

Also, Lance, away in the Marines, was becoming disillusioned. "Those D.I.s," he wrote once in a hastily scribbled note from boot camp, "Dad, they're the living end. When you swat one of those mosquitoes that cloud around us, they ask you to tell its sex. It doesn't matter whether you say male or female, they always say you're wrong and mark you down for special guard duty. Tripoli, my neck! They forgot to put Parris Island in that song!"

There was the worry about our son. Alarming newspaper stories about a careless D.I. leading a squad of raw recruits into a swamp from which a dozen never came back.

Now the worry because there was no business. And there was the worry caused by Merikay's doting mother.

LB kept suggesting that the simple answer was for me to get a job "and start supporting my daughter in the style to which she's accustomed." There were bitter remarks made in front of friends or strangers, or anybody, about how much money the Howards had put into my "get-rich-quick-Wallingford" schemes. What a promoter I was! Dick's campaign against me was paying off. *How he must be snickering,* I thought, *as he sees how everyone's turning against me.*

"God," I cried in the darkness of the night, "are you going to let him get away with it?" Of course I prayed for his soul every day. My last encounter with him was in his New York eyrie, when he had fired me illegally from the board of directors for single-handedly raising the couple of thousand dollars that saved our mining lease from being canceled. I had told him I detested his unethical conduct, but I loved him in Jesus and was going to pray for his wicked soul every day, that he would come to know Jesus, too.

He had foamed at the mouth, leaped from behind his desk and tore the air between us wordlessly. "I forbid you to pray for me!" he raged.

But I prayed, almost every day. Most of the time between gritted teeth, "Lord, give me love for the unlovely!"

Then Merikay, healed by the magnificent power of God, but still ungrateful, turned again to the bottle. LB encouraged her. "Doctors!" she scoffed vigorously, "What do they know about it? Even if Merikay had a problem, which of course she doesn't, the psychiatrists advise treating such people in a normal way. They say you should keep on serving drinks to your guests. After all, people expect to have cocktails when they come to my house."

"Yes, but they don't advise you to sneak drinks to your alcoholism-prone daughter."

"Just one won't hurt her." A baleful glance at me. "After all, with a no-good husband like you . . . "

She'd talk right over me like a tractor going full blast when I'd remind her that the family doctor had warned that even a teaspoonful was enough to set Merikay off on another drinking bout.

Sometimes our verbal battles became so fierce I wondered how a Spirit-filled Christian like me could completely lose his cool. Almost to the point of hitting LB. The dark thoughts that flooded my mind! Constantly I fought for control over my thought life. Nor did I always win. I used up my fair share of

God's wonderful forgiveness. Jesus who always has His tender hand stretched down to lift us up again. To forgive, to forget.

So it was with desperation that I seized the sudden invitation from my new friend, Henry Carlson, to go with him and a small group of Full Gospel Business Men on a crusade in the Caribbean. The group would accompany the famous evangelist and pioneer in divine healing, William Branham.

Perhaps in the day by day exposure to Spirit-filled Christians, Merikay would find final deliverance from the bondage of alcohol. And of course there was always the fear of cancer, the monthly mounting apprehension, the inner fear she fought to conceal.

Not quite realizing it was anything more than a pleasure jaunt, Merikay pulled herself together enough to make the trip. Barely.

The first night we wandered through the lush gambling rooms of the Carib Hilton ("Why couldn't we have stayed at an elegant hotel like this instead of that crummy, second-rate dive your creepy friends put us in?"). And we visited the Rose of Sharon Orphanage run by big-hearted blonde, Sally Olsen. Now Merikay's slender store of energy was exhausted. She kept to her hotel room during the crusade, in another world. A world of fog and nameless, haunting terror. If she could only realize that, instead of helping, the alcohol only made matters worse. Her drinking seemed so senseless. If only she would come to one of the meetings. If only she could see the power of God in action. Why, one night about nine hundred blind and deaf Puerto Ricans had stood to their feet in the midst of the meeting. They were healed instantly as Branham, under the power of the Holy Spirit, called upon them to stand and receive their healing.

Sometimes I could prevail on Merikay to go swimming on the sunswept beach beside the hotel. But more often she clung to the darkness of her room, shades drawn, covers pulled up to the tip of her nose, now swollen from drink.

Days were something like hell. Nights in the open air meetings with William Branham came close to heaven. My job was to help make a way for him through the crowds. He didn't even know my name. Didn't know I was married. Didn't know my wife was in Puerto Rico. Or that she was deathly ill in her hotel room. It was an iron-clad rule that nobody should speak to him either just before or just after the meetings. He often staggered away, exhausted from praying for the sick.

Now on the last morning the ministerial association of San Juan gave a farewell breakfast for us. William Branham preached about Zaccheus, the little tax collector who had climbed the sycamore tree to see Jesus. I was sitting at a table directly in front of the speaker's table. Suddenly I began to see queer green diamond shapes on the white tablecloth. Thinking perhaps that migraine, of which I had long ago been healed, was trying to come back on me, I got up and went to the rear of the banquet room. I had forgotten to take a picture of William Branham during the crusade. So I raised my camera by the door where I wouldn't interfere with his preaching.

Suddenly he broke off and said, "I feel the spirit of prophecy coming on me." He pushed away his veteran interpreter, Frank Hernandez, who interprets for Billy Graham, Oral Roberts and other evangelists. Then he jerked to his feet a young man sitting nearby and had him interpret. I wondered why because he was not a very good interpreter.

"There's a man sitting here this morning," Branham said slowly, "whose son is the victim of epilepsy attacks. He is pray-ing for this son who is beyond the sea. Every time this man gets into an evangelistic campaign, the devil puts an epilepsy attack on his son and he has to return home." His voice rose com-mandingly. "But now, at this very instant, that demon power is broken in the name of the Lord Jesus Christ. Be *free!*"

A rather stolid Norwegian who had driven the evangelist every night to the meetings, rose up from his seat, clapped his hands to his head, and fell to the floor with a shout, as though he'd been hit by a sledge hammer.

"There's another man here this morning," Branham continued, "who's praying for his wife who is lying near death in a hotel nearby."

Startled, I looked at Branham to see if he could possibly mean me. He looked blind. Between us and above our heads I saw a blue-green oval cloud in the air. I remembered that this is the way Branham has often described how he sees the Holy Spirit manifested where there is strong faith among the people present.

Suddenly it was as if some gigantic flash bulb exploded inside me. The force knocked me off my feet. My camera went in one direction. I sprawled across the floor in a skid that took me perhaps fifteen feet from where I had been standing. The feeling I had was of absolute cleanliness, holiness.

Like the time I had been healed by the power of God in Wesley Hospital.

From a long way off, as if under water, I could hear Branham saying, "His wife is the victim of a horrible disease. But God is going to heal her. And the healing will be manifest in the fullness of His time."

As I got to my feet, to my surprise I found that my hands were not the least bit dirty. I did not even have a skin bruise. I felt light, as though my feet were about a yard off the ground. In fact, for the next twenty-four hours my body had no feeling. I had to watch with my eyes as I planted my feet, as if in a dream, and as I turned the doorknob, moving my hand as my eyes directed.

"There's another man here," continued Branham, "who's

140

been praying for his daughter. She's been mentally afflicted by Satan for nineteen years. But she is now free and healed."

With a loud shout Frank Hernandez whirled like a top and fell on the floor. Later we learned that this daughter, unknown to anyone but his wife and himself, had lived with them all that time, hidden away from the world.

Unable physically to attend the Branham meetings in which I had prayed she'd find immediate deliverance, Merikay did make some of the dinners with our group. Even fellow Christians can be harsh at times. As I steadied Merikay, often wild-eyed and wobbling from drink, I overheard biting comments about any woman who would disgrace herself that way in public. And how inconsiderate of her husband to embarrass the group. But when Merikay, my love, summoned up the courage to join us, how could I further hurt her sensitive soul by telling her she was in no condition to appear in public? Instead, praying under my breath all the time, I tried to act as though nothing was wrong and she was the lady she really was at heart.

Merikay was a truly sensitive spirit. So many alcoholics are. Sensitive, fragile spirits so easily bruised by this world. Perhaps that's why so many artists and musicians turn to alcohol as a solace and escape. But she tried! Only God knows how she tried!

One afternoon she even pulled herself together and went with us to the penitentiary where our missionary friend, Sally Olsen, ministers . When the fathers are put away, she gathers the children, abandoned by their mothers, into the Rose of Sharon Orphanage. In daily visits she keeps the fathers informed with little pictures and crayon sketches.

Warmed by Sally's love, Merikay sat in the chapel with a few of our group, Demos Shakarian and his wife, Rose, and Henry Carlson. Inside she might have been shaking with the hang-over of the night before and the quick pick-up drink before we left the hotel, but outwardly she appeared calm and alert. With the depth of compassion that comes from prolonged suffering, Merikay identified with these men who might never walk again through sunlit flowers. Or feel the ocean's breeze. Or the lips of a loved one on their cheeks.

The last Sunday was the spiritual pinnacle of the whole trip for me. Again Merikay was in no shape to come with me. For many months I had been fighting off the leading of the Holy Spirit to lay hands on the sick. I'd joined a weekly prayer group at our new home church, St. Elisabeth's, and we prayed for the sick by Christian name alone. We never knew what the problem was. Only our minister knew.

But me lay hands on the sick? I was too much of an engineer, too much of a stiff Episcopalian for that. But I had finally asked God to confirm to me if He really wanted me to lay hands on the sick. Then this sudden invitation to go on my first healing mission. The group hadn't trusted me as mature enough to give a message, so they sent me along with Paul Wichelhaus, who was more experienced.

Only the Lord sent his taxi to the wrong part of San Juan, and I ended up alone at the first Pentecostal church I'd ever seen. It was plain inside like a box. No cross. No stained glass. Not even a real pulpit. A big bass drum and two trumpets instead of an organ. And the minister was a woman.

I'd never seen a lady preacher before. I kind of agreed with St. Paul about women keeping silent in church. She embarrassed me by asking me to "give the message." I declined. Then she asked me to give the altar call. I explained we just didn't do that in the Episcopal church. Her question stung me, "Can't you do *anything* for the Lord?"

I offered to give my testimony. At the end my mind finished

telling my lips what to say. But my voice went right on. With a shock I heard myself saying, "If anybody needs healing for body, mind or spirit, come forward." Urgently I asked God to heal them all right where they were in the pews. When I opened my eyes forty men and women had surged forward.

I asked the Lord to make the first one something simple like a sore tooth, or a headache, something I could believe for. But a deaf mute came first. In desperation I inwardly threatened to throw my Bible away and never set foot in a church again if God did not instantly heal him.

And God performed the impossible when we laid our hands upon him. God enabled him to hear and speak for the first time in his life! Every one of those sick and suffering people received healing at the touch of Jesus. Paralysis, heart attack, cancer . . . . I thought of the Scripture telling how the dying and diseased lined the streets, and of those magnificent, ringing words, "and Jesus came. And He healed them everyone."

He did not heal the one woman, however, who had no faith but said belligerently that she had come forward because "everybody else is being healed. Why not me?"

But through her reaction, the Holy Spirit gave me the reason why many are not healed. I didn't know this verse, but later found it in the eleventh chapter of Hebrews. "He who comes to God must believe that He is, and that He is a rewarder of those who seek Him."

I sighed deeply. "God, You've healed others through me. Why not the one I love most in all the world, Merikay?"

# 12

# Yes, Lord?

Weeks had passed since our return from Puerto Rico. My faith to believe God for His best had flowered. I began to think I could believe God for anything. Or anyone. But why did I have so much trouble believing God for delivering Merikay?

These thoughts troubled me as I sat at the breakfast table that snowy morning. Merikay sat slumped in the pink bathrobe that had been her uniform for several years. I loathed the sight of it. She wore it day and night, seldom took it off unless we were going out. And we rarely went out. Except to Sunday dinner at 1015 Pine Street. Sometimes she made it to church with me, but most times not. Usually I sat right under the preacher's nose in the first pew, soaking in spiritual strength for the ordeal that seemed to go on endlessly.

And nobody seemed to understand the depths of our suffering. Or even care. The preacher was a good man, and once in awhile he'd pay a house call. His youngest son, Billy, adopted Merikay and always sat between us, snuggling into her fur coat. His love made Merikay feel needed and important. They had a real affair going. After service we'd have a penny hunt. There was an old, broken-down safe in the church basement back among the cobwebs. We made up a game. By sticking pins into a lock for which there was no key, a penny, or pennies, which Merikay and I had previously planted, would come clinking out.

Many months later the minister asked Merikay if he could borrow Billy back from her. He needed him in the choir. But even in the choir the love affair went on. Billy winked during the sermon and when he passed our pew in the processional, he'd reach out and pat Merikay's sleeve lovingly. When Merikay fell and broke an arm, Billy fell and broke his arm months later. He smiled up at her when she visited him in the hospital.

"Gosh," he sighed happily, "you and I do everything the same, don't we, Merikay? We even broke the same arm."

One friend at church, an investment banker who had found God and deliverance from alcohol through AA, tried his best to help Merikay. But she steadfastly refused to admit she had a drinking problem. Then I realized that our preacher really loved Merikay. That love touched her. Our families would have picnics together on rare occasions. Strangely enough, LB liked these people too, and would take us all swimming at the Glenview Country Club on hot summer days.

"Father Baar," she'd say over and over again, "I want you to preach my funeral service. You're the only minister I can stand."

He was able to love Merikay, without condemnation,

unreservedly. But he seemed unable to tap Jesus' power to deliver.

It was time for me to end this early morning reflection and catch my train for my office in Chicago. Yet a strange impression came over me that I would get a long distance telephone call. I tried to shrug it off, but the strange feeling persisted. Thoughtfully I stirred my coffee. Merikay urged me to get started. The road to the station would be slippery. It seemed wise not to tell her of my strange feeling. She didn't believe the Holy Spirit speaks to people today. Not to me anyway.

So I dawdled, asked for another cup of coffee. For years I had taken only one. I thumbed through the paper again. Finally Merikay pointed accusingly at the wall clock. I had missed my train. Yet no phone call. Just a silly idea. Now I had an hour's wait for my next train. Just then the telephone shrilled demandingly. A strange tingling sensation swept over me. Something wonderful was about to happen.

"You don't know me," a soft female voice began. "But as I was sitting here in Dallas reading your testimony of how God raised you from a deathbed, I suddenly thought of my best friend's daughter, Jane."

She went on to say that Jane had five small children and was dying of cancer in a hospital west of Chicago. She asked if I'd go and pray for her. She was sure God would heal her if I did.

*If this is you, God,* I thought, *then let Merikay agree right away to go with me.*

So it was that the two of us embarked on the strangest experience of our life together.

When we arrived at the hospital, the receptionist informed us that we were too late. Jane had died. Then the receptionist left the room. At that moment the Holy Spirit seemed to say to me, "Follow Me." Up one corridor and down another, through doors, the Holy Spirit led us. We came to a stop before one door. I knew I was supposed to enter. Merikay stayed outside to wait for me.

There was a single cot in the room. On it lay a silent form covered with a sheet. As I walked toward the bed, I brushed against the dresser. A sheet of paper lay near the edge. The ink was still wet. It was a death certificate.

I read it without any feeling. Then I went to the bed and pulled back the covers. Already the body was stiff and cold as marble. I felt the wrist. No pulse. I looked closely at her throat. No throbbing. There was a small hand mirror on the dresser. I held it close to her lips and nostrils. Even after several minutes, there was no trace of moisture. I put the mirror back.

All during this time I moved slowly, deliberately. I felt an other-worldly calm within. It was as if the Lord were giving me instructions. Just one step at a time. Do this. Do that. Never seeing or thinking farther than the next move.

I took both of Jane's cold hands in mine and prayed a prayer to match my faith. I asked God to restore the woman to consciousness.

Color came to her fingertips, moved slowly up her arms, and finally reached her cheeks. It was as though she were receiving an invisible transfusion. Suddenly she opened her eyes and smiled.

I could hardly believe my eyes. Joy mingled with the inexpressible peace within my breast. Then suddenly I felt humbled, awed. I knew that I had no power in myself. God really had *all* power. How He could restore life to a woman given up by medical science I did not know. But He had done it, before my very eyes. How wondrous to be an instrument in the hand of the Almighty! My only responsibility was to be obedient. To do as the Holy Spirit directed.

"I'm hungry," said Jane.

Joyfully I left the room and shouted to a passing nurse, "Bring some food. Quickly. She's hungry."

The nurse nearly dropped her thermometer. She stared at me as if I had gone mad. My mind was so full of joy at seeing the power of God manifested that I didn't stop to think what a shock it would be to the hospital staff. Here I was, just stepping out of a dead woman's room and ordering dinner for what by all their training was a fully accredited corpse.

Would they drop to their knees in wonder when they saw her?

"You've hypnotized her," cried one.

"You injected her with some chemical."

They practically threw me out of the hospital. Such is unbelief. Nothing will convince those who don't *want* to believe in God.

Jane went back to her home and her devoted family. There her recovery was swift beyond belief. Soon she resumed her duties as wife and mother. Happiness bloomed in that plain frame house in the countryside.

*When,* I kept crying out to God, *will this be for Merikay? When will William Branham's prophecy, if indeed it was from You, come true? When will she be my laughing darling again?*

There was the testing of my patience again. I'd stopped praying for patience when I discovered that every time I prayed, it would be tested. Merikay had begun smoking again. With the keen sense of smell of those who have been delivered from the bondage of nicotine, I noticed it right away. But I asked the Lord to give me the wisdom not to mention it. I tried thanking Him, though there really didn't seem anything to be thankful about. But the Scripture does say to praise God in everything.

Then suddenly one day she burst into the livingroom in a shower of laughter. We had been to early mass. It was Ash

Wednesday and the priest had marked our foreheads according to age-old custom. He made a tiny cross from the ashes of the palm leaves burned after the previous year's Palm Sunday.

"I was sitting at the vanity table," she chuckled, "and when I opened the drawer to get my powder, I found a long-forgotten package of my favorite brand of cigarets. I thought I'd light one up just to see if they tasted as bad as I remembered. Just as I raised the lighted match to the cigaret in my mouth, I glanced in the mirror." She paused. No laughter now. "And I saw the cross of ashes on my forehead!"

That was the end of that. God had taken care of that matter far better than I ever could. "But why don't You take care of the alcohol problem the same way, Lord? Why? Why? Why?" I asked in frustration.

Then Lance swept in and out of our lives briefly again. This time in his Marine's dress blue uniform with the red stripe down the pantleg. Sparkling white cap. Bright, ruddy cheeks. There were new lines in his face. He had been hurt. When you looked deep into his eyes, it hadn't been all that great. But he never mentioned that part.

There was some bright chatter about his Sharpshooter's badge.

"Great, Chief!" I patted him on the back, gave those stiff young shoulders a squeeze.

No response. No emotion. After all he was now a United States Marine. He belonged to an elite outfit. And Marines never show emotion. Well, hardly ever. Something that looked suspiciously like a tear glistened briefly in his eye.

He pulled the peak of his cap further over his nose. "Oh, that," he said, gulping. "That's nothing, Dad. Lots of other guys made Sharpshooter, too." But not, I discovered much later, with 100 percent bull's eyes.

Merikay laughed and joked with him. It was great to see how close they had become. He spent hours in the bedroom with her, sharing all his heartaches and disillusionments. Later, much later as Merikay and I lay in bed, arms wrapped around each other, she would tell me all that she—in her motherly wisdom—thought I should know.

Then he was gone again. The memory of his presence floated in the air for a long moment. All the longing sadness of the night song of the whip-poor-will.

Out of the ache in my heart rose a poem.

*Goodbye, Son . . .*
*For goodbye is the first step toward, "Hello, again."*
*You stood there, bright and shining with all the minted new-*
*    ness of a silver dollar.*
*You wouldn't compromise your art, Son . . .*
*Never compromise your actions or your thoughts or your*
*    ideals.*
*Keep them all bright, shining banners in the world around*
*    you . . .*
*Don't let the world muddy you or dirty you . . . . Your soul*
*    is beyond all mire . . . in the safekeeping of God, the*
*    Holy Spirit.*
*So many words, so many thoughts to share . . .*
*Yet like a giant glacier frozen solid stiff . . . only a trickle*
*    manages to escape . . .*
*Where there is a silent roaring in my heart.*
*Everything in me yearns to throw my arms around you, to*
*    hug you close, to kiss your cheek . . . to pour out the*
*    deep thoughts . . . the warmth of love inside . . .*
*And so, a quick, firm handshake . . . a banal quipped, "Good-*
*    bye . . . Take care of yourself,"*
*And off you go, straight and true as an arrow glistening . . .*
*    speeding through the sunlight . . .*
*"Goodbye" . . . and yet, "Hello, again."*
*And yet sometime . . . somewhere . . . somehow . . . I know it*
*    will be, "Hello, again!"*
*And that is only how it's possible to say . . . "Goodbye, Son.*
*Goodbye, Son . . . ."*

# 13

# Calling Hades

It's steamy hot in Haiti. In the tiny cubicle at the short wave radio station, Haiti's only communication connection with the outside world, I was trying to reach Merikay back at our Glencoe home.

"Hades?" the American operator asked Merikay. "Where's that?"

I could hear Merikay's velvety laugh faint in the distance. "Oh, some people call it Haiti."

"Well, Haiti or Hades. Anyway Hades is calling you."

So for a few fleeting moments of, speak a few words, listen, speak again, my darling got the message.

"Only one out of every four telephones here works," I reported. "I'm talking with the government about installing a modern communications system."

Haiti was just about the first nation in the world to have an automatic dial phone system. It was installed by the U.S. Marines back in the bloody revolution when they had come in to restore law and order. They'd also built highways, hospitals, and public office buildings, including the sprawling "White House" or Maison Blanche; and had trained the proud Garde d'Haiti, the president's elite guard.

But time had passed. Maintenance had deteriorated. When I looked into the Telephone Exchange Building, I found the doors of the sealed glass compartments, in which the delicate mechanism was supposed to operate in vacuum cleanliness, wide open. Worse yet the windows of the room were also thrown wide open, and the dust from the dry, unpaved streets below hung heavy in the air. It was a minor miracle that anything worked.

Then there were the "no-see'ums," almost invisible little bugs whose appetite for metal was insatiable. So many microscopic holes were eaten in the metal cables that the copper wires were severed. All these had to be replaced by plastic, which the microscopic bugs found distasteful. Meanwhile, as the Haitian businessmen would say with a shrug, the useless telephone standing in colorful glory on the desk was an "objet d'art."

Getting things accomplished in Haiti was like walking through hip-deep molasses. In my first interviews with the government officials I made it clear there was to be no *pourboire,* money passed under the table. Together with an experienced U.S. independent company we surveyed the chaotic communications situation, made a presentation. But it had to stand on its own merits.

Merikay had made the first business trip with me to Port-au-Prince. The city nestled whitely—that is, at a distance—beneath towering mountains on whose heights straggly mahogany trees stood out like hairs on a bald man's head. But close at hand Port-au-Prince was something else. Along the waterfront the tumble-down shacks assaulted the visitor's nose with violence. Las Salines smelled like a giant latrine.

That first night in the hotel I felt a great compassion for these gentle, smiling black people. They picked their way gracefully between the holes in the dusty streets, baskets brimful of plantains, grapefruit and mangoes on their heads. Most of the people were skinny as shadows; children big with bloated bellies from malnutrition.

As I sat there the Holy Spirit seemed to be asking me to help these needy people. I asked the Lord to confirm it in His word. But I had lost my Bible, the same Bible I had lost six other times in various parts of the world. It had always supernaturally come back again. But not yet this time.

A thought came to go ask at the desk. The clerk stared at me haughtily. "A Bible? What do you think this is, a church?"

Back in my room, again the Spirit told me to go to the front desk. Again the haughty stare. "No, M'sieur. We have no Bible."

On my knees again in my room the Lord seemed to impress me that somewhere in that hotel there was a Bible. Again I approached the clerk. He was becoming impatient. Behind the desk in a corner I suddenly noticed a package wrapped in brown paper.

"What's that?" I asked.

The clerk shrugged. "It's been here for days."

"May I open it up?"

He shrugged again. "If you wish. It'll save me the trouble. I've been too busy."

Inside were forty Gideon Bibles.

"May I have one of these?"

"After you put one in every room."

When I opened my precious Bible after praying that God would show me what He wanted me to do, it fell open at Galatians 6:9. "Be not weary in well-doing. For in due season ye shall reap, if ye faint not."

So I struggled with bureaucrats who smiled and smiled with gleaming white teeth, and said, "Yes, yes, yes." Only nothing ever happened.

But I made many good friends, especially a fine Christian senator named Artur Bonhomme. He helped every way he could to cut the red tape. But every time we thought we had our communication package neatly put together, it would fall apart at the last moment. There seemed no way to get around the *pourboire.*

So I made trip after fruitless trip to Haiti, always hopeful, always disappointed. Then one fall day in Chicago one of my black friends flew up with the Haitian delegation to the Pan-American Games. He confided to me a "delicate situation." Haitians considered any matter involving money as delicate. The delegation had exhausted their meager funds. They had no money for "uniforms" or dress clothes. They would be unable to participate in the closing ceremonies in which the various delegations would march, national flags held high, around Soldier's Stadium. They would lose face.

So I phoned several Americans who had business interests in Haiti. And the Haitian delegation paraded proudly with the others, all resplendent in newly hired tuxedos. "If we can ever do anything to repay you," swore Andre Rousseau, attorney general of Haiti, "just let us know. Anything. Anything at all!"

Little did I realize that I would be coming to them, hat in hand, within a few months. Through the tireless efforts of Senator Bonhomme, the Full Gospel Business Men's Fellowship International had received a personal invitation from the president, Dr. Francois Duvalier, to come and "evangelize the nation."

Since I personally knew many key Haitian officials, Demos Shakarian, president of FGBMFI , asked me to fly down ahead and make arrangements for the crusade. The biggest place available was an open air theatre which held only a few thousand. The ideal location was the huge stadium with twenty-three thousand seats. But it had never been used for anything but the Haitians' national madness—soccer. So my friend, Andre Rousseau, told me.

"But who's in charge? Whom do I have to see, Andre?" I asked.

"The president of the National Football Association."

"And just who is that?"

*"C'est moi,"* he replied, his chest swelling proudly. I could see he considered this position far more important than his high office of attorney-general, important though that was. In French he explained to his conferees how I had befriended the Haitian delegation to the Pan-American Games. He could not refuse our worthy group this small favor. So we got the huge stadium for half the usual rental.

I flew back as soon as we'd shaken hands on the deal, picked up Merikay and joined the two dozen businessmen and their wives who had converged on Port-au-Prince. The Riviera Hotel was one of the newest and had the largest swimming pool. Mourning doves cooed in the nearby tropical underbrush. Shaggy goats tinkled their way down the mountainside in the early dawn. And all night from midnight on, the gamecocks prematurely heralded the dawn.

But my hopes for Merikay's complete deliverance from alcohol during the crusade were shattered. Day after day she steadfastly refused to attend even one of the nightly meetings.

"It's bad enough to be in this God-forsaken place," she

snorted after a short visit to the great Iron Market. There we threaded our way through the gay merchandise sprawled on the hard-packed ground. It was hot work ducking the clutching, screaming vendors. "But this stink! It's enough to make me throw up from here to yesterday."

Yet she was sweet to our "personal waiter," as gray, shuffling Jeffrey called himself. Then there was a group of ragged urchins she laughingly called my "army." They lay in wait for me at the overseas short wave radio station, knowing I'd be there once or twice a day. Then they'd climb all over my car like a swarm of black ants and ride back to the hotel. Or the stadium. Or anywhere. She lovingly hugged them to her heart, handed out gourds and candy and what they needed most of all—love.

But she never attended any of the crusade. Thousands were healed and delivered of all manner of diseases, but how could my love be delivered when she refused to admit she even had a drinking problem?

One day an old hag was dragged to the stadium, handcuffed to two men. Their muscles bulged with the strain of controlling her. I was giving my healing testimony at the evangelist's request while he went to answer an urgent overseas radio call. At the mention of the name of Jesus this horrible creature snapped those links like thread. As she rushed towards me, I remembered how at dinner a few nights before, the Episcopal bishop of Haiti had told me of the power in the sign of the cross.

"Stop in the name of Jesus!" I cried.

Quickly I made the sign of the cross between us.

"Stop in the name of Jesus!" I cried.

To my surprise she hung there in the air, clutching claws frozen. With the active help of a nearby Haitian preacher, we cast out the seven demons that had bound her for ten years. As a youth, she had been taken to a voodoo witch doctor by her mother. The witch doctor had dedicated the young girl to these demonic spirits. In voodoo the worshippers dance madly under the full moon for hours crying out to various demon spirits to "ride them like a horse." To possess them.

This was my first face-to-face experience with naked demon power. I knew Satan existed. I'd met him that night in the little Nazarene church in Deming. But I really hadn't *believed* in demons. Not till then. I hadn't known how to protect myself by covering myself with the blood of the Lamb.

That night under the bright arc lights, Catherine testified as to how Jesus had set her free from the demons. Thousands were also set free as she continued to testify night after night.

During the three week crusade many thousands of people came to know Jesus as their personal Savior. Several of us had a private audience with President Duvalier, who thanked us for coming to help Haiti. We even held hands in a circle in his ornate office and prayed for the future friendship of our two nations. He remarked at the miracle of that one special night when seven thousand men had come forward and committed their lives to Christ. Among them was the radio engineer who had been broadcasting the crusade. We had bought one half hour for twenty-five dollars—our entire budget. But he became so caught up in the meeting, he forgot to turn the program off and later offered us a bargain we couldn't refuse: he would broadcast each meeting from start to finish, even if it lasted four hours, all for the price of one half hour. We had the longest half hour programs in the history of radio!

Thousands had been healed. Thousands had been delivered from the bondage of alcohol and other evil spirits. But not my darling Merikay. What about William Branham, Lord? What about his prophecy of Merikay's complete healing? Or was it indeed a prophecy? Someone once said, "A prophecy is only an opinion until it comes true. Then it becomes a prophecy."

I became indignant with God. Here I'd been working so hard for Him. Helped set up this mighty crusade. Helped thousands find health and healing and Him. Wasn't the laborer worthy of his hire?

"Haven't you been blessed, my son?"

"Yes, Lord."

"Hasn't it all been My work, My power?"

"Yes, Lord."

Into my mind the Holy Spirit brought words of comfort: "Commit thy way unto the Lord. Trust also in Him. And He will bring it to pass."

"Yes, Lord, but . . . "

"Didn't I deliver her once before? When you stopped struggling and turned her over to Me?"

"Yes, Lord, but . . . "

"Is there anything too hard for me?"

Into my heart came a deep peace. I was to need it in the months ahead. "Yes, Lord!"

# 14

# Prayer Duet

Endlessly, the months dragged on. Lance had finished his active duty and now was attending the Art Institute. From his mother, Maggie, he'd inherited real talent. It was too far, he said, for him to commute by train the thirty miles to Chicago. But I suspected he wanted to get away from our drink-clouded life. Meals were seldom on time, if at all. And everything else was topsy-turvy, and completely unpredictable. He never felt safe having his friends around, with the sudden outbursts of temper, the wild ranting and raving without reason. So he moved into an apartment on Chicago's near north side with a friend. He loved Merikay deeply, but he couldn't stand the constant strain. Often I wondered how much longer I could.

How heavy my cross! Then, as I nearly sank under its

weight, I heard a soft voice whisper, "Don't you think My cross is heavy, too?"

"Forgive me, Lord, for my selfishness." My cross suddenly felt like a feather.

In the fall of 1960 I prevailed on Merikay to come with me to the annual conference of the Order of St. Luke, to which we both now belonged. Headquarters was St. Stephens' Episcopal Church in Philadelphia. I thought gratefully of the joyous experience of the baptism in the Holy Spirit which I received at the Full Gospel Business Men's Convention two years before. What joy it had brought. Yes, and what sorrow. Someone once said that the sign of the baptism in the Holy Spirit is trouble.

Trouble aplenty I'd had with Merikay, who fought this experience savagely. I still had to hide in the bathroom to worship the Lord in my prayer language. "How long, Lord, will it be until You let me meet someone else who has the same prayer language as mine?"

"Soon," He seemed to say. "Soon."

I didn't know whether I could hold out much longer. And Merikay was still concealing her problem, still stumbling and faltering, and still failing. Her healing progress seemed to have stopped. She was still weak and thin.

Then Lance phoned late one night, hardly able to talk. It seems that he had said something unflattering to a neighbor as he pushed past him on the stairs. The drunken man had swung at him with a bottle and smashed his jaw. So for months Lance lived on Sego and learned the wisdom of keeping silent.

This incident upset Merikay, of course. It was another excuse to reach for forbidden fruit.

About this time I went on a speaking tour. Hadn't I promised the Lord I'd witness for Him whenever asked? And wasn't I being asked more and more? However, I was finding it more and more difficult to speak of the victorious life in Jesus while haunted by the turmoil in my own home.

I was sitting in the kitchen of David, my Full Gospel Businessman host, in Baton Rouge, Louisiana one day. With us was a Jewish businessman of some stature in the community. He suffered from emotional and physical problems. He had wealth, but no peace. He had tried to find Christ in the Methodist church, and then the Baptist church. Now in his desperation he was even willing to try the Episcopal church.

As we prayed, David suddenly looked over at me and said, "Don't you think we ought to pray for this brother in the Spirit?"

I knew he meant in a prayer language but I pretended not to hear. I prayed louder in English.

A little later he asked the same question. The Spirit within me told me he was right, but I hurriedly assured him there was no need to. I was afraid of being embarrassed by those pitiful monosyllables. I had often asked God to increase my language beyond the "ma" and "la" when I heard linguistically illiterate brothers and sisters pray in beautiful sentences.

Finally David looked me right in the eye. "You have received the baptism in the Holy Spirit, haven't you?"

I nodded.

"You do speak in other tongues, don't you?"

Again I nodded unhappily.

"Then let me hear you."

The words sank into my soul like a harpoon. I bowed my head and out came the same old "la ba ma da."

No thirteen-year-old girl ever blushed redder than I. A shout of "Hallelujah!" made me open my eyes. Like an echo came the identical sounds I was making. Only these sounds were flowing from David's open mouth.

We prayed in unison, and the sounds tumbled like a musical waterfall. I went fast. David went fast. I slowed down. David slowed down. It was incredible. It was supernatural. The Jew, kneeling there on the floor between us, looked from one to the other like a man watching a ping pong match. He realized that no amount of human planning, practice or coordination could do such a thing. After about ten minutes, he cried out, "Now I know God is real. I accept His Son, Jesus, the Christ, as my Messiah."

Tears of joy streamed down his face. I asked if he wanted us to pray for his crippled leg.

"Oh no," he cried, the radiance of God upon his face. "That doesn't matter any more. I've got healing where it counts." He tapped his heart.

I had the joy of seeing this Hebrew Christian again about a year later in New York. He was active in the Brotherhood of St. Andrew, the evangelical arm of the Episcopal church, a lay reader, and a powerhouse for God throughout the whole state of Louisiana, until his recent death.

On my return home I told Merikay about this supernatural confirmation of my experience, and how that had been a confirmation to David, too. He also had been praying that God would let him meet someone who spoke the same language as his.

Merikay's reaction was typical. She shrugged, totally unimpressed. "So what else is new? Besides, I wasn't there. How do I know it happened?"

I cried out silently in my soul. "Oh, Lord, help me to convince her of the truth—that the baptism in the Holy Spirit with tongues is valid. If it is a known language let me know what it is."

This time the Lord didn't make me wait so long.

Three weeks later, at about two in the morning the Holy Spirit awoke me and led me to a book in the library. It was *The Silent Billion*, by the famous literacy expert, Dr. Frank C. Laubach. I had purchased it about a year before, but had never opened it. Just as the Holy Spirit sometimes leads me to open the Bible to find an answer to a problem, I opened this book to page 35. There were the words, *ma-ma* for man, *a ma*—father, a la—God, *ma la*—large, *la ma* for yard.

The tingling sensation that so often breaks out all over my body when I sense the presence of the Lord burst upon me. I could hardly read the rest of the page because of the joy and praise I felt. It was the Maranaw dialect of the Philippines, language of the fierce Moslem Moros. It was the very first language that Dr. Laubach had ever put into written form.

Again Merikay lifted her nose in disdain. "Oh, you read that when you first bought that book. It just welled up out of your subconscious."

"Lord, you made this woman." I prayed. "What is it going to take to convince her?"

More problems crowded in. Dick, the New York magnate, was turning the screw tighter. In thirty days Florida Manganese would be entirely out of business. No way out. Our fellow directors gave up. Our own lawyer advised throwing in the sponge.

Every day I prayed desperately, "Lord, throw dust in their eyes."

It was all I could think of. At that time it was the "in" thing for wealthy Jewish people to make the trip behind the Iron Curtain into Russia. The head of Dick's legal firm wanted to make this trip. He called in his forty-two lawyers, told them to prepare everything, all the legal papers, but to hold up final action until he returned. Dick was not only his valued client, but a Harvard classmate and best friend. He didn't want any slip-ups. As soon as he returned, he would take charge and see that I was wiped out once and for all.

On his return he called in his forty-two lawyers with all the papers. Now he was ready for the kill.

"Telephone Deming!" he barked. "Call our cooperating attorney."

A few minutes later, a white-faced lawyer rushed up. It was too late. By the mysterious providence of God, the chief attorney had gotten mixed up on his time during his trip. God had indeed thrown dust in their eyes. So we had another chance to fight the take-over scheme.

# 15

# Where There's God's Will ...

For many months the Holy Spirit had seemed to be urging me to undertake an incredible task. I felt God wanted me to go to India and tell Prime Minister Nehru about Jesus. I had many reservations. Billy Graham had met him. Surely he'd told him the good news. Besides I didn't like the man. Never had.

"He's a hypocrite," I told the Lord.

"But I love him, too."

"He's arrogant."

"I love him."

"He's an agnostic."

"I still love him."

"Lord, I don't have the money to go to India."

"I have all the money in the world, son."

"But how do I know he'll even be in New Delhi? He travels so much."

"My son, the times and the seasons are in My hands."

"But Lord . . . my wife is ill. I can't leave her for such a long time."

"My son, lovest thou Me?"

"Lord, You know I love You."

"More than husband or wife or family? More than anything? More than anybody?"

I sighed and got up off my knees. "Yes, Lord. More than anything . . . or anybody. I'll go."

But I had to be sure it was God speaking to me. Gideon in the Bible had asked for supernatural confirmation that he was going to win that big battle against the Philistines. He had only set up two conditions for God to meet. I set up seven. God is still God, I reasoned. He can meet seven conditions as easily as two. And after all, He's asking me to cut out my heart.

About this time a new problem surfaced. Doug, the boy we had wanted to adopt and raise along with Lance, had gone AWOL from the Marines. He was caught and promptly tossed into the stockade. Somehow he escaped. They caught him again. This happened five times. Then an anguished late night phone call came from somewhere on the West Coast.

"Larry," he sobbed over the phone. "The Shore Patrol and the FBI are after me. I won't go back to that stinking stockade. I've got a gun. I'll shoot myself first."

Click. He hung up. I had no idea where he was.

"Lord," I prayed, "send him here to me in Chicago. I don't care if he has to spend the rest of his life in prison. But send him here so I can tell him about You. I want him to spend eternity with You."

I had a great plan worked out. Senator Everett Dirksen was

a good friend. He'd help. And one of the officials of International Christian Leadership in Washington was my friend. There were a lot of strings I could pull.

"Lord," I begged, "You don't want me to leave Doug in a mess like this, do You? I love him as much as my own flesh and blood."

"Don't you trust me?" There was a long pause as the words sunk deep. "I gave my only Son for you." Another pause. "Have you forgotten?"

"No, Father. I haven't forgotten. But it isn't easy . . . "

"I never said it would be, son."

It was the first good night's sleep I'd had in months. I had decided to follow Jesus—all the way. Before I drifted off a Scripture verse floated into my mind: "There is no man that hath left house, or brethren, or sisters, or father or mother or *wife* . . . for my sake and the Gospel's, But he shall receive a hundredfold now in this time, houses, and brethren, and sisters, and mothers and children, and lands, with persecutions; and in the world to come eternal life" (Mark 10:29, 30).

*With persecution!*

I sat up suddenly, wide awake. Oh well, there were still those seven conditions. Somehow I hoped the Lord wouldn't meet them all.

And yet, if He really wanted me to go . . .

Months before, the Haitian communications project had temporarily bogged down in red tape. I had turned to helping Haiti build badly needed highways. The U.S. government had approved a multimillion dollar loan, based on an acceptable engineering feasibility study. So it was that I became a technical consultant to Meissner Engineers of Chicago.

On their behalf I made several trips to Haiti. Eventually the contract between the Republic of Haiti and Meissner crawled towards completion. All that remained was for Haiti to sign. It would be a double blessing. Haiti would be helped and I would make a sizeable commission.

Then one night as I returned home from a late vestry meeting at St. Elisabeth's, Merikay met me with a tear-stained face. "It's Zookie," she sobbed. "He gave me a long look and got out of bed kind of stiffly. I thought, after all he's eleven. That's like being seventy-seven years old." She took a deep breath. "Then he went slowly from room to room, looking around at all his favorite places. Just as if he was saying goodbye to each." She took another deep, quivering breath. "And, oh Laurie, he *was*."

She pointed to the favorite corner by the front door where he always awaited my return, curled in a fluffy ball. His nose was pointed toward my anticipated footsteps. But the usual cheerful bark would never greet our ears again.

Merikay turned to the bottle for solace.

Then the Lord began answering my seven conditions. My first was that somebody should invite me to go to India. Nobody ever had. But suddenly out of the blue came an invitation from a friend who was president of a Bible college. Unknown to me, they had arranged a Christian round-the-world witnessing mission.

"This morning in our prayer time," Dr. Harrison wrote, "your name came up. We realized we did not have an Episcopalian in the group. Nor an engineer. Nor anybody with an outstanding healing ministry like yours. All our places are taken. But we will put you down for the first cancellation."

Invitation to India? They'd be in New Delhi one whole day. But would Nehru be there that day? I had asked that Merikay be able to accompany me. A seat turned up. That there be some friend close by who would be able to help her as I'd be flying west with one group, and she'd be flying east later with a second group. Our groups would meet in Cairo. Two members of our Winnetka Prayer Band, unknown to us, had reserved seats.

Another condition that the funds would be provided. Unexpectedly some mining equipment I owned was sold in El Paso—$10,000 worth. A fifth condition, that Meissner Engineers would give me the two months off.

But the answer to that was a flat no. Didn't I realize that this multimillion Haitian contract was coming up for signature? I had nursed it all the way. I must stay for the signing. And that date kept being postponed from week to week. "But it's only a signature," I kept pleading. "Anybody can witness that."

Finally they agreed with me. "Guess we don't really need you for the signing," they said. "But if you go on this trip, then you're through with Meissner. No guarantee of a job when you get back. And you'll forfeit your commission." Well, anyway, a fifth condition met. The sixth—that even though I had the cash in the bank, I'd be able to "go now and pay later."

"Where do you want to go?" the ticket man asked.

"Around the world."

His eyebrows shot up. "You'll have to pay 10 percent down."

"No problem."

"And give two references, a bank and a personal one."

Once outside on LaSalle Street, I realized with a sick sort of feeling that my personal reference, Bill Horstman, was out of town three weeks out of every four. And I'd been having an argument over interest with the Jewish banker whose name I'd given. Worst of all, it was now about four thirty on a spring afternoon. Nobody in his right mind would be in the office at that hour.

But surprisingly both men were. The Jewish banker said that there must be some good in me because I'd borrowed substantial funds from the bank a year before to put on some kind of

Christian TV program. The tickets arrived by messenger in Glencoe Saturday afternoon, the day before our scheduled departure.

But what about the seventh and most important condition—that Merikay would send me off with a smile?

Obviously quite impossible. Just a week before departure time for his world trip, an evangelist friend had implored me to help him with a crusade in Haiti, since I knew the country so well. After considerable prayer, I flew down. Following a successful meeting one night, the burden of intercessory prayer came upon me. My friend and I prayed in our prayer languages for an hour. Then the leading of the Holy Spirit came to me loud and clear. I must return home at once. So I took the next plane.

Merikay was in the hospital. She had fallen in the kitchen that very night, struck her eye on the edge of the stove, and suffered a compound fracture of her arm. Shortly afterwards, as we prayed in Haiti, God had answered our prayers by sending our family doctor by to give her a vitamin shot. And he had hospitalized her.

"Lord," I prayed, "all bets are off. Surely you can't expect me to leave my darling under these conditions?" There was only silence.

I have found two important prerequisites for seeing God meet my tests. First, we must be willing to do whatever God wants us to do, if He meets the condition. Second, the answer must come supernaturally in a way we cannot affect by our own actions.

Now there was no way Merikay was going to send me to India with a smile. If it had been difficult before, now it was plain impossible. But I got ready to go. Often we miss God by not being ready to move when He answers. But I was determined not to ask her anything. If the Holy Spirit didn't move on her, I would not go off and leave her. Already all my Christian friends had advised me not to leave her in this condition. Only one friend, Hubert Mitchell, had any word of encouragement. He'd been one of the first Youth for Christ missionaries, started the Interchurch Ministries in Chicago, and the Go Ye Fellowship in Los Angeles. He asked the key question, "Are you sure it's the Holy Spirit and not Larry Hammond?"

"The last thing I want to do is go off and leave Merikay. I love her. But I know God wants me to go."

"When God calls and you know it is God, then be obedient. I believe if you commit your wife to the Lord, then He will take care of her until you return."

Breakfast passed pleasantly in Merikay's hospital room. We laughed at the funny little things a husband and wife enjoy, like how I'd started calling her "Buzzie" and then "Snuzz-Buzz," and when she began calling me "Big Buzz." I looked at my watch. The plane was due to leave in just two hours. But Merikay had said nothing about the trip as yet. I felt it only fair to remind God that He only had a few minutes. It would take me over an hour and a half to drive to the airport. I really didn't want to go unless He met this seventh condition. I was just going to sit there.

Suddenly she turned to me in the middle of a sentence. "Do you think God wants you to go on that trip to India?"

"Yes."

"Do you really think He wants you to go off and leave me here?"

"Yes."

"You mean to sit there with your big, bare face hanging out and tell me God wants you to go off and leave me? When they may have to operate on my eye—maybe even take it out? When we may never see each other again?"

"Yes." Under my breath I was praying.

A long pause seemed to go on forever. Finally, Merikay's worried face burst into the most beautiful smile I've ever seen. "Then I want you to go, too."

As I put on my overcoat and started for the door, I remembered Abraham bargaining with God about Lot. "Lord," I prayed, "I'll be gone for months. Maybe never see my wife again. Couldn't we have an hour together before I go?"

The telephone rang shrilly. It was the airline. Equipment trouble in Boston. There'd be an hour delay. "Thank you, Jesus." I took off my coat and sat close beside Merikay on her bed, holding her good hand in both of mine. About fifty minutes later the phone rang again. It was the airline. Another delay. An hour later, another phone call. Another delay.

Suddenly an anonymous phone caller with a deep masculine voice said, "Take a different airline. There's a sheriff with a warrant for your arrest waiting at the airport. Take another airline, a different airport."

The phone clicked. After the initial shock, I began thinking. Was this call really being used by the Holy Spirit to warn me? Or was it a hindrance from Satan? I decided to follow my original plans. If there was any ambush ahead, God knew all about it. Let Him take care of it.

It doesn't usually snow, even in Chicago, on April 9. But a raging blizzard suddenly swept in from nowhere. In minutes both O'Hare and Midway airports were socked in. Nothing coming in. Nothing going out.

During all the years of my wife's illness I had never been able to spend the night in any hospital with her. I prayed I might stay this last night. Nobody came for the dinner dishes and tray. At check-up time, no intern, no nurse. So I slept through the night in a straight chair beside her bed.

The dawn came clear and crisp. Schedules were in chaos. So

I took a different airplane from another airport. It wasn't until six months later I found out that there had been a sheriff with a warrant waiting for me. It seems LB suspected I was running off with a blonde, and the $10,000 in our joint bank account. I asked God for the grace never to mention it to her.

Somehow between Chicago and Los Angeles, all my baggage disappeared, so I traveled throughout the Orient in just the clothes I was wearing. I drip-dried through Japan, Hong Kong, Formosa, Vietnam, the Philippines, Thailand, Burma, and into India.

God fulfilled my life-long desire to see the Taj Mahal, that poem in stone. At midnight I went to bed weary but happy. "Delight thyself in the Lord, and He will give thee the desires of thy heart."

Within just a few minutes I awakened sharply. Was it a voice? Was it His voice? I was to take the very first train to New Delhi, hours away. I must not wait to go with our group on the afternoon train. At the desk the sleepy night clerk informed me that there was a combination freight-passenger train coming through Agra enroute to New Delhi at four that morning.

Just then a taxi screeched up with a tipsy passenger returning from a night club. The cab driver offered to sleep in his taxi until time for me to leave. A few hours later his soft scratching at my screen awakened me. At the teeming station the driver deposited me in the crowd, telling me the train would be coming in just five minutes.

Among the smells and crying babies I waited five, then ten minutes. I decided there'd been some mistake and started up the stairs. A voice said, "Go to the other side of the tracks." I asked the man next to me what he had said. He shrugged blankly. I took another step up the stairs. Again I heard that soft voice. And then again. I remembered God calling Samuel three times. Quickly I crossed over the tracks. In seconds an express train came puffing into the station, seven hours behind schedule.

At the Janpath Hotel in New Delhi I phoned the U.S. ambassador. "Everybody wants to see the prime minister," he scoffed. "But he doesn't want to see anybody."

The prime minister's secretary, Mr. Khana, was more hopeful. But it would take at least two weeks to set up an appointment. I didn't have two weeks. Our group was passing through the city that afternoon on the way to Kashmir. Three days later we'd return to New Delhi for only one day, Saturday. That, the secretary pointed out, was impossible. It was the worst day of the year to see the prime minister. It was the anniversary of his father's death. It was the anniversary of Rabindranath Tagore, the great poet. It was also the closing day of congress. Every single moment was packed with official functions.

I sat dejected. Maybe I had misread the signals. I was here. Nehru was here. But all doors seemed closed. I'd left Merikay behind critically ill. Had lost all contact with her from the time I reached Tokyo. Every time I called the hospital they told me she was no longer there. Every time I phoned 1015 Pine Street, the phone would be abruptly hung up. Even Lance would give me no information.

"Lord," I cried in the anguish of my soul, "if I'm here on Your business, then show me the key!" Into my mind came the name of a young Indian diplomat. Merikay and I had befriended him when he was a junior member of the UN delegation nearly ten years before. The embassy told me there was a man with a similar name in the defense ministry. In India every secretary has a secretary, and that secretary has a secretary. No important official ever answers his own phone.

But this one did. When I explained who I was, he exclaimed,

"Ah, Larry Hammond, my friend. I am Ramesh. What do you want? India is yours."

It seems he was one of the twelve men who ran India. But Saturday was absolutely impossible. Any other day, but not Saturday. I told him how I had come to know God personally through Jesus since we last met. I pointed out that he was the key provided by God. I would go on with my party to Kashmir and return Friday night, knowing he would have the appointment made somehow.

The Vale of Kashmir is as beautiful as the songs and poems glorifying it. While there I bought an emerald bracelet for Merikay and a jeweled brooch for LB. That was the price a friendly jeweler required to arrange a breath-taking moonlight visit to this fabulous beauty spot. Over the towering Himalayas shone a full silver moon. It bathed the lilting fountains of the Shalimar with a dreamlike mist.

But my joy faded from time to time as doubts crept in. Could even Ramesh arrange the appointment? Was the impossible really possible? Even if I did meet the prime minister, what was I going to say?

I hadn't the remotest idea. Yet I felt absolutely convinced that God had sent me and that He would give me the right words when the time came.

Friday swiftly came. We waited long at the airport. Finally our chartered plane swept in through the lofty Himalayas. We started to board. But the pilot pointed warningly. Way up in the peaks a storm had broken out. Black clouds filled the pass. Lightning flashed ominously.

"You are lucky, my friends," he laughed. "You now have three more days to spend in this paradise."

These high mountain storms, we had been warned before, often spring up unpredictably and usually rage for three days.

"But I have to get back to New Delhi tonight," I urged,

"to keep my appointment with the prime minister tomorrow morning."

He just laughed, the way an adult laughs at a child.

"If the storm stops," I asked, "will you fly us back?"

He stared at me as I told him about Moses, how, when Pharaoh's chariots were behind them and the Red Sea before them, God had made a dry path through the sea. I emphasized that God is the same today. What He did yesterday, He will do today. What He does today, He will do tomorrow.

Then I took a deep breath. Either the Word of God was true, or it wasn't. I told the pilots I was going to pray that God would make a way through that storm. I knelt down among the baggage and prayed out loud so they could hear me. It was one of the shortest, most desperate prayers I ever prayed.

"Oh, Lord," I cried, "You made a way for the Hebrew children through the Red Sea. Make a way through this storm. And we thank You now that You have answered before we called upon You."

The Indian pilots were smiling. Their teeth gleamed white against their dark skins. I prayed for the gift of wisdom or the word of knowledge. The thought came to invite them all into the restaurant to have a cup of tea for fifteen minutes.

My eyes were glued to my wristwatch. The hands suddenly seemed to be moving with the speed of light. I got up and walked out onto the verandah. I didn't dare look up at those towering peaks.

"Let's go," I managed to squeak out.

The first pilot started to laugh. "Crazy Christians . . ." Then he looked up over my shoulder. All the color went out of his face. He began to shake. The second pilot acted the same way. When the navigator also began to turn white and shake, I recovered enough nerve to turn around and look.

Then I began to shake. The clouds still towered above the tops of the peaks and billowed blackly between them, blocking the high, narrow pass. But right through the center of the clouds there was an opening. It was like a highway of light through the storm, a tunnel of light.

"Let's go," I cried again, this time with a loud voice.

"No, Sahib, no!" they protested. "The pass is narrow. There is no place to turn. The clouds will close in and we will all crash and die," the crew members protested.

I was feeling bold. "God doesn't need you to fly the plane," I said. "He can take us without the crew. Or He can take us without the plane. Which way should we pray?"

Perhaps I was tempting God. But He is so merciful and long-suffering. "No," they cried. They had had enough of the supernatural for one day.

It's a good thing that plane was equipped with an automatic pilot. Our two pilots sat shaking all the way. At some spots the wing tips seemed to graze the sheer mountains as we flew between them. Two hours later we emerged from the pass. I looked behind us and saw the black clouds fill the opening like a cork. Later we learned that nothing and nobody came through that pass for the next seventy-two hours.

At the Janpath Hotel there was a message from my friend, Ramesh. The prime minister would see us at his palace the next morning at eight. We had planned to take the whole twenty members of our tour. But the bus had a flat tire. Some began to think of shopping. Others wanted to go sight-seeing. Some doubted we could really see Nehru. Where was the official invitation? All we had was a scribbled note in pencil.

Finally it looked as though I was the only one going. *What ingrates,* I thought! *Here I've arranged a prized appointment with a famous statesman, who controls the non-aligned nations—one-third of the world.* I was so discouraged that I just about decided not to go either. But the Holy Spirit reminded me that *I* was the one asked to go, not the others. But what about the message? I had no better idea now that I was in New Delhi than back in Chicago.

On seeing me alone, the prime minister's secretary was upset. "Where is the group—the twenty businessmen?" I really began to pray. If they didn't come in the next few minutes, the prime minister would have to go on to congress. Ours was the first appointment of the day.

Just then a taxi drove up. Out stepped two of our party. Then another taxi came from the opposite direction. And another. Now there were six of us. We were promptly ushered into the huge reception hall. Scores of diplomats in red silk sashes and swallow-tail coats. Generals and admirals in full dress uniform.

My friends wanted to know what message I had for Nehru. I told them I had nothing to say unless God gave me the words.

"Let's pray!" urged all of them at the same time. So we knelt to ask guidance. Suddenly I saw some white pantaloons stop by us. It was the prime minister himself. Embarrassed, we scrambled to our feet. On the way in the taxi I had been rehearsing a few Scriptures. Isaiah tells us, "The Word of God shall not return void . . . it shall accomplish that which I desire." If all else failed and the message from God did not come through, I would quote the Scriptures.

Around and around in my head those words went like a merry-go-round. "The Word of God will not return void." In my spirit I cried desperately, "Yes, Lord. But what is the Word? What is your message to this leader of one-third of the world?"

Everything stopped. My mind became quiet and blank. I gazed into the dark, burning eyes of this man. I claimed the promise of God in Luke 21:15, "I shall give you utterance and wisdom which none of your opponents will be able to resist or refute."

I opened my mouth in faith with no idea what, if anything, would come out. My blood froze as I heard these words, "Mr. Prime Minister, the Lord Jesus Christ has no use for fence-sitters, neutralists or mugwumps." I tried to stop but could not. "In His Holy Bible He says, 'Be ye hot or cold, but not lukewarm or I'll spue you out of my mouth.' " It was as though Someone else were speaking through my voice.

How I wished I could have disappeared into thin air. Nehru frowned. "Spue?" he asked threateningly. "That means spit, doesn't it?"

*Spit* is a dirty word in the Orient, especially to a high class Brahmin. I started to apologize. But the very same words came out of my mouth again. Nehru's face flashed white with anger. He raised his arm as if to strike me. Then he whirled away, striding down the hall.

I certainly had opened my big, fat mouth and put both feet into it. My friends looked at me in horror. Here I had come halfway around the world as an envoy for the Prince of Peace, and I had insulted a great world leader right in his own palace.

I prayed that God would give me a second chance. This time, I promised, I would get the signals straight. Into my mind came the thought to take his picture. Silly! I rejected it. The official press photographer had already taken a dozen pictures of our group. But the thought came again. And again, softly persistently. I know it's not going to work, I said to myself as I followed the prime minister to where he stood deep in conversation with high dignitaries.

"Mr. Prime Minister," I said to the leader I had just insulted, "each of us has a different make of camera. We'd like to take your picture as a souvenir." Such a stupid thing to say. I blushed with embarrassment.

For an endless moment Nehru stared at me. Then his face broke into a broad smile. He was not a man who smiled easily. Or often. "Where would you like to take it? Here or on the palace steps?"

"Outside." I grasped the chance to go anywhere to get away from all these people. A dozen of his personal staff followed our group closely. There on the steps, I said something like this, "Mr. Prime Minister, you've sought after truth all your life."

"Yes, and I'm still searching. What is Truth?"

"A man named Pontius Pilate asked that same question of Jesus nearly two thousand years ago. And Jesus answered him by saying, 'I am the way, the truth and the life.' I've come halfway around the world to share with you the good news that God by whatever name you call Him, is Truth. The invisible, mighty God who made all this—built these magnificent Himalayas . . . hung the galaxies in space, reached down and took a handful of dirt, moulded it into human form, and breathed the breath of life into him. God Himself is invisible, but we see His power and presence everywhere."

"In the past few years," mused the prime minister, "I've had an increasing sense of inner emptiness. There must be something beyond what we can see and touch."

"There's God," I repeated. "The God who loves you so much He sent me around the world to tell you about His Son, Jesus Christ, who is Lord of Lords and King of Kings, and the only way to salvation."

Nehru's dark eyes burned into mine.

"God created man in His own image and asked man to love Him. But early in history man yielded to temptation, to pride. As a result we are separated from Him. All through the centuries man has been trying to get back to God. People didn't understand Him as a God of love. They saw Him as a God of judgment, of authority, of vengeance, a Holy God. But they didn't understand His love. So He sent His only Son, Jesus Christ, to walk among us as living love. When we break a law, we have to pay a fine or go to jail. Jesus did that for each of us. He paid the penalty for our sins by dying in our place upon the cross. He is our substitute, our way back to a Holy God who loves us enough to sacrifice His only Son."

The prime minister seemed lost in thought.

"Mr. Prime Minister, you're a man of compassion. You love your people. You've gone to jail for freedom and human dignity here in India. You've passed laws so that the untouchables—whom everybody scorns—might be treated like human beings. You've tried your best to do away with the caste system. But all your efforts have failed." I paused. "No law can make one man love another. It takes the transforming love of Jesus Christ to make us color-blind and caste-blind. This will bring the world the peace you've sought so hard all your life."

"Yes," Nehru said with a sigh, "the world needs peace. Must have peace. But how?"

"Jesus is the Prince of Peace," I answered. I reached out and took his right hand in my left. "Why don't we pray right now."

The prime minister, the men in my group and I held hands there on the palace steps in front of his retainers. We prayed that God would become real to him through an experience with Jesus Christ.

As we finished the prayer, he squeezed my left hand. Though I was disappointed that he did not get down on his knees and cry out to God with tears, I believe that the squeeze may have been a sign that he opened his heart to God.

From India we flew to Egypt. In Cairo my lost luggage miraculously appeared. It had been unlocked, a big rip down the side of one piece. Fifty one dollar bills were spread over my clothes. Gold and silver cufflinks. Not one thing was missing. All during our trip the little widows whose baggage I'd been toting thought I was God's special bellboy. Now that I had my own bags to carry, my popularity suffered.

In Cairo I received another surprise, or rather a shock. I'd made all the arrangements before leaving Chicago for Merikay, accompanied by my sister, Mary, to join us in Cairo. I'd hoped against hope that she'd be strong enough to join the group going east one month after our first group started west. And an airport immigration official had informed me that my wife was enroute to the Nile Hilton. So my heart sank when I saw Mary by herself. All she could tell me was that LB had emphatically stated, "Merikay is going on this trip over my dead body." Mary had been utterly unable to find out anything else.

My heart was heavy. Where was Merikay? And Doug? Was he in jail? Had he been court-martialled? Had he carried out his threat to shoot himself? I needed to get away to think. I walked out into the desert in the darkness. "Under these same heavens in this same desert," I prayed. "You spoke to Abraham and guided him. Lord, I need an answer tonight. Right now. I must know. I spoke to Nehru even if I didn't do too good a job. Are You through with me on this trip? Can I now go back to my family? Or is there something more you want me to do?"

In the blackness of that desert I literally ran into another tour member, James Brown. In the darkness the Lord had brought us together.

I poured out my heart to Jim. He put his arm around my shoulder. "My son, Jamie, was far from God, too. He was running a rock and roll band. He was on drugs. Right under my nose. But God mercifully blinded me to the situation, or I couldn't have faced my congregation. When I did find out, I reached for the stick like any good Calvinist. But my wife, Marianne, spoke a word of wisdom. 'Jim,' she said under special anointing, 'the least we can do and the most we can do is to put our trust in God. Let's commit him to the Lord.'

"So we did. Within a matter of months a miracle happened. He was converted in one of my out-of-town meetings. He had come along just for the ride on one of those new jets. Larry, my friend, commit your wife and son to the Lord and trust in Him."

So once more—this time in the inky blackness of an Egyptian night—I gave Merikay to the Lord, thanks to Jim Brown's counsel.

# 16

# The Road Back

Back in Chicago, my in-laws had the door barred. They wouldn't even talk to me on the telephone. The hospital gave me no information. It was six months before LB would even say a gruff hello. And it was several months before I saw my wife again—then it was twice as long before she finally forgave me for being away so long. She had nearly died. They'd put her in the Milwaukee Sanitarium again, behind locked doors this time.

I needed a pass to make my weekly visits. There was no privacy. Someone always was watching through the glass in the door. But, little by little, she gained strength. And, little by little, our love bloomed again. After some weeks I was able to take her out for a few hours and we could kiss each other in the privacy of my nearby motel room.

The emerald bracelet and ring helped. My frantic, scrawled postcards and letters should have told her that I had thought of her and loved her every one of those twenty-two thousand miles. Only LB had kept them. She released them only after a jeweled brooch from Kashmir softened her heart.

If I had dropped everything and flown back from Tokyo, I couldn't have done anything to help Merikay. Again I learned that when we're doing what God wants us to do, He'll always take care of our loved ones.

While I was overseas, Doug phoned friends in New York. They sent his airfare. He voluntarily turned himself in at the Brooklyn Navy Yard. So I knew where he was, in solitary, awaiting his court-martial. I wrote to him and sent tracts. There in his cell he met Jesus. Then through another miracle he was given an honorable discharge. It was the first time in the Marines' 150-year history that anyone ever got such a discharge. Suspended sentence. Five years. Ordered to go back to high school. Merikay and I had been praying he'd return to school. He also had to stay within fifty miles of the Brooklyn Navy Yard. Our hearts nearly burst with gratitude to God, who does all things well.

After a few trial weekends at home during that winter, I decided to take Merikay with me on what I hoped would be my final trip to Haiti regarding the new telephone system. The road feasibility study was proceeding under Meissner Engineers, but they still wanted me to keep some supervision over it. I'd helped them with political contacts and in the engaging of reliable Haitian personnel.

Our family doctor warned it would be taking a big chance for Merikay to stay at the hotel. It had the biggest bar in the city, and the bar had to be passed to reach the dining room. "Even one teaspoon," he warned ominously, "even smelling the cork could start your wife off again on a binge that could be fatal with her damaged liver."I decided to trust the faithfulness of God. It would be impossible otherwise to keep her away from alcohol in the exotic land of rum and rumba.

Breakfast portions of fruit were overwhelming at Castle Haiti. Mangoes, grapefruit, plantains in colorful profusion. But when I'd return from my daily trips to the government offices, there was never any fruit left, even though there'd always be an ample supply left over from breakfast. When I'd hungrily eye the empty dishes and ask what happened, Merikay would answer, "Quien sabe?" (Who knows?)

One day I returned unexpectedly. I found her laughing on our little balcony as she threw, one by one, our treasured mangoes, papayas, and grapefruit down to two little black boys. They were dancing in excitement. For them it was Christmas every day. I smiled. Merikay loved children—any kind of children, the more raggedy, the better.

The days passed in dreamlike sequence—always deep, blue skies, always bright sunlight, and the nights full of Rada voodoo drums and crowing gamecocks. I began to appreciate how much missionaries in heathen lands need prayer support from those at home. And prayer partners where they are. Merikay was behaving herself. Hadn't had a single drink in the weeks we'd been in Haiti; passed right by the bar with its clinking ice and sweet rum smell. She was reading her Bible daily, too. We were sharing the *Upper Room* daily reading. But she didn't do much praying. At least we seldom prayed out loud together.

Then darkness pressed down upon us as the Mardi Gras season started. Banging drums, ear-piercing whistles, and shrill chanting seemed to go on night and day. I found it almost impossible to pray. Never did I appreciate the church more. Each Sunday we'd go to Holy Trinity Cathedral, with its comic strip murals. Bishop Voegeli had commissioned

Haitian artists and then, in a moment of apprehension, had fled to Florida. When he returned he saw a new concept of The Last Supper. The apostles were of every race and color. Jesus looked very Haitian. And the one white man? Judas, of course!

The first visit was during 4 A.M. mass. The early morning darkness hid the pitifully ragged members from the eyes of the curious as they slipped like shadows down the twisting alleys. Merikay's sharp elbow nudged me during the first hymn. "They don't have any hymn books," she whispered. "They must know all the hymns by heart."

Another sharper nudge. "Look, over there." She nodded discreetly to where three black-garbed nuns were kneeling. Beside them two French poodles, black out of deference to sensitive Haitian feelings, as the nuns later explained. In another corner a tiger cat arched its back and yawned lazily. Overhead small, yellow birds chirped to the organ music and flitted about the vaulted ceiling.

"This is the church for me," Merikay giggled. "The church of the cats and dogs."

Every day I would set out, hopes high, that today the long-promised contract would be signed by the appropriate officials. Hadn't President Duvalier himself okayed the contract and in our impressed presence ordered the appropriate cabinet officer to execute it forthwith?

Sadly, I learned that the Haitian word for forthwith is *demain*, which means tomorrow. "Demain," they would say, teeth gleaming whitely in their black faces. But tomorrow never came. So after nearly three fruitless months, Merikay and I flew home where tomorrow becomes today.

For several years now I had belonged to a dedicated prayer group affiliated with the Order of St. Luke. It met weekly at Trinity Episcopal Church in Wheaton, Illinois, a suburb west of Chicago. Its primary function was intercessory prayer and the ministerial laying on of hands for the healing of the sick. Over the years we had seen almost every conceivable disease healed this way, either at the altar during the laying on of hands, or far away by what is called "absent" prayer. In "absent" prayer the only contact between the prayers and sufferers is spiritual.

After the main healing service, many of us would meet in private homes for deeper fellowship in the Holy Spirit. All the gifts of the Holy Spirit were manifested during such times. Also Father Dick Winkler would pray for any seeking conversion, healing or the baptism in the Holy Spirit.

Since the group had faithfully prayed for Merikay for some five years, I thought they'd appreciate seeing for themselves the great things God had done. She reluctantly consented to go one night shortly after our return from Haiti.

"On the one condition," she said, with a penetrating look, "that nobody knows I'm your wife."

But then the third person we met innocently asked, "And is this your wife?"

I replied with a straight face, "No, she's just a friend."

Merikay exploded like a volcano. "I am not his friend, I'm his wife."

Then two ladies in garden-party hats came up. "You look tired," one said. "Wouldn't you like to relax in the minister's study?"

"Anywhere so long as I can get out of this insane asylum!" she blurted.

Shortly afterwards the rector came in. He didn't waste any time getting to the point.

"Merikay, it's so good to meet you after all these years. Wouldn't you like to receive the baptism in the Holy Spirit?"

To her great surprise, she admitted later, she said, "Yes."

As Winkler laid his hands upon her head and asked Jesus the Great Baptizer to come and baptize her according to his eternal, unchangeable word, Merikay opened her mouth wide. When I entered a few minutes later, I heard my wife speak five beautiful languages, such as I had yearned for. Merikay, who had pooh-poohed tongues for so long. Richard Winkler recognized one as Aramaic, the language of our blessed Lord when he walked on earth. Another was Hebrew. Still another, a Chinese dialect. And two that nobody knew.

Instead of rejoicing I complained in my spirit. "Lord, how could You do this to me? She never even wanted tongues. And here I am with this stupid ma-ba-la deal."

The Lord chastised me thoroughly. For several months, until I came crawling back in repentance, He took even that away from me. Over the years He has spoken Turkish, Ukrainian, Hebrew, and a dozen other languages I don't know through my lips. And people have been converted and healed when He has spoken to them in their own language. But He has never spoken a word of any language I know: Latin, French, Spanish, German or Italian. Yet, I have many times heard persons illiterate in these languages speak them more perfectly than I, who studied them for years. Nor does He ever speak Maranaw through me any more. I memorized basic Maranaw. But God does not want us to have intelligent control over what He is saying through us in our spiritual language. Apparently this is His way of using the foolish things to confound the wise.

After this, life became heavenly. Now Merikay had the supernatural strength to resist alcohol. Every Thursday night she drove the 100 mile round trip to the prayer group in Wheaton, rain or shine. What a burden lifted from my shoulders! No more fear of what she might do while I was away from home. No more worry about bringing in friends. No more embarrassment. Merikay even offered to host one of the Winnetka Prayer Band monthly meetings. How those dear people rejoiced at this marvelous answer to prayer. Now at last she was really one of them. Gerda and Elsie, the cook, had tears in their eyes.

What a joy to read the Bible together, to worship in our prayer languages. Oddly, when Merikay confided this experience, LB excitedly and proudly began telling everyone who'd listen how her daughter didn't drink any more, wasn't even tempted by the ever-present cocktails at 1015 Pine, and that Merikay even spoke in tongues! She may not really have understood what that meant, but she did know what it meant to have her old "jolly dolly" back again, laughing and bright-eyed instead of bleary and thick-tongued. To my added joy, Merikay shed that pink houserobe, began to dress each day, and to go out for lunches, concerts and lectures at Lake Forest with friends.

More and more I was being called for speaking engagements around the nation. Now I felt free to accept most of them, though Merikay was not yet strong enough to accompany me often. There was the time in Denver when the Holy Spirit urged me to stay a few days longer, though I was due in Rockford, Illinois, for a long-announced FGBMFI dinner meeting. I told the Lord I would stay if He would provide a substitute for me. He did this through a long distance call I made to a friend. Unable to go himself at the last moment, he reached evangelist Charles Trombley, who had arrived unexpectedly in Chicago. So Trombley skidded over seventy-five miles of sheer ice to speak to one hundred twenty people. One of them was a Jehovah's Witness. A former Jehovah's Witness himself, Trombley brought that man to the Lord.

Later I learned that even if I had flown in, I couldn't have gotten out of O'Hare. Meanwhile, a fierce ice storm struck

Glencoe. Some seventeen thousand homes were without heat or light during those several bitter days. But our little ranch home was warm and lighted, an oasis in the dark. So I learned again that God takes care of His own when they're doing His business.

When Merikay traveled with me we ministered together. One time we prayed for Debbie, who was what the world calls a Mongoloid. Unable to find medical help, her Southern Baptist parents had even dared to attend the ceremony of laying on of hands at the altar. Merikay and I laid our hands upon Debbie's head and asked Jesus to touch her. Debbie's face glowed like an angel's. Along the altar rail she went with us, wriggling happily and putting her rosy cheek against those of the other troubled and diseased people.

"Jesus loves you," she'd whisper, throwing her chubby arms around their necks. "He'll make you well, just like He's making Debbie all well."

Scores were healed through the pure love of this five-year-old. Later when the doctor examined Debbie, her mother told us, he was amazed to find her IQ had gone up 27½ percent. Once a year at the annual conference, or on our rare visits to her home in Alabama, Merikay and I would lay our hands on Debbie. Each time there would be marked improvement. Today as she enters adolescence, our "angel unawares" has entirely lost that pinched-head look and is in her proper school grade.

As I participated in healing services in churches of most major denominations the Lord used my increasing absences from home to teach Merikay His way. She began studying the Bible, started going to St. Elisabeth's every time the doors opened, even to morning mass at seven. One day in winter a Moody Bible School graduate, a retired missionary to China, phoned to ask me to come pray for his wife, Alice.

He had heard me speak about my own miraculous healing at a recent Full Gospel Business Men's dinner in Chicago.

"I'm sorry. He's not at home right now," Merikay said.

It didn't matter that I wasn't there. It didn't matter that Merikay protested that she couldn't pray for the sick without me. It didn't matter that the snow was hip deep. Out he came, scooped Merikay up, carried her off to his home, and into his wife's upstairs bedroom. Alice had been bedridden with curvature of the spine for some years. Piled high around her bed were heaps of books on divine healing. It was Merikay's moment of truth, just as it had been mine in Puerto Rico.

"Do you believe what you read?" Merikay asked, gesturing at the heaps of books.

"Why yes," replied the startled invalid.

"Do you believe God can do anything?" Merikay persisted. "Even for you?"

Taken aback by Merikay's blunt approach, Alice nodded wordlessly. Merikay took her firmly but gently by the hand. "In the name of Jesus, rise up and walk." And that's just what she did. Real faith came into her heart. She dressed herself, got hold of her vacuum cleaner, went downstairs and cleaned house for the first time in years.

Then there were Ray and Eloise, two very mixed-up young people. Eloise was married with two children, but her husband was not living with her. A family friend, Ray, was. "Uncle Ray," as the adoring youngsters called him. They loved him more than the absent father they never saw. In this instance, Merikay was projected into a telephone counseling ministry.

"It's easy to tell people in trouble what to do when they're just bodiless names over the wires," she laughingly reported to me.

"Just what did you tell them?" I asked.

"Told them they ought to stop monkeying around and get married."

"Did they?"

"Not yet. Ray says, as a born-again, Bible-believing Christian, he doesn't see how he could marry her."

"Why not?" I asked.

"She's divorced. And Ray says St. Paul says not to marry a divorced woman."

It took months of counseling, but Merikay finally found a compassionate minister to marry them. She and I were matron of honor and best man. Later when a little boy arrived, we were asked to be godparents.

Meanwhile the Lord had been speaking to me about living by faith. For nine months I resisted. "Lord, I'm giving you about 75 percent of my time now. I go all over the country speaking for you, holding healing services. I'm only spending 25 percent of my time working to support my family." I thought I'd better remind Him of what He's said in the Scriptures in case He'd forgotten.

" 'He who neglects his family is worse than an infidel,' " I quoted back to Him.

This monologue went on for months. Every time I returned from a speaking trip I would remind the Lord that I had taken off several days from my business, turned the love offering back to the church from which it came, and paid all my own expenses, too. It hadn't cost the Lord a dime.

Suddenly one day He broke His silence. "My son, you're patronizing me. Whose money and whose time is it, anyway?"

I looked in the mirror and cried out to the Lord to forgive me. Imagine me patronizing the God who had given me life; all I had; the God who had raised me from a deathbed, healed my wife so many times. It broke my heart.

"Didn't you trust me for your salvation, My son?"

"Yes, Lord."

"Didn't you trust Me for your physical healing?"

"Yes, Lord."

"Is it so much to trust Me for three meals a day? Clothes? A bed?"

Contrite, I promised the Lord I'd do it. But I had to be sure it was He speaking. I knew He could take care of ignorant itinerant preachers. But me? I was smart. I could earn a good living. There were plenty whom He had to take care of. It didn't seem right to add myself to His gravy train.

Usually I received an invitation every week or so. Wise words from my old friend, David Duplessis, evangelist and well-known ecumenicist, had helped me know God's will. I followed his example. I went where I was invited: that was usually north to Canada in the winter and to steaming New Orleans in the summer. As a confirmation that I was in the right place at the right time, I asked God to let me see at least one miracle every day that I was away from home. Somebody who would come to know Jesus either as Savior, or Baptizer in the Holy Spirit, or as the Great Physician. I empathized with the well-known evangelist who used to say, "I couldn't have a fat, old wife with a moustache, whom I'd be glad to get away from. My wife is beautiful. It costs me every day I'm away from her."

That's exactly how I felt about my Merikay. But the Bible tells us that a gift that does not cost us anything is not pleasing to God. So I set up another test for God. If the Lord really wanted me to start a faith life, I would. But I wanted Him to give me a sign so big I couldn't miss it. Any sign.

"But soon, Lord."

That night I had my first peaceful sleep in many weeks.

The issue was settled. It was up to the Lord now.

He didn't waste a moment. I was whistling when I walked into the office of Meissner Engineers the next morning. It was bedlam. Sheriffs and bill collectors everywhere and weepy-eyed secretaries sniffling at their desks. The company had just announced bankruptcy. The news went through me like a flaming sword.

"Lord, forgive me," I cried out getting down on my knees, "for being so slow to obey You that 278 innocent people have to lose their jobs. Make it a blessing, Lord."

The company's president had broken or bent a few laws. It was an immoral leadership. Out of the wreckage came a half dozen smaller engineering companies under moral leadership. I also remembered that they owed me about $5,000.

"I don't care if I never see a penny of that commission," I told the Lord.

That prayer was answered. I never did. But as the day wore on, doubts began to cloud my mind. I remembered I had done a study of the company six months before and recommended measures which could have cut the overhead by nearly $250,000. The president had rejected my study.

This bankruptcy really had nothing to do with my "test," I decided. It was just a coincidence that it happened right after my prayer.

Or was it really a coincidence? Or the hand of God?

I had an uneasy feeling deep inside, so I decided to set up another test. I asked the Lord in the next two weeks, to send me so many invitations to speak that it would take me exactly six months from the first to the last—to the hour, to the minute, to the second.

I sighed with relief. It might be dirty pool, but this was one condition it was impossible for Him to meet. I'd made it too tough.

That very night I got a long distance call from California. Or somewhere. The next day, an airmail letter. The next, a telegram. Then the invitations began pouring in like Christmas mail.

I refused to open any more until the two weeks were up. Then I put that big pile next to a calendar and started matching up dates. I nearly fell off the chair an hour or so later when I saw it was exactly six months from the first to the last. To the very day. To the hour. To the minute.

Then I started looking for an out. Here was the fourth of July. Open. Labor Day. Open. Thanksgiving. Open. Christmas . . . "Lord, is this Your answer? What about these six open days with no invitations?"

I heard the voice of God: "I can fill those, too. Don't you ever want to see your family?"

My first invitation was from a church in Wisconsin. The minister asked the congregation to give me a generous love offering. I protested. I really didn't need it. Let them use it for their church. But they insisted the Lord had told them it must be for me personally to help in my faith life. So I crammed into my pocket the whole thirty-five dollars. From the look of the preacher's clothes, he needed it worse than I. I couldn't wait to give it away.

As soon as I did, I heard that soft, sweet voice, deeply hurt now. "Is this the way you spurn My love, son, when I start to take care of your needs?"

From that time on, I've accepted anything that's been given me in the name of Jesus. Anything from a penny to a paper clip. And there've been some paper clips, too.

# 17

# One Soul—
# Worth $5 Million

Life with Merikay became heavenly. No more battles with the bottle. Everywhere she went she drew everyone to her as a lush flower garden attracts swarms of bees. She had a lightness, a gaiety about her. A simple childlike wonder at the world. And a deep compassion born in the fires of her own suffering. She gave Jesus full credit now for the many miracles He'd performed in her life. She was a bouquet of miracles herself. She inspired confidence.

But while life at home improved, affairs at the mine came to a crisis. Dick and his New York group had been putting increasing pressure on me to release to them several mining claims which I had staked long before they had come into the picture. The claims were adjacent to the forty some patented claims which we had originally leased from the Pittsburgh owners. Both the Southwest Manganese partners and their successors, Florida Manganese, had rejected my offer to sign them over. They figured they had enough claims. Their problem was making money out of those they already had.

Dick also had brushed my offer away when he first joined the company. He was now milking the company according to plan. Suddenly he was all afire to acquire those claims. His idea was that I should cede them to the company, which was now his company. So he sued me for a million and a half dollars. Over the months secret engineering reports fell into my hands. They contained all sorts of information I could never have learned otherwise. I discovered that Dick and his company had trespassed on my mining claims. That's as bad as horse stealing out West.

To add to the pressure, my father-in-law, Tex Howard, also was sued for a million and a half dollars. Now seventy years of age, and without Jesus, Tex's health failed under the added pressures. His attorney kept warning him it would cost him a quarter of a million just to defend himself. His estate might be tied up for years, his successful Waylite Company crushed under legal onslaught. Tex was a big warm-hearted man with the highest ethical standards. He came as close to living by the Golden Rule as anyone.

At his request I had allowed his attorney to represent us both. But when a year had passed and the attorney had not even put in a legal answer, I realized we could lose the case by default. I was led to a Christian lawyer at St. Elisabeth's, Kirkpatrick Dilling. He started a countersuit for damages for the million dollars worth of ore we believe had been illegally mined from my claims. Through God's help many things came to light. Tex's attorney had used stock of which I was the equitable owner to aid Dick's group in taking over.

My attorney exulted, "We've got them cold. Open and shut case. There's no way they can wiggle off the hook."

Meanwhile, wilting under pressures from the New York group, Tex stopped playing his favorite game of golf. He lost weight. One day he turned anxiously to me.

"I thought you were a Christian."

"I am."

"Then why don't you help me? I'm dying."

I tried to comfort him. "Don't worry about legal fees. My lawyer will represent you and I'll pay him out of the damages. You've nothing to fear."

"But I am afraid." There was real agony in his voice.

"If you only knew Jesus, you wouldn't be afraid. He says that God has not given us a spirit of fear but of power and love and a sound mind."

His eyes beseeched me. "Help me, please."

Home I went, arguing with God every step of the way. The engineering report estimated a gross worth of nearly ten million dollars. That meant the stock Merikay and I held was worth nearly five million. I was a millionaire. Didn't the Bible say that the workman is worthy of his hire?

Silence from above. Desperately I cried out, "Am I my brother's keeper?"

Still silence. "Lord," I agonized, "I've put You before my wife. I've put You before my son." I took a deep breath. This was heavy. "I'm even willing to put You above My mine." Pause. No answer. "But do I really have to, Lord? Lord?"

As usual when facing a major decision, I set up a test. If my beloved father-in-law were really dying, and this were really necessary to save his life, I'd give it up gladly. Well, anyway, I'd give it up. But I wanted supernatural confirmation. I asked the Lord to speak to me out of His Word the next morning at eight, wherever I happened to be.

The following day was beautiful, sunny. As I drove in the heavy morning traffic to Chicago, I was singing the favorite hymn of both Merikay and myself, "Amazing Grace." The music on my car radio stopped abruptly. "What does it profit a man," an unusually vibrant voice said with great emphasis, "if he gain the whole world and lose his own soul?"

*Strange,* I thought, *on this popular disk jockey's program.* Suddenly another voice announced, "It is now exactly eight o'clock."

Then the music came on deafeningly. It couldn't have been God speaking to me! Or could it? A strange uneasiness came over me. I had been praying for Tex's salvation for seven years. Could my attitude have been blocking his accepting Jesus? If this were God, then I wanted Tex's family physician to tell me personally. "Before ten tonight, Lord," I said.

When I returned home that evening as I was undressing, the doorbell jangled. Pulling my dressing gown on, I went to the door. There stood our personal physician, Dr. Cummins.

"Been trying to get you all day."

"Did you come to give Merikay a vitamin shot?" I asked hopefully.

"No, this is about Tex. He's dying. If something doesn't happen fast . . . well, he can't last much longer at this rate."

"What can I do?"

"I don't know." He sighed. "But you're a Christian. If there's any way you can help him get over his fear, you had better do it."

God had spoken. I repented of my rebellion. Then I dressed and drove to 1015, two miles away.

"It's the lawsuit," Tex said. "I'm afraid of what will happen."

He was a big-boned man. Normally he weighed about two hundred and sixty. Right now he looked shrunken. The chair seemed too big for him. There was desperation in his voice.

I prayed my way back home. "Lord, I've been praying for

Dick for years too. How will he ever come to know You if he continues to reap fortunes?" I knew of at least three or four other multimillion dollar companies he'd taken over with the same tactics.

The decision was difficult, but in the end God won. I agreed to give up the mine. But like Abraham I wanted a little favor. "I've torn this mine out of my heart, Lord. But don't let Dick profit by it. Give my lawyer wisdom to handle it. Wake him up at two in the morning, Lord, so I'll know it's You."

Next morning about seven my attorney phoned me exuberantly. "I've got it!" he shouted.

"You mean you just woke up with the answer?"

"Usually that's what happens. But this time I woke up in the middle of the night."

"What do you call the middle of the night?"

"Funny you should ask that. I turned the table lamp on. It was exactly two o'clock."

"Don't tell me any more," I said quickly. "That was God giving you wisdom."

"You're putting me on."

"Just do what God told you."

Kirk did. In the end, Dick was so anxious that I never have any possible claim on the mine that the mine fell into the hands of a third party. Every time I think of it, I thank the Lord.

After I gave up the mine, I asked the Lord to make good His side. Hadn't He said one soul is worth the whole world? Then I wanted to see my father-in-law commit his life to Jesus. Immediately after I had made my decision to throw in the towel, Tex recovered so quickly it was astonishing.

I invited him to a Billy Graham Crusade. Reluctantly he agreed to accompany me the last night. I thanked God—until I came by to drive him into town and he appeared in his housecoat and slippers, pipe in hand.

"I forgot," he explained hurriedly, eager to get back to the TV. "There's a championship prize fight tonight on TV. You wouldn't want me to miss that, would you?"

It was a great meeting. Afterward, at nearly two in the morning, I drove past 1015.

*Well,* I thought, as I saw the lights burning in the TV room, *I'll drop by. Maybe some of this joy will rub off on Tex.*

Tears wet Tex's cheeks. This last night of the crusade had been televised. And he'd seen it. My heart rejoiced. Tex had met his Master! All I had had to do was get out of the way.


During that fall, Merikay had been doubling over in stomach pains I thought were cramps. She was so nonchalant about the problem, I was convinced it was not serious.

"Nothing must keep you from participating in this first FGBMFI airlift to London," she said.

When I returned several weeks later, Merikay greeted me with warm and open arms. Her green eyes had never looked more beautiful. "Thank God, you're home again safe and sound, Big Buzz. I prayed for you every morning and every night. Set my alarm clock six hours ahead so I'd be having breakfast with you in the morning and going to bed with you at night." She giggled. "Now my ice-cold feet will thaw out. I'll put them on your back when we go to bed, just like I've done every winter. Now I don't mind having to go to the hospital and having my gizzard chopped out. I've got you back again."

Then she told me she had been losing blood. Sometimes she had been so weak she had fainted. And all alone! How guilty I felt!

"Snuzz-buzz, you know I'd never have left you, if I'd known," I said.

"I know," she nodded, kissing me into silence. "That's why you didn't know."

LB was beside herself with concern. Their family gynecologist had been forced to stop operating. But for his favorite patient, his "Pogo pal," a comic strip they both shared together, he would. Didn't trust anybody else, he said.

But LB didn't trust him. "Not that doctor!" she shouted. "I'm not going to have him faint over my daughter's body! Why, he has to wear a complicated corset and use a cane even to walk. Takes him an hour and a half just to get dressed. My daughter's going to have the best! The very best!"

As a Christian who had experienced the divine healing power of Jesus in both our lives, I wanted to trust Him and His promise for Merikay. Especially since the experts weren't even sure she could survive such a major operation. But Merikay wanted to trust the Lord for the healing through the surgeon. Trusting God to heal someone else is usually easier than trusting Him to heal oneself. Since I felt that husband and wife should be of one mind—I agreed to the operation.

"Get any doctor you want," I told LB. "It's Jesus who'll have to do the healing anyway."

LB picked the top surgeon in abdominal surgery.

Merikay had wanted to enjoy Christmas at home before entering the hospital. "What a way to start the New Year," she sighed. Then she brightened up. "But it's better than ending the New Year before it begins. So many times while you were overseas, I wondered if I'd ever see the start of this New Year."

"Darling, why didn't you call me? I'd have dropped everything and have flown right back."

"But you were on the Lord's business, Big Buzz," she chided me. "What kind of a Christian would I be to interfere?"

LB's choice of surgeons was perfect. He was young,

appeared strong as an ox. But he had an unexpected heart attack.

"Pick another," I suggested. "But I still believe God wants to use our gynecologist."

Her loud reply had to be censored.

Her next choice was the next best surgeon. One week before the scheduled operation, the second choice was called to be on the staff of the same hospital where the family physician was department head. Now it was out of the question for him to operate on his superior's patient, if the superior wanted to. And the superior wanted to—wouldn't trust this delicate operation to anybody else.

So the operation was moved up a day because of Merikay's now-critical condition. I first heard about it when I telephoned the hospital with my usual good morning.

"Buzz," she said, trying to sound calm, "I wish I could kiss you goodbye first . . . but it's too late."

"Hold everything," I reassured her. "I'll be right there."

"But it's too late," she repeated forlornly. "They've needled me already. They're coming with that stretcher on wheels any minute."

"Hold everything. I'll be right down."

"But you're too far away."

It was too late and I was too far away. Breathless, I burst into her hospital room. It was empty. *Oh, God, let me kiss her just once more before* . . . On the pillow lay a note.

"I love you. Pray I'm back beside you soon. Snuzz."

Madly I dashed into the hall. I had to find her. I had to pray with her once more. I bumped into a physician I knew.

"George!" I grabbed the lapel of his white jacket, "Where is she?"

"Take it easy." He patted my shoulder. "She's on the way to the operating room. Maybe you can catch her at the elevator. It's around that way."

I dashed around the corner following his finger. The elevator door was closing. I spread my arms to break the light beam. "Snuzz!"

There she lay all wrapped in white. So little. So vulnerable. And in just a few moments the surgeon's sharp knife would slice deep into that warm body I loved beyond all the words in all the languages in all the world! I bent over tenderly and kissed her. It was a long kiss. I stepped back. The elevator door slammed noisily shut. She was gone.

*It will just be a few hours,* I told myself. In the back of my mind the nagging thought, *But what if... what if this really is goodbye? Forever?*

I dropped to my knees in that sterile, unfriendly corridor.

"God . . . please . . . Lord, she's in Your hands."

What better hands? The hours dragged by as I waited in the family room near the operating room. I wished I had a cigaret. "Forgive me, Lord! I have You. And You're enough. But strengthen the doctor. Give him wisdom. Guide those trembling hands. Don't let him tire. Renew his strength as the eagle's. Lord, You can use him. Glorify Yourself by proving You can give him the strength."

Merikay needed an unexpected intestinal operation. One our doctor had never performed. Delicate. Dangerous.

Suddenly, a frantic summons squalled over the loudspeaker. They didn't have to use the word *emergency.* It throbbed underneath the words. "Surgeon needed in Op 13 . . . right away . . . a general surgeon." The voice rose a few notes. "Any surgeon."

Twenty-five operating rooms. All in use. A six-hundred-bed hospital. And not one single surgeon available. The call shrilled out a second time. A third time. Back in the operating room, the physician's scalpel was poised. He couldn't wait any longer. Heavy blood loss. Danger of cardiac arrest.

Just entering the hospital at that moment for a routine

checkup on a patient, a young surgeon heard the emergency call, bounded into the operating room. He thrust out his hands for the sterile rubber gloves, seized the scalpel, did an operation only he had ever done: a pie-shaped niche in the colon.

Back in bed a day later, wan and white, Merikay smiled at me. In a few days she was up hobbling about, carrying her intravenous bottle in her hand. She flitted from bed to bed, cheering the other patients.

# 18

# Slip-ups Enroute to Sainthood

Swiftly the years slipped past. Merikay often counseled with me as a team at the rapidly growing Tennessee-Georgia Camps Farthest Out. Out of her suffering was forged a compassion that God mightily used for the healing of sick bodies and minds. However, I felt I should cut down on my extensive traveling ministry and spend more time at home with her.

I had been living a faith life. But LB criticized me for this increasingly, and Merikay parroted her comments. Now I decided to prove that I could make money *and* serve God. I got involved with an outfit called Era International Development Corporation. Many Christians hold jobs and still serve God, I told myself. But I was to learn at great cost never to pattern my life after any other man, only to obey the will of God for me.

Before long I became president of the corporation. Then I

found that I had inherited a morass of concealed debts. I tried to put the company on sound financial footing, but I finally became convinced I had to visit the Asian offices personally.

My stay in the Orient stretched out beyond the originally planned ten days. At times it reminded me of Haiti. The calm impassive Oriental face. The formal bowing head. The toothy smile. A very pleasant but frustrating way of saying "no."

The lengthening pressure of my absence, plus the constant criticism of LB—highly seasoned descriptions of where I came from, what I was, and where I was going—caused Merikay to reach again for the bottle. On some of our transoceanic conversations she became embarrassingly vituperative.

But a multimillion dollar mahogany deal was at stake. I was determined not to return without wrapping it up. It meant at least two to three million dollars a year profit to our company. I would get a big salary and a hefty chunk of stock. I'd be a millionaire again. And just look at all the good I could do spreading the Gospel with that kind of money!

But I ran out of money as the weeks turned into months. Our Washington office had promised to send funds. They never came. A Texas oilman had promised to stake me to optioning a new oil site in Indonesia. His money never came. I lost the oil deal.

In fact I owed the hotel so much I couldn't afford to move out, and I couldn't afford to stay. Every day the pressure to pay my bill increased. It appeared that I was facing jail. No jail is pleasant, but an Asian jail is at the bottom of the pile. One night I made an urgent collect call. I told LB that if I didn't have x-number of thousands within twenty-four hours, I'd never come back—probably spend the rest of my life in jail.

As usual LB responded. A couple days later, just as they were about to throw me out of the hotel, the funds came through. That revised many of my former thoughts about LB. No matter what, she was a tower of strength in time of need.

It was one of a number of four-figure checks she wrote for me as she loudly proclaimed to anyone who'd listen, "My daughter isn't going to embarrass the Howards by being married to some no-good jailbird!"

Her bark was always worse than her bite. "After all," I said once when her vocal fury subsided as she sucked in a large breath, "I'm your favorite son-in-law."

"Favorite!" she exploded. "Thank God, you're the only one I've got!"

It wasn't easy for me to be a Christian around LB. Or even to sound like one. "Here comes Jesus," she'd rasp in that cold voice that never seemed to thaw out even in summer, even when she spoke to Merikay.

The ridicule in front of anyone and everyone was more than I could take. One day as I was licking my wounds and complaining to the Lord, He seemed to say, "Aren't you proud to be called by My name?"

That was a whole different ball game. Next time she sneered in front of her sophisticated guests in minks and evening gowns and tuxedos, "Here comes the Jesus man," I bowed slightly.

"Thank you, LB," I said in an innocent voice. "I'm so glad you recognize the Spirit of Jesus in me."


More weeks of negotiating passed. The mahogany concesssion was finally signed, and I went home.

Merikay cautiously welcomed, and LB tolerated, my homecoming. But my wife's initial coldness melted as she forgave my protracted absence. Too late I was to learn that whenever I planned a long trip away from her, internal pressure would build up like a head of steam in a boiler. The worry about what LB would say. The dark pressures she would have to face alone. No wonder she slipped from time to time.

Now I know I spent too much time away from home. Not just on the Lord's business, but also on my own. That senseless pursuit of the will-o-the-wisp called fortune. As if I didn't know better by now. But I was blinded by pride and the hurt caused by LB's harsh verbal barrage.

"Never did a decent day's work in your life. You've been sponging off the Howards ever since you snatched Merikay out of the cradle. Why you're old enough to be her father!"

"Not quite. Just fourteen years older, LB."

"Why, she could have married the son of the president of the second biggest steel company! She could have had a prominent politician. He proposed when he was just an ensign at the Great Lakes Naval Base. And look at him now, a leader in the House of Representatives! Why some day, who knows, he might even be president of the United States! But you," she'd spit out in naked disgust, "you're worse than nobody. You get-rich-quick-Wallingford. You cheat . . . you liar . . . you leech . . . you skunk! And I *mean* it!"

Yes, she meant it all right. And even if Merikay didn't mean it, even if sometimes her thoughts were too blurred to realize what she was saying, too often she echoed those barbed words. But more often, when her natural sweet self, Merikay would defend me in a white-hot fury of her own.

"Stop it," she'd cry desperately, digging her long sharp nails into LB's wrist. "Or I'll never come back here again!" However, she was as effective as a butterfly beating its fragile wings against a tank.

Gentle Tex would look up with pain-narrowed eyes from the big red chair facing the TV set where he spent nearly every moment of his waking hours. He watched football, golf, baseball, basketball, or "As the World Turns"—almost anything that would help him escape the world around him.

"Now, LB," he'd begin in that big voice that was always soft and gentle when he spoke to her. And that's as far as he'd usually get.

In spite of all my efforts, Era did not make it. Associates whom I brought into the picture took over the sure-thing mahogany concession. We lost our money and I lost the faith of those who had risked their money in reliance on my integrity. I was sued by fellow Christians. The cruelest cut of all. The Law of Compensation, Emerson calls it. Even though the men were finally sentenced to prison, I learned a hard lesson through it all. If God wanted me to live by faith, then that is what I had better do.

Some time later our friends, Chet and Mary Weirich, were driving us back from ministering at a Full Gospel Business Men's meeting near Chatauqua. The Holy Spirit had moved in great power through me. A number of people had been visibly healed. Perspiring and thirsty after a couple of hours of this, I grabbed a nearby pitcher of ice water and gulped down its contents. Later Merikay reminded me we had a drive of several hours back to Buffalo and it would be wise to visit the rest room. I turned that way. Somebody stopped me to ask a question, and I completely forgot about it.

Unfortunately there were no gas stations along the New York Throughway. Pride kept me from asking Chet to stop the car anywhere along the snow-heaped highway. I waited until we got back to the Weirichs' house.

Once there I discovered to my consternation that I had developed acute urinary retention. That could require catheterization in the hospital. I was considering what to do when my eye caught a framed verse on the wall, "You shall serve the Lord your God and He will bless your bread and your water; and I will remove sickness from your midst" (Exodus 23:25).

It was as though God were saying to me that I could be healed either way. I could go to the hospital and be catheterized. Or I could trust God. It was a hard decision. But I had trusted Him before and He had never failed me. All that night as the whole house slept, the Lord showed me the blotted pages of my life . . . broken promises . . . self-will, carelessness of other people's feelings . . . page after page. With tears of regret, I begged for forgiveness. I prayed in tongues, sometimes softly, sometimes almost shouting in my anguish. Couldn't say a word in English.

The next morning I was to speak at a Fellowship breakfast. Chet urged me to go to the hospital or at least try to take it easy in bed. My stomach was too swollen to fasten my belt. Mary and Merikay had to lace my shoes. I couldn't bend over. I wrapped my heavy lined raincoat around me to cover my bulging stomach.

At the Holiday Inn, Chet suggested I just greet the people who had been praying for me. There were several speakers there who could substitute. I insisted on speaking as advertised. "You shall serve the Lord your God . . ." I must serve Him to claim His promise.

I wavered as I struggled up from my seat. The pain caused perspiration to pour down my face. I claimed another promise, "Open your mouth and I will fill it." Instantly strength came back. With every forced word, my voice became stronger. Later when we listened to the tape, Merikay shook her blonde head in awe.

"Nobody would ever guess in a million years that you were suffering such pain."

When I invited people to come up for prayer, again Chet

urged me to let the other ministers pray for the crowd. It looked as though the whole room had surged forward. I knew in my heart I had to pray, had to finish serving the Lord even if I burst in two. With a couple other men, I moved through the crowd for over an hour, until the last seeker had been touched by the power of God.

For about ten days I sweated out the promises of God, hardly able to leave the bed. Each night moisture seemed to seep out of my body. Just about the same amount of liquid I drank so prayerfully and sparingly. Each morning our saintly hostess, Mary, would have to change all the sheets.

It was a time of great testing. Everyone urged me to go to the nearby hospital. Death comes fast from uremic poisoning. My stomach burned with a fierce fire. It felt hard, as though filled with cement. The pain was excruciating.

God sent Dr. Winston Nunes to encourage me. Wise in the ways of God, he laid hands on me and urged me to believe God but suggested I not be too proud to seek healing through doctors and hospitals when they were so available. However, in my heart I had determined to trust God.

To me the issues were clear. The last time I had trusted God to raise me up from a deathbed, I had had no choice. The doctors had given me up. I was beyond human help. This time I faced a test at a higher level, a greater challenge to my faith. I could choose to accept human help, or I could choose what I felt to be God's way—trusting Him.

During those days, I continued ministering wherever the Lord opened up opportunities. I experienced unusual blessing on those times. Many people were helped.

Then I capitulated to Merikay's pleas to go in for a long-neglected physical examination. The doctor took one look at my bloated stomach. Before I knew what had happened, he had catheterized me. Almost one gallon of urine came out. My stomach went down.

"You've destroyed the architecture of your kidneys," he said gravely. "You may have to wear a catheter the rest of your life."

He sent me to a top urologist who promptly had me admitted to Evanston Hospital. When the urologist came to see me next day, my urethra had ruptured. He tentatively diagnosed it as cancer of the prostrate. He postponed the operation for eight days. During that time I fasted, drinking only a vegetable cocktail of carrot, beet and celery juices brought me each day.

Then I discharged myself from the hospital, much to Merikay's consternation. She was upset by the doctor's dire warnings as soon as he found out I'd escaped. So believing I was healed, but for her peace of mind, I returned to the hospital, underwent a painful exploratory operation and biopsy which proved that if I ever had had cancer, I didn't any more. For months I suffered slow recovery, many times regretting I had yielded to Merikay's persuasion.

My feelings about this whole experience are mixed. I feel that I was right to hold out for God's way as long as I did. God worked a deep spiritual cleansing in my life during this time. He blessed many other people—through my suffering. I am only sorry that I was not permitted to trust God to the end—even to the point of death. But He knows my heart.

# 19

# Vienna

Merikay's tongue had become swollen. She put off going to the doctor, fearing what he might find. At last she could stand the uncertainty no longer. She made an appointment. The biopsy confirmed her worst fears. It was cancer. Now she almost came unglued.

The doctor recommended surgery, and Merikay agreed. In a five-hour operation the surgeon removed about one-third of her tongue. Through the torturous days and nights that followed, I wondered, would she ever be able to talk again? Would I ever hear that throaty velvet voice again?

Finally, bandages and stitches removed, she began to make noises. Thank God, her larynx was okay, but it was hard to understand her. She had to learn how to talk all over again.

Just before the operation, a friend had told me about a new

nutritional approach to controlling cancer, called Laetrile. I had urged Merikay to try this, which might make the operation unnecessary. But she had been psyched up and went ahead with the mutilating surgery.

The FDA was making it difficult to use Amygdalin-Laetrile in the United States, so I had been praying to be able to take Merikay to Germany for possible treatment. The FGBMFI was planning another airlift, but Merikay was uninterested.

Then a good friend phoned when I was out one day and interested her in going to East Germany on the airlift. When she found that we could also visit Vienna, Merikay became enthusiastic. Her great-grandmother, a countess, had emigrated from Vienna.

So it was that a number of weeks later, we stood before the open door of a candle-lit apartment in Vienna. Vienna State Opera singer, Reid Bunger, and his wife welcomed us graciously. We had never met them, but we had some mutual friends.

Before we entered the living room Bette Bunger lowered her voice in a warning. "We're born-again Christians like you. We also believe in the baptism in the Holy Spirit and divine healing, but not for today. We'll have to ask you not to even talk about Jesus to the friends we've invited tonight. They're intellectuals. Opera singers, diplomats, scientists. We don't want to frighten them off."

"I will pass your request along to God, but I'll have to do what the Holy Spirit wants," I said. Out of my mouth that night came the whole Gospel—the full Gospel. How we can know Jesus in any or all of his three manifestations, as Savior, Great Physician and Baptizer in the Holy Spirit.

The room became very quiet. I asked the Lord what to do next. He said, "Go lay hands on each one of them."

Merikay and I went around among these intellectuals, scientists, and opera singers, laying on hands. Some of them jumped nervously, some of them dodged, but a few seemed to yield. The last ones we prayed with were Reid Bunger and his wife, Bette. They both began to speak softly in tongues.

"I knew God sent you to answer the hunger in our hearts," Bette whispered, face radiant. "At first when I got your letter, I wasn't sure. Speaking in tongues is so divisive."

God also moved in other ways that evening. During the afternoon there had been an urgent call from the wife of a high U.N. official. She wanted to bring Christina, the nineteen-year-old epileptic daughter of another high official. I was reluctant because in my experience I had found many epileptics to have a demonic problem. You can never tell what they're going to do. She came in before the meeting started. Silently in the Spirit Merikay and I bound the demon spirit in her, and commanded him to be silent during the meeting.

As soon as the other guests began departing, this wild-eyed girl rushed over to us.

"What's the matter with free love? What's the matter with getting high on pot? What's the matter with drinking?" she demanded.

I just put my right hand on her head and commanded, "In the name of Jesus Christ I cast out this spirit of epilepsy and all other foul spirits of Satan!"

Instantly, the girl's eyes changed. She became warm and loving. She threw her arms around Merikay's neck, and asked us not to leave her.

Christina had suffered from grand mal epilepsy for seven years. She was on heavy medication every hour. She couldn't go to school, couldn't work. Her mother had become a slave, hardly ever left their luxurious apartment.

Next morning her father telephoned, very upset. Christina was refusing to take her medication. Georges Tchamitch expected his daughter to have an attack at any moment. He urged us to come right away and undo the damage we had done and persuade her to take her medicine.

"Look at her, look at her! She's going to have an attack any minute," her father said when he met us at the door.

"Has she had an attack?"

"Not yet. But she will any minute."

"I didn't tell her to stop taking the medicine. It must be Jesus."

"She keeps saying that Jesus healed her."

"He is the Great Physician," I replied slowly. "If Chris feels that way, and hasn't had an attack, it seems to me that she is healed." I thought for a moment. "Has anything else happened that is different?"

"Any time Christina wrote her name she went into an epileptic fit," the father said. "But this morning she wrote a four-page letter to her brother in London."

"Looks like pretty good proof that she's healed." I smiled.

"I don't know about that. I don't know anything about angels and demons and Jesus," he answered, softening. "This is all beyond me. But if your prayers did so much good, maybe you should pray with her again."

We sat her on one of those big cushion stools. Merikay and I laid hands on her and prayed that Chris would be baptized with the Holy Spirit. Immediately she began to praise God in another language. After a few minutes I turned around and looked at her father.

Tears were trickling down his cheeks. I went over to him. "Wouldn't you like to meet the Jesus that healed your daughter?"

He nodded. So we led him to the Lord and prayed for him to receive the baptism in the Holy Spirit. Georges Tchamitch, diplomat, linguist, cosmopolitan, began to speak a language he had never learned.

Across the room his Swedish wife sat stoney-faced. The Holy Spirit said, "Go over to her."

She seemed a very unlikely candidate, but Merikay and I walked over and asked, "Would you like to know Jesus?"

She nodded and we prayed with her. She also came into the kingdom of Christ.

Georges Tchamitch couldn't do enough for us. "Have a martini!"

"Thank you, but I don't drink."

"Then have a cigar." He thrust it at me. "Pre-Castro."

"Thanks, but I don't smoke."

His face fell. "Isn't there anything I can do for you?"

I looked around the spacious room. There was a beautiful grand piano. The score of a Beethoven concerto lay open on the stand.

"Beethoven is a favorite of mine," I said. "Would you play that concerto?"

"Oh," he replied, hands trembling, "I'm too moved. I couldn't play right now."

"If you play under the power of the Holy Spirit," I replied, "you'll never play better in your life."

So the little man sat down, and rolled up his sleeves. As we looked out the picture window at the city of Vienna, we'd never heard that concerto played as well by Rachmaninoff, Rubinstein, or any other.

Later Christina wrote a poem for us to express her gratitude. Previously, this girl could not even write a letter. How great is God's power!

### White—and Red and Black

*Turn and look, and learn from little children what is love, what is truth.*
*Babes are we all, all staining our swathing robes of trusting innocence hourly as we grow.*

*And when we are full in the flesh, then indeed we wear black.*

*For black is the color of earthly knowledge. And in knowledge is no trust.*

*Therefore, black is the color of mourning throughout the world.*

*Black is the color of fear.*

*And out of this darkness which is black can come nothing but pain.*

*Learn from children, for all are afraid of the dark.*

*We do not wear white when we are old.*

*We say, "White is for the virgin, for the good, for the innocent."*

*Therefore, we cannot wear white, we are too old.*

*For we are afraid of God's wrath upon us, if we disguise ourselves in a color opposite to our proper natures, for before Him we are naked.*

*And so, round and round, like squirrels in a cage we go, in an ever-widening circle as we shrink before God.*

*And is the circle not our own symbol of the human ego?*

*Red is the color of blood.*

*Reveling in red and laughing a crazy poisoned laugh—signs of nature rejoicing in sin.*

*Red is a color we like because we "remember" we are not our brother's keeper.*

*Therefore, red is the color of evil, though it is the color of blood.*

*God is the center of the circle, the great Light of every soul.*

*God always gives, and love is giving. God always accepts, and love is acceptance.*

*God has infinite patience, and love is waiting in trust.*

*For what child refuses a sweet, even if it is poisoned? It does not know.*

*Only the child says simply, never shyly, "I love you."*

*For we are hard and dark, and blush to say, "I love."*

*We think, "Oh, they will laugh with scorn!"*

*And such laughter kills the flame of light and hope, and then we die.*

*For love is not only giving, but taking also.*

*But because we strive, in "love," to trust, we endure in relative content in the whole, with the whole, and for the whole.*

*And so, therefore, is white the color of Love.*

We ministered to a number of other individuals in Vienna. Some were healed. Some were baptized in the Holy Spirit. Some came to Christ for the first time. Peter Bronson was one of the notable converts. Leader of the International High School, he had set the pace for his fellow students in hashish, speed and other drugs. Within a few weeks as a Christian he turned the school around, led ninety students to Jesus.

The opera star, Reid Bunger, and his wife were to start a prayer group for the international set and another for the young music students who throng Vienna from everywhere—spiritual pebbles whose ripples still go out today, spreading across Europe in the fields of music, the arts, science and international politics.

Just before leaving Vienna, the Lord led me to seek a courtesy meeting with the Archbishop of Austria, Franz, Cardinal Koenig. For three-quarters of an hour we discussed the charismatic renewal sweeping the world.

Then he asked why the Full Gospel Businessmen's Fellowship International did not hold a crusade in Austria, as we were doing in Scandinavia and Germany.

"We have not been invited," I replied. *After all,* I thought, *Austria is the most Catholic of nations, about 98 percent, the site of the ancient Holy Roman Empire.*

The Cardinal leaned forward, opening his arms. "I am inviting you."

"But do you know what we believe, Your Eminence?"

"Tell me."

"We believe every person should have a personal relationship with Jesus."

"So do I." The Cardinal sighed. "I wish all my people knew Jesus in this personal way. What else?"

"We believe in divine healing, that Jesus still heals today just as when He walked the shores of Galilee."

"So do I. There's no reason why people have to go all the way to Lourdes for healing." He sighed again. "They could be healed in our churches right in Vienna. In their hospital beds, even at home. If they'd just believe. What else?"

This time I took a deep breath. "We also believe that the baptism in the Holy Spirit, as on the day of Pentecost, is for today. For whosoever will."

A long pause. "I am for anything that will make our people stronger Christians." Another pause. The Cardinal rose, taking both my hands in his. "When can you bring the Fellowship to Austria?"

I could hardly believe my ears. Even in 1970 it was early in the move of the Holy Spirit among Catholics. Merikay and I took the plane for new adventures in Berlin. We virtually were walking on clouds.

On Sunday, Merikay went with me to the Assembly of God church in the heart of Berlin.

"The morning service," Pastor Spitzer explained, "always lasts exactly two hours, from ten to twelve. This allows the worshipers time to get the bus or subway home and still return in time for the five o'clock evening service."

The Lord led me to share my healing testimony and to point out the need for coming to God with clean hands spiritually.

When the invitation was given for those who wanted spiritual or physical healing to come forward, the whole church started coming, five hundred people. They formed a big U from the rear of the church past the platform and over to the other side. The pastor and I began at the rear and laid hands on each one. Deaf ears were opened to hear. Blind eyes were opened to see. Hard hearts were opened to receive the love of God. It was glorious. It was a special delight for me to see Merikay sharing her faith in Christ with women in the line.

We prayed and prayed. Finally the last person had been

prayed for. It was three-thirty. I was exhausted and I marvelled at Merikay.

But after lunch and a half hour's rest we were back again. It was almost a totally new congregation. Those from the morning service hadn't had time to eat and return. But this time Dr. Clarence Fast and Jim McLendon arrived when the time came for prayer. Since they spoke German, Dr. Fast and Jim took one half of the long line. But it was still nearly ten o'clock that night before we wearily left. Merikay stuck with it to the very end, exhausted though she was.

In Hanover we visited Dr. Nieper who is pioneering in nutritional treatment of cancer with Amygdalin. He removed several stitches overlooked in Merikay's throat and gave her a strict dietary regimen. He said that if she would faithfully follow his instructions, he was sure cancer would not recur. It would stay under control. But, he warned her, any deviation or even short suspension of the daily treatment could result in recurrence.

Much encouraged, Merikay plunged into the divine healing ministry with zeal. The experience of the mass healings that Sunday in Berlin had reassured her that Jesus wanted to use her in an even greater way in the healing ministry.

# 20

# Four Stars in Our Eyes

Back home again, faithfully following the Nieper treatment, Merikay's health bloomed. She went nearly everywhere with me on my missions. In July 1971 I was one of the speakers at the annual retreat of the Buffalo Fellowship chapter. Merikay came too. Since I was an Episcopalian, the retreat chairman asked me to go to the airport with him to meet Ralph Haines, the Episcopalian general who was to preside at the military prayer breakfast the next morning.

With the general was his wife, Sally, and a staff aide, a major. As we rode back in the limousine, I figured I should cushion the shock they might have at what they would see at the convention. So I began to share about the lengthening of legs and other miracles that were going on. The "Doubting Thomas" miracles I call them. God in His mercy lets us see a crippled back straighten or a short leg grow out right before our eyes. It makes it easier to believe for the healing of things we can't see, like heart attacks or cancer. I told how, just the year before, my own right leg had miraculously grown out one and one-eighth inches.

The major got stiffer and stiffer, turned into an icicle beside me.

At dinner the Holy Spirit led Merikay and me to talk to the general about the baptism with the Holy Spirit and what power it brings into a Christian's life. Sally Haines became excited. "Wouldn't you please give the baptism to my husband?" she asked.

"There's nothing I'd rather do," I said. "But no man can give this. It's from Jesus. He is the Baptizer." I thought to myself, *I should lay hands on a four star general? There might be another war and where would I end up?* But we prayed, the four of us, holding hands over the coffee cups, that the general would have a sovereign experience.

At the head table that night I sat at the general's right side. Harald Bredesen, the speaker, sat on his left. Harald gave a message on the power and presence of the Holy Spirit, one of the most beautiful sermons I've ever heard. The crowded room became intensely quiet. As we stood, God's glory came down and encapsuled the general. His face began to go through contortions. He began to mumble a sound or two. I put my arm around his shoulder from the right side, and Harald from the left, and with over three hundred people watching, he began to speak in other languages.

Later the general described his experience: "All of a sudden, I heard this voice coming out in some strange language. Then I realized it was my voice, and I knew I was on a special wave length up there."

Our wives were sitting at the table directly opposite.

Suddenly Sally Haines leaped up from her seat, rushed across the floor, and threw her arms around his neck. "Oh, Ralph, darling, I'm so glad." And she began speaking in tongues, too.

It was a beautiful moment. The general hugged and kissed her. Then he turned around and grabbed Major Allinder and squeezed him in a big bear hug. Over the general's shoulder, Major Al's face turned red as he choked out, "I'm the first Marine major to be hugged by a four star general!" Then he hugged Harald Bredesen and me (almost breaking our ribs), and Merikay who had followed Sally.

As she slipped out of his embrace, Merikay looked ruefully at the four long scratches left on her bare arm by the stars. "I'm the first girl to be scratched by a four star general."

After the meeting Harald, Merikay and I went up to the general's suite. We spent several hours with him going over the Scriptures, praying with him and encouraging him to pray at will. As Harald said wisely, "The devil is going to fight this one with all he's got."

It was nearly five in the morning when we left.

After that convention General Haines began to talk about Jesus everywhere he went. As commander of the Continental Army Command (USCONARC) with the four continental armies and the military district of Washington under him, he went everywhere. His responsibility was to direct, coordinate and inspect the training of the army in the field within the continental U.S. He would call a meeting of all chaplains and noncommissioned officers and talk to them about Jesus. He would tell them there had to be a spiritual renewal in the army.

He spoke at the Washington Fellowship military prayer breakfast, at colleges, at Explo '72 in the Cotton Bowl in Dallas, and at the presidential prayer breakfast. At 6 A.M. each Friday in his office he held a prayer breakfast for a dozen generals on his staff.

He talked so much about Jesus that a Jewish reporter on the *Washington Star* wrote a scathing interview on the front page. It asked suspiciously who was paying for the general to fly around the nation talking about religion? The church and state are supposed to be separate, it stated. Something ought to be done about this.

Something was done. A congressional committee in charge of military affairs called the general in and asked him what he was doing. He explained that he was not making special trips for religious purposes. But as he inspected various bases around the country, he was taking his free time to speak at meetings and to talk to troops. He felt that the spiritual dimension was the most neglected in the military, and improving it was just part of his job.

Later he described the meeting to me. "I gave them my whole testimony from beginning to end. They became uncomfortable. Some of them said, 'That's enough, General. We've got the picture.' "

This testimony was printed in the *Congressional Record* in July 1972.

When the general retired six months later, he began to travel and speak about the Lord everywhere. Almost every major military base in the country invited him to address their troops. He was featured speaker at the Easter sunrise service at the big El Paso base. He spoke at West Point, the Air Force Academy, even Annapolis.


Summer came, and we had an invitation to speak for the Fellowship in Davenport, Iowa. The night before, Merikay had been visiting at 1015 and apparently yielded to LB's idea that "one little drink won't hurt you." She staggered into the bedroom, slipped off our bed and broke her kneecap. I had to leave her at 1015 and go on to Davenport. So I would not have to travel alone, I asked our missionary friend, John Childers, to accompany me. We arranged to meet on the freeway near the Brookfield Zoo. Getting Merikay taken care of and settled had taken all morning. I had to hurry, as there was a five to six hour drive ahead.

At the appointed place where the freeway branched off, I found myself starting down a turn marked "To Chicago." Once I took that I'd have to drive for miles before I could turn around. So I backed up carefully and parked on the overpass near the intersection. With its siren wailing and red light revolving, a police car swooped down. Two officers slowly unfolded from it. One flipped his pad open.

"Don't you know it's against the law to back up on a busy freeway?"

"But, Officer," I weakly protested, "I looked. There was nothing coming."

"And you're illegally parked on an overpass."

"But . . ." I started to remind him that he had pulled in front.

I fished around in all my pockets. All I came up with was the morning's mail I had taken from our box unopened. The policeman shook his head. "Doesn't prove a thing. Don't you have any identification?"

"Must be a hot car," added the other officer darkly.

"It's my wife's car," I explained. "All my papers and my driver's license are in my wallet."

"Where's your wallet?"

"That's what I'd like to know." Now I was searching desperately, turning all my pockets inside out. I found a printed testimony with the picture of our Fellowship group and Nehru on his palace steps.

"That's me," I pointed.

"Must have been a long time ago. Doesn't look anything like you."

I found a *VOICE* magazine at the back of the car seat. Inside was a group picture. "That's me."

"Hah!" grunted the first officer. "Too small to tell. Where's your license?"

"In my wallet."

"Yeah." A knowing wink. "What wallet?"

"It's red leather and . . . " I was still fumbling desperately. "It's been an upsetting day. My wife broke her knee last night, and I just took her to the hospital this morning and . . . "

"Why'd you wait so long?"

"She didn't want to wake up our doctor, so . . . "

"So . . . " The officers had me sitting between them in their patrol car. "You say you live in Glencoe?"

"Yes. 574 Woodlawn."

"Where are you going anyway?"

"To Davenport, Iowa. I'm late now. You see this missionary friend is supposed to be meeting me here to drive out. He'll have a license."

"Yeah?" The freeway along the overpass was empty. "Where? I don't see no missionary."

Neither did I. But I was praying desperately. "Dear Lord, send John. Hurry up, Lord. Can't you see I'm in trouble?"

"What are you going to Davenport for?"

"To speak at a Full Gospel Business Men's . . ."

"Full what?" The officer sneered. He reached across me and tapped his pal's shoulder to get his attention from the radio. He was scrunched down talking to someone. "This guy thinks he's really somebody! Well, let's show him. We treat 'em all alike: mayors, big shots, loud mouths."

Just then John's red hair appeared at the car window.

"There he is!" I cried with relief. "There's my missionary friend, just like I told you. He can identify me . . . "

I stopped short when I realized John had a rakish green beret sloping over his red hair. A bright yellow sports jacket. Green slacks. And he was wearing the black and white genuine snakeskin shoes from Hong Kong I had given him. His eyes blinked owlishly behind his Granny glasses.

"That's a missionary?" the officer exploded into laughter.

"Prove it, John!" I urged. "Show him your identification." John handed him his minister's credentials. Assembly of God.

"Never heard of it!" barked the officer. "Where's your driver's license?"

My heart stopped as John opened his billfold and took out a license dated at his home city, Las Vegas, Nevada. Both cops roared with laughter. "Probably some con artist!"

"Okay," said the first officer, starting to write on his pad. "First violation. Backing up against traffic. Then illegal parking on an overpass. And driving without a driver's license." His voice was ominous. "What else can we lay on him, Joe?"

Joe put the radio away. "What's the number of your driver's license?"

"It starts with H something," I faltered. "I really don't know."

Over the radio blared a police call. A green Cadillac was going ninety miles an hour the wrong way down the tollway. It was a calling-all-cars alert.

"Better go after that guy," I suggested hopefully. "He might kill somebody."

"What about you, buddy?"

"Oh, I'll wait till you get back."

The calling-all-cars summons shrieked again. The officer with the pad closed it up and put his pencil away.

"Joe, how are we going to write a ticket when he doesn't even know his license number? Let's go after that green Cadillac."

Both John and I sighed with relief as they pushed me out of the patrol car, and zoomed off. John took over the wheel. "I've traveled around the world on faith," John said, shaking his head. "But this is the greatest miracle I ever saw. No license. No fine. No arrest. God must really want you in Davenport tonight!"

At first I didn't think so. Nobody in the banquet hall looked as though he needed healing. But when I walked into the next room, a little nun with a hip-long metal brace on one leg hobbled up.

"Please pray for my leg," she said sweetly.

"Do you have faith to believe God, Sister?" I asked.

"Yes," she answered firmly.

"Then take off that brace." I was surprised to hear the words come out of my mouth. She sat right down in a chair and unscrewed the heavy metal brace. I picked up her left leg and almost regretted having done so. It was lifeless and cold. It appeared about seven inches shorter than the right leg. I got down on my knees and prayed as hard as I could. Nothing seemed to happen. Five, ten, fifteen minutes went by. All the time I was telling God He had to perform a miracle for His own sake. Then I realized I was operating by sight, not by faith. I changed my prayer.

"Thank you, Lord, that You are answering our prayers, Your way."

Warmth began to come into her leg, but I couldn't see anything visible.

"Lord, I know you're healing her. But please let me see something," I said. Suddenly her leg began to grow across my palm. About two inches. Then it stopped. I prayed. Perspiration poured down my face. But no matter how I prayed nothing seemed to happen.

"Lord, what's the problem? Is it me?"

God said, "There is a Baptist minister out there who needs to be in on this miracle. Call him in."

Months before, Paul Vogel had been sent home to die from multiple sclerosis by the Mayo Clinic. He had driven a couple hundred miles to get us to pray for him as a last resort. Jesus had touched him as Merikay and I prayed. He had begun to walk and leap.

So I called Paul in, gave him the leg to hold and told him to pray. In about ten minutes the thin, shriveled leg grew another two inches across his palm, then stopped. He couldn't give it back to me fast enough.

I took it again. "Lord, it's only grown out about two-thirds of the way."

God answered, "That missionary traveling with you never has seen a physical miracle."

So I called John Childers. He prayed loudly, and in four or five minutes her leg began to grow. John's red hair almost stood up on end. When the leg stopped growing, he handed it back to me.

For forty-five minutes altogether I'd been praying on my knees. "What do I do now, Lord? I'm about prayed out."

The nun asked, "Can I get up and stand on my leg now?"

I said, "You can do anything God tells you to do." So she got up. Leaning on the arm of another nun, she began to walk around the room, rejoicing.

In the meantime I asked out of curiosity, "How long has your leg been this way?"

"Since I had polio at the age of two," she answered. "And I'm thirty-five now."

After she walked out I said, "Lord, You're a God of perfection. And that leg is still about an inch short. How do You account for that?"

Then God said, "She's a teaching nun. I want the five hundred students at her school to watch the end of this miracle."

And that's the way it happened.

Merikay was staying at her mother's while recuperating from the broken kneecap. When I was in town I stayed there, too, but I left frequently on the Lord's work.

Esther, LB's cook-housekeeper, loved Merikay like a sister. Up and down the stairs she flew with breakfast, with lunch, with dinner, with snacks, with everything. She tried her worried best to prevent LB from bootlegging liquor into Merikay; showed me secret hiding places in dresser drawers, under dresses, under underwear, under everything. Every bottle we found I'd toss into the garbage can. But the stream—slowed to a trickle—flowed on. Even when I was in bed beside Merikay, LB would manage to replace the bottles. Sometimes I'd wake in the late night to see her drifting by like some ghost in negligee, bottle cuddled babylike in her arms . . . or in the early dawn slipping silently through the hallway connecting the two bedrooms.

So many times we had thought that the battle with alcohol was won, only to be plunged into the thick of it again. Sometimes I wondered, will we ever win?

# 21

# Teeth of Death

Could I praise God in the face of disaster? This question had plagued me for many years. Suppose my house burned down? Suppose I lost my job? Suppose my wife died suddenly? Could I really praise God? The Bible tells us to "in everything give thanks; for this is God's will in Christ Jesus for you." But could I really praise God? Then on a snowy December afternoon I discovered the answer.

Our propjet plane had made an emergency landing on a handkerchief-sized airfield at Le Mars, Iowa. The ceiling was low and getting lower. Falling snow was being swirled by a brisk wind. The pilot was eager to fly back to Chicago before the weather closed in. I was involved in a business discussion with a friend who had driven down for the meeting. We sat in the car, parallel to the plane. Several times the pilot ran over and urged us to conclude our conversation.

After a while my friend and I walked over to the plane and found the rear door on the left side closed. We went up to the cockpit and called to the pilot through the small hatch, "What about the door?"

"Hurry up, we have to make a fuel stop," he answered. "We've got to get going."

So I walked around the nose of the plane, thinking that there was a door open on the starboard side. With a shock I saw that the propeller was revolving. I turned to walk away from the propeller. Suddenly I was struck from behind and thrown violently onto the runway. The pilot had leaned over to shake hands with the other man through the hatch. In so doing, he had relaxed the pressure on his right brake pedal. The plane had swerved around and caught me from behind.

Blood gushed out of my torn body. The propeller had cut the overcoat and clothes from my body and severed the bones, muscles and tendons of my leg. My left foot lay about six inches from my left cheek. My left arm was mangled. The elbow joint was destroyed, I had fourteen compound fractures, and the radial bone was completely gone. My hip joint was broken, the ball smashed into powder, the neck of the femur broken. Four pieces of bone, one inch long, landed a hundred yards away.

But great joy flooded through me. Within a few minutes I would see Jesus face to face. I began to praise Him. First in English and then in a heavenly language, which enabled me to express the inexpressible. I wasn't interested in a physical healing. But if the Lord had any reason to keep me on earth, I prayed that I could keep a clear mind. For what seemed like hours I lay outside in weather fourteen degrees below zero. Though I lost almost all the blood in my body, I was never faint, never dizzy and never went into shock. Around the plane came my friend, moaning and groaning about how awful the situation was. I told him to stop it and begin to praise God.

Then the pilot came running out, clasping his head and saying, "My God, my God, forgive me!"

It was bitter cold lying there. My friend made a little pillow out of his coat and put it under my head. It seemed as though my spirit was out of my body watching everything. Like a movie, the whole scene unfolded before me. In a few moments the sheriff's car arrived, followed by the state highway trooper. Time seemed to stand still.

Some forty-five minutes later the ambulance came clanging up. The teenage driver leaped out with a rubber disposal bag in one hand and a whisk broom in the other.

At first glance he thought I was dead. "He doesn't need a doctor, he needs a preacher," he said.

"Where's your stretcher?" I asked.

"Didn't bring one," he said. "I heard the news on the radio and there's never enough left to fill the bag. But there is too much of you to put in the bag."

He had a problem.

I believe the Holy Spirit enables us to manifest any one of the nine gifts of the Spirit needed at any particular moment. Right then I needed knowledge, so I asked for that gift. I told him to go look in the back of his ambulance behind the brown blankets. He protested there was nothing there. But when he looked he found a stretcher.

"It looks long enough," he said, "and I hope strong enough." But the problem was how to get my broken, bleeding body onto the stretcher without leaving behind an arm or leg.

At this moment up drove a car with a Spirit-filled Catholic chiropractor. A patient had broken an appointment in his office six miles away, so he had decided to come out and fly his Piper Cub. Through my lips I heard directions coming which by-passed my mind, an act of the Holy Spirit. With no medical education, I gave such technical directions that they were able to get me on the stretcher intact. The chiropractor told me later that would have been impossible without such guidance.

The ambulance rushed me to a small clinic six miles away. My blood is a rare RH negative type. In that little town of 10,000 they had one unit. The nurses clustered around me trying to stop the flow of blood. I gave the doctor my mother-in-law's phone number. I wanted LB to cushion the shock for Merikay. When the doctor telephoned my mother-in-law, she remembered an old family friend whom she hadn't seen in thirty-five years. This man seldom returned to his office after lunch. But this day he was in the office when she called. He urged her to send me immediately to St. Joseph's Mercy Hospital in Sioux City, and he promised to get the best orthopedic surgeons to try to save my life. So the nurses trundled my bloodstained stretcher back into the ambulance.

"I was never so glad to get rid of a patient in my life," said the doctor later. "There was just no way to stop the flow of blood."

Off we went over those icy Iowa roads. Every time we crossed a railroad track the ambulance dropped about eighteen inches and my body bounced up. *They ought to make these things more comfortable,* I thought. Then I realized I was riding in a combination ambulance-hearse, and I wasn't even dead. I burst into laughter. I laughed all the way into the emergency room in the hospital. The doctors met me with their sleeves rolled up, scalpel ready. For a starter, they wanted to remove my arm and leg. I stopped laughing. I refused to let them. They warned me that I would die.

"Praise God," I said, "I'll see Jesus all the sooner."

"He's out of his mind," said one of the doctors and went to telephone my family.

Merikay, who didn't even know I was out of Chicago, picked up the telephone to hear a strange male voice urge, "We must have your immediate permission to amputate your husband's arm and leg to save his life."

She refused permission and hung up the telephone. Then she called the nearest prayer group. They called another group in Buffalo. In turn, they called the Christian Broadcasting Network. All over the country the wonderful electricity of Christian prayer went up. For the next six hours Merikay clung to the phone. California, Texas, Florida, Chicago, New York . . . she called them all.

Back in the hospital emergency room I could feel the prayers enfolding me, like the waves of the ocean lifting me up. Still the doctors were insisting that they had to amputate my leg and arm. Just then, in came the family friend. I asked for wisdom through the Holy Spirit. Out of my mouth came words that hadn't passed through my mind. In front of all the witnesses I gave the family friend the verbal power of attorney to sue the doctors for every penny they were worth if they amputated my arm or leg and I didn't survive the operation.

About this time a minister friend, Hugo Zerbe, began to pray in the Spirit in his office outside Chicago. My name came to his mind, He called my home. No answer. Then he called my mother-in-law. She told him she just heard the news I'd had a horrible accident in Iowa. Hugo asked Jim Smith, a minister in Sioux City, to look after me.

The next day as I was regaining consciousness, through the blur of pain I saw a tall man with a silly grin enter my hospital room.

"Thank God, brother," he said in a loud, cheerful voice, "you've come to Sioux City. For six months my church has fasted and prayed for a revival. Nobody has been saved, nobody healed, nobody baptized in the Holy Spirit. But God has sent you to start a revival."

I have met some strange people in my time, but this man was the strangest.

"What can I do in this broken, bleeding condition?" I asked with just a trace of self-pity.

His face shone with enthusiasm. "You can do anything and everything," he replied, "that you're willing to let Jesus do through you."

So through the weary weeks that followed, as I lay in the hospital on a Stryker frame, flat on my back, my left arm mangled, an IV needle in my right arm, my left leg in traction with a twenty-pound weight, I learned that we are never too weak, never too insignificant to be used by God if we are willing.

The hours dragged by.

Deep in the night I asked the Lord what the meaning of all this was.

"It's the answer to your prayers."

"My prayers, Lord?"

"Haven't you been praying for more time to pray and read the Bible?"

"Yes, Lord."

"What else do you have to do now?"

The combination radio-tape recorder which the minister left helped me hear more gospel messages over the local Christian radio station than I had heard in all my life. That night a Presbyterian banker, sent by the minister, came to my Intensive Care room. Rules permit only close members of the family five minutes out of each hour. The nurse asked if he was a close relative.

"Sister," I replied, "he's my brother."

She let him in. Five minutes later she told him his time was up. I told her we were still praying. She went away and came back in five minutes. I told her we were still praying. She returned the third time and said, "I know, you're still praying. That's the longest prayer I ever heard."

Soon the head nurse bustled in and accosted the banker. "Don't you realize this man is fighting for his life? You are sapping his strength and energy."

"We are praying to God," I reminded her.

She went outside and called all the nurses together. "The man in there is dying," she said. "He's out of his mind. Let him die happy. Don't go near him, no matter what he does or says."

For the next seven hours we had an uninterrupted prayer meeting in the Intensive Care unit. The banker was heart-hungry for more of the Christ who said, "he who believes in Me shall never thirst." In spite of my pain, the Holy Spirit brought to my mind Scripture verses which finally convinced the banker that the baptism in the Holy Spirit is for today, is even for Presbyterians, even for bankers, even for him.

As I lay flat on my back, my arms outstretched in that awkward position, the banker knelt beside the bed. So, Jesus the Great Baptizer, baptized him, according to His promise, with the Holy Spirit. He jumped up, raised his arms toward the ceiling and began to walk around and around that little hospital room, praising God in a language he had never learned. He became louder and louder.

"Not so loud," I said, "or we'll both be thrown out."

Outside the hospital room the nurses listened in awe. But they had been told not to interfere. So our prayer meeting lasted the remaining seven hours of that shift.

The next night the banker brought his ten-year-old son, who received Christ in simple childlike faith. The son also spoke a beautiful language that he had never learned. Amazed, the banker looked at me. "What took me so long?" he asked.

"That's what the Lord has been asking you," I replied.

However, there was much agony in those endless days. I hurt in so many places I couldn't count them. It's a traumatic experience to be catapulted from adult self-sufficiency to infantile dependence. For many days, I couldn't even scratch my nose. I was utterly dependent upon the care and the love of those ministering to me. When I asked the doctors about my condition, they shook their heads grimly and said that gangrene was bound to set in in my hip joint. Eventually they would have to amputate my leg anyway. Even if by some miracle I lived, I faced two years of lying in a hospital bed before I could even hope to be able to get into a wheelchair. I'd have to wear an artificial leg and arm the rest of my life.

During those dark days I kept proclaiming the healing promises of God, found throughout the Bible. Psalm 103 came alive for me. "Bless the Lord . . . Who heals *all* your *diseases; . . .*" In Isaiah 53:5 He promised me, "by His scourging we are healed."

When another dear friend, Arlie Pierce, drove all the way from Chicago in a blizzard to see me, I asked him to go to the newspaper office and get the reporter. I wanted to make sure that Jesus Christ got the credit for my healing.

"But you're not healed yet," protested the nun.

"Sister, that big, black book over there tells us 'by His scourging we are healed.' I can't stand upon the Word of God, but I'm lying full length on it."

Faith, the Apostle Paul tells us, is the evidence of things unseen. We must witness before the evidence of our senses confirms our faith.

Twice the hospital refused to admit the reporter. Finally I threatened the head nun that I would send for a stretcher and an ambulance and go to the newspaper office if they didn't permit the reporter to enter. Then my banker friend warned me that the reporter was a cynical woman who would write a bad report. She was bitter, hated everybody and everything. She was an agnostic.

*Doesn't God love agnostics?* I thought. *Weren't all of us at one time agnostics?*

Lying on my back on the Stryker frame I shared the wondrous works of God in my life with this gray-haired reporter and her photographer. During that hour the Holy Spirit melted her hard heart. She accepted Jesus Christ as her Savior. A few days later her interview appeared on the front page of the daily newspaper, *The Sioux City Journal,* with a banner headline.

In her interview she related with warm enthusiasm my personal experiences with Jesus as my Savior, as my Baptizer in the Holy Spirit, and as the Great Physician; that I believed that in His own time and place and way, He would manifest a complete healing of my broken body. I also stated that I was going to take part, with the FGBMFI, in a planned crusade in Vienna, Austria, in a few months, even if I had to be carried on a stretcher.

After that I felt better. Now I was committed. There was no turning back, impossible as it then seemed.

I knew no one in Sioux City except the banker. I was a stranger and they took me in. Through reading this newspaper interview men and women from as far as a hundred miles away flocked into my hospital room, averaging six to twelve a day. Out of compassion they came, and out of curiosity. They brought flowers, candy, cards, and love. They also brought problems.

Some needed salvation. Some needed physical healing. Some needed a deeper experience with Jesus. In His marvelous, compassionate way Jesus met every need. There was no power in my body. I lay there broken and bleeding. But the matchless power of Jesus was manifested through my broken body. It was clear to all that it was His power, not mine.

Late one snowy evening an eighty-year-old farm couple arrived. She could hardly see and he could hardly hear. Five years before, they had listened to a tape of some meeting in which I had spoken and had prayed that they would get to meet me before they left this life. People pray the strangest prayers. That night they left the hospital room seeing and hearing and praising God in a language they had never learned.

Among the scores of others who found healing was a Methodist minister named Don. He had been seriously injured in an automobile accident nine years before. His body was twisted out of shape from double curvature of the spine. One leg was several inches shorter than the other. His kidneys, his heart, his liver had all been affected. He already knew Jesus as his Savior. When he understood that he could meet Him as the Great Physician, he asked me to lay hands upon him and pray for him.

The glory of God filled the room like golden rain. Brother Don's crippled body straightened out and his short leg lengthened, as Jesus performed an invisible osteopathic treatment. He was the happiest Methodist minister I had ever seen.

Two weeks later he was back again with a long face.

"What is the matter, Brother Don?"

"The healing didn't last. I knew all along that it wouldn't last."

"How long did it last?"

"Only three days," he replied.

"Did you tell anyone about your healing? Did you buy a new pair of shoes?"

"New shoes are out of the question on a poor preacher's budget. No, I didn't tell anyone about the healing because I was afraid I might be ridiculed. I wanted to be absolutely sure that it was real."

"Your unbelief has lost you the healing," I explained, "but if you will repent, we will ask the Lord Jesus in His compassion to heal you again. Only this time you must tell the very first person you meet. And you must buy a new pair of shoes."

Again the glory of God filled the room. Brother Don's crippled body straightened up miraculously in an instant of time. He began to praise God in a new language. The door opened. A nun stuck her head into the room. Brother Don looked at her, then he looked at me. "Her?"

I nodded. "Her."

He straightened his jacket and awkwardly walked over to her. Embarrassed, he said, "I'm a Protestant minister. I don't expect you as a Catholic to really believe what happened, but when that man on that frame laid hands upon me and prayed, the power of God straightened out my crooked body and healed me."

The nun's face shone. "Isn't our Lord wonderful!" she exclaimed.

So Brother Don went, walking, leaping, and praising God in a new language down the shining corridors of St. Joseph's Mercy Hospital. When I saw him a year later his body was still healed. It will still be healed at the end of time. What Jesus Christ does lasts forever.

After the first few days I refused to take sedatives because I wanted to prove that the grace of God was sufficient for all my needs. Sometimes the pain became blinding, almost unbearable. I thought of the Scripture that tells us that the Lord chastens those He loves.

"Lord," I prayed, "You must love me more than anybody in the world. And I appreciate that. But couldn't You love me a little less? Turn down the back burner for a few minutes?"

Each time, out of the rich treasurehouse of His grace, would flow the healing balm. The pain lessened to a bearable amount. During those endless nights I proved the truth of God's promise. He was present in that little room like a light in the night. "I will never, never leave you or forsake you. I will be with you always, even to the end of the world."

*Perhaps,* I thought once, *He has forgotten that I've been active in the divine healing ministry for many years. How can I be used in this condition?*

"I'll send people to you. Haven't you prayed to be used in a greater way in the healing ministry?"

"Yes, Lord. That's my heart's desire. What does it take to be used?"

"Faith."

"What else?"

"Compassion."

"How do you develop compassion?"

"By observation and experience."

Again it was an unexpected answer to my prayers. Into my hospital room came Methodists who were seeking a deeper experience with Jesus. There they met Presbyterians, who met Catholics, who met Episcopalians, who met Pentecostals. Out of these meetings about a dozen charismatic prayer groups were formed, including one in the hospital among the nuns.

During the months, I must have prayed for nearly a hundred of Jim Smith's congregation. A real revival started in their midst.

One night I heard God's voice. "How do you want to be healed—your way? Or My way?"

I took a deep breath. "Help me, Lord, to have the patience to be healed Your way."

Several times during those months my lovely Merikay flew

in to comfort and encourage me with her prayers and her love.

Later our son Lance flew in from New York and spent the night on a cot in my room. I asked him to forgive me for the many times I had put other things before his needs— my work, my love for Merikay, myself, the whole world. He forgave me everything. The hurts, the bruises, the scars of all the years melted away.

My recovery was miraculous. The main reason was because of my willingness to allow the Lord Jesus Christ to use me even in that battered condition. We cannot be a blessing to others without being blessed ourselves, as the power of God flows through our bodies. There was no doubt in anyone's mind. It was His power, not mine.

In the natural, the situation was ridiculous—sick and suffering people coming in to seek healing through someone more ill than they. It had to be God. We serve a God who will not permit others to steal the glory that belongs to Him.

Then in the midnight hours as the nurses were turning me on the Stryker frame, the impossible happened. About every two hours a board was screwed down over my face. The frame was then rotated on a large metal wheel so that I lay on my stomach. This was to prevent bed sores. I had made that upsetting trip a thousand times and never did enjoy it. This night I was turned so that I was lying face down at the top of this metal wheel. Suddenly I fell. Someone had forgotten to fasten the safety catch. "Don't let me break anything already broken," I prayed.

I fell upon my right side, breaking a rib and developing an embolism, or blood clot.

For forty-five minutes, while the nurses shook with fear, I couldn't say a word. Then, when I finally got my breath back, I told them not to report the accident. I realized it was merely human error, just one of those things.

Next day my general doctor, who had stopped seeing me in order to save me the daily charge for his visit, came in to find out what had happened. He had given the nurse strict instructions a couple of weeks before to remove the bandages from my right donor leg, where the skin had been removed to be put on the left side. The nurse had not followed his orders. Angrily, he ripped the bandages off. With them went my skin. A culture was taken. It showed I had two infections, both of which are fatal in 90 percent of serious burn cases. Over the next few days, heroic efforts were made to save my life. But nothing seemed to help.

Every day I became weaker. I knew I was dying. But I was determined not to let Satan destroy my healing. Over and over I claimed the promises of God. But nothing seemed to help.

Then a retired nurse, whose husband I had helped to find Jesus some weeks before, came. She stayed in my hospital room two full days, reading the Bible, praying.

On Sunday I knew that death was not far away. I had been asking the Lord, through the Holy Spirit, to have my friend, evangelist Kenneth Copeland, telephone me. His prayer would be my point of contact. Then I would reach out and touch the hem of Jesus' robe and be healed.

Two days dragged by. About nine o'clock Tuesday night, the telephone rang. It was Kenneth Copeland. He apologized for calling me so late at night.

"The Holy Spirit has been dealing with me for two days to call you. I can't go to sleep tonight without being obedient."

I asked him to pray. As he prayed, I made that my point of contact and released my faith. Immediately my body began to mend. In a couple of weeks I was back where I had been before the infection began.

The Fellowship airlift was leaving soon from Chicago. As

the time approached I wanted to be closer. So I arranged to be carried on my stretcher to the Sioux City Airport and flown into Chicago. There at Passavant Hospital I'd wait out the three weeks before our departure. During those weeks I was so weak I could hardly raise my head from the pillow. I could stand on one leg for only brief moments, supported on either side by strong interns. When I told the doctor I wanted to be released in time to go on the airlift, he shook his head. It would be many months before I could even think of leaving the hospital, he said. I told him I had promised God to be there if it was humanly possible and that I intended to leave with the airlift. If he would not give me an official release, I would release myself. He finally agreed to let me go if I could find a nurse who would accompany me. My resourceful wife found such a nurse.

On the day of departure God told me to get to the airport six hours before departure time, although we were only required to be there three hours ahead. Angrily, the ambulance drivers who brought me to the airport told me they could not wait three hours to put me on board the airplane. They had other things to do. I told them to go about their business.

"Who will put you on the plane?"

"If human hands don't, divine hands will," I said.

My friends gathered at the airport were happy to see Merikay and me. Most of them thought I had come to see them off. When I said I intended to go on the trip, they just shook their heads in disbelief.

The airline was not insured to carry passengers on board in my condition in wheelchairs.

"It's too bad. You'll have to stay behind," they said.

"God has not brought me this far to leave me," I told them.

I had myself wheeled up to the chief executive of SAS Airlines. Claiming Psalm 81, I opened my mouth and the

Lord filled it with words that had not come from my mind. "There are 190 men and women waiting to go on this trip. But if I am not put on first, nobody will go."

The executive just looked at me. "Is that so?"

I was as surprised as he was. I really believe that God would have stopped or postponed the airlift if I had not been allowed to go.

The executive summoned six stout Swedes. They carried me backwards in the wheelchair from the runway up the steps of the 747.

On the plane were some Jesus people who helped Merikay and the nurse stretch me out on four of the seats, belting me down. A doctor had agreed to go along to help me. But he was a slight man. So I prayed for other help. Along came a stout professor from Nebraska who offered to help also. He had had experience lifting amputees in and out of wheelchairs. Together the doctor and the professor lifted me in and out of the wheelchair, in and out of bed, all over Europe.

Among the priests I had invited to accompany us was Fr. Hal Cohen, S.J. chaplain of Loyola University, New Orleans. The Holy Spirit led us to encourage Fr. Hal to stop by Brussels where he spent three hours conferring with His Eminence, Leo Joseph, Cardinal Suenens. For several years I had been sending the Cardinal the *VOICE,* official magazine of the FGBMFI. Out of that interview the next year came the participation of Cardinal Suenens in the Sixth Catholic Pentecostal Conference at Notre Dame. He was the special guest of the steering committee, to which Fr. Hal belongs. Since then Cardinal Suenens has become the spokesman among the Cardinals for the charismatic renewal in the Roman church. He has authored *A New Pentecost.*

Being pushed in a wheelchair along the cobblestones of Europe by Merikay and the nurse was an experience I would not like to repeat. I think I have personally bumped into every cobblestone on the streets of Vienna, Copenhagen and Stockholm.

I learned another great lesson out of this experience. There is a blessing in dependency. Always I had been very independent, not liking other people to do things for me. Now I found that if we are willing to allow others to minister to us in the name of Christ, we can be a blessing to them. As the Scripture says, we save our lives by giving them away.

Sometimes I feel nostalgic because Jesus does not seem to be as poignantly close to me as He was during those soul-testing nights in the hospital. Then I seem to hear that soft voice, "You don't need Me so much right now. But when you do again, I'll be there."

Yes, His grace is sufficient for us. I would gladly go through every moment of agony in that hospital for the joy of knowing in a deeper way that Jesus, whose love never fails and whose compassion knows no length, no breadth, no height, no depth, no end. Yes, Jesus Christ is the same yesterday, today at our point of need, and forever.

# 22

# Cancer Again

Back in our own home again after our airlift experience, I was almost helpless. I was in a hospital bed. Pillows propped up my damaged left side, so I could half lie on my right side. This eased the mind-blowing pains which geometrically increased every minute I lay immovable on my back. Pillows were placed under my knees, with more pillows between my knees to relieve the pressure on my crushed hip area. Pillows supported my fractured left arm. Pillows were everywhere.

Clucking about me like a mother hen, Merikay located a male nurse, Pat Edwards. It took a man to lift me in my totally helpless condition. Later maneuver me into and out of the wheelchair—my island of hope. Some day . . . some day . . . .

Again, as in the hospital, my life contracted to the narrow confines of an eight-by-ten room. But the room was sunny and looked out on the street. Through the screen of pines I could not only hear, but actually see the autos on their way to and from the railroad station. The laughing children on their way to school. Bounding, barking dogs.

I depended on Merikay or Pat to raise and lower the bed. Then as the weeks passed, I managed to operate the electric control myself. Now I could see the trees leafing out in that delicate green of spring . . . the little buds of the star magnolia bursting pinkly open in front of my window . . . the sudden flash of scarlet or blue song birds feasting on the seedball Merikay had hung on the magnolia.

Therapy was every-other-day torture. My left knee had frozen from the months in traction. Yet, little by little, inch by inch, Neil tenderly worked it loose. He would turn me on my stomach. Then grasping my leg against his chest foot up, he would put the strength of his back against it, pressing, releasing, pressing a bit more. Progress was dishearteningly slow. And painful. At times, to keep from crying out with pain, I would pray loudly in tongues. At St. Joe's, this had been the only way I had been able to keep from screaming. The therapist there thought she was a man—"if it don't hurt, it don't help." She threw her weight against my locked knee and crunched my stiff fingers with zeal.

Then there was church. TV is great if you are a shut-in. But my soul was hungry for worship at St. Elisabeth's. Finally one Sunday morning I decided to try to make it to the service. Hours ahead of time I began the painful process of dressing. Then Pat eased me onto the great, green cushion in my wheelchair and pushed me along the streets. Cruising at almost stalling speed just ahead of us, Merikay drove our tan Catalina.

As Pat finally wrangled my wheelchair between the first pew and the altar steps, I burst into tears. The familiar hymns, the robed choir, the loved faces of friends. Being able to join in the singing as Merikay turned the pages. Being able to worship again. How many times I'd dreamed and prayed for this impossible moment as I lay in the hospital. It was like heaven.

As I grew stronger, I began to make an occasional sortie out in God's service. First, stretched out on pillows on Hugo Zerbe's back seat, we drove to a meeting in Wisconsin.

Then our first journey into Chicago to Faith Tabernacle to thank all our friends who prayed so long and hard. What a blessing, they said, to see me—long ago given up by the doctors, but not by the Great Physician—roll in, sitting in a wheelchair. And there were a few meetings where God was able to use me in prayer and counseling.

Then came the time to make good my promise of the year before to speak at the mayor's prayer breakfast at Sioux City. I had yearned for the chance to thank personally all those who had prayed for me and cared for me so lovingly at St. Joe's.

Waiting excitedly in the lobby were my doctors, Dave Paulsrud and Don Boyle, and Sister Mary Siena, the directress. Sister Mary greeted me with a warm hug and kiss. The doctors were like little boys discovering presents around a Christmas tree. Their expert eyes devoured the X-rays I had brought to show them the new pieces of bone that Jesus was growing in my leg. Then that lunch, specially prepared in the staff cafeteria. Nurse Mary Shoemaker, nurse's aid Frances Closter, and Sister Mary Lenore—everyone from "Third Main" was there, beaming. And there were tears in most eyes.

By Easter I was attempting a few steps with a crutch. Two crutches wouldn't do because of the lost elbow joint on my left arm. That arm was almost useless. Our friend, Dan Uhrig, was helping Merikay out of his car. Again pride proved my downfall. Thinking I'd show her how I could get along without them, I started ahead up St. Elisabeth's steep, stone steps. As I swung my right leg, the tip of my shoe caught the top of the first step. I spun helplessly, crutch clattering. "Please, dear Lord," I gasped. "Don't let me break anything on my good right side!"

Full length on the six stone steps I fell, with a sickening crack. Again it was my left side. Dan rushed me to Evanston Hospital. It was like coming back to my Alma Mater. After examining me, the doctor found that my humerus was broken.

Meanwhile inside stately St. Elisabeth's the collection plate came to Merikay. The usher had seated her right under the preacher's nose. She was stewing about what had happened. No news. Yet she could hardly get up and leave from her prominent position. She was praying as the plate was held out. She dropped her envelope. The plate remained.

"It was almost as though," she laughed about it later, "the plate had X-rayed my contribution and said, 'Not enough.' "

The impassive usher nodded his head slightly. Merikay looked into the plate and saw a hastily-penciled note. "Don't worry," it said. "Larry's gone to the hospital. But someone will see that you get home."

This last accident was a little too much for Merikay, however. She weakened under the added strain; reached again for the bottle. Now it was more necessary to have the night nurse for her than for me. We arranged for faithful Ethel Peterson to keep Merikay company. Ethel was not only a nurse, but a friend.


One night Merikay's father pushed away his dinner tray and sank back into his big red chair. For the first time in his life he seemed disinterested in the exciting baseball game on TV. Not at all like hearty, life-loving Tex. When he did get up, he seemed disoriented and turned the wrong way for bed.

I had just been helped to bed myself when the phone rang.

"Come quickly! Get Merikay over here right away! Her father's dying!"

Merikay cringed. "Daddy . . . not Daddy!"

The shock was too much for her. She wilted under this latest pressure, escaped in the bottle, and knew no more.

A quick conference on the phone with LB. "Do you think I should send him to the hospital?" It was the first time she'd ever seriously asked my opinion about anything. "Tex hates hospitals. What do you think?"

I felt in the Spirit Tex's time had finally come. Tex had celebrated his eighty-second birthday earlier that year. A ripe old age. I remembered how, long years before, he'd asked the Lord to let him live until he was at least seventy. How gracious God is!

I counseled against the hospital, sent my friend and current therapist, Art Fry, over to help. Art made him comfortable, aspirated him to help the labored breathing. LB tried to reach the family doctor. He'd gone to his private hideaway in Wisconsin. Dr. Case, who'd faithfully come night or day for twenty-five years, also was at some convention. LB took it as a personal insult.

"How could they, at a time like this! They knew Tex was feeble, might go at any time." Yes, that's what she'd been saying for all of the twenty-three years I'd known her.

It was no surprise when Art's calm voice came over the phone about three in the morning. I'd awakened a few moments before with a strange feeling that Tex had slipped into that larger life. He had.

LB moved calmly through the gathering commotion of the next few days in majestic efficiency. But Merikay had come all unglued by the day of the funeral. I tried to keep her from the bottle. But there always seemed to be a hidden cache. Finally her brother came, when I phoned for his help. After much struggling, we managed to get Merikay dressed and into the car. As we drove up to the cemetery, almost everyone had gone. Only the minister, Dr. Baar, was left loading some flowers into his car. The grave diggers were beginning to throw the dirt back.

Grabbing my crutch I hopped as fast as possible over the ground. The minister turned at my frantic yells. I knew if Merikay did not attend this last farewell to her beloved Daddy, she'd never forgive herself. The minister in his compassion understood.

So under the little canopy among the empty, circled chairs, Father Baar conducted a second service just for Merikay. And me. And Art Fry, who'd made it possible for us both to be there. Unread, in my pocket, unheard by anybody, but beating within my heart was the tribute I had written for Tex at my brother-in-law's request:

"His was indeed a life of love. Tex Howard is the only man I ever knew who never said an unkind word. His was indeed a life lived out in love . . . 'Faith, hope and love . . . but the greatest of these is love.' Tex believed on Jesus Christ and these beautiful words spoken by Jesus apply to him, 'I am the resurrection and the life . . . whoever liveth and believeth in me shall never die.'"

After the funeral Merikay's struggle with the bottle continued off and on. Speaking invitations came for me, and opportunities to attend charismatic conferences. Sometimes Merikay was able to come with me. Most often, she was not. When I felt that God wanted me to go, I left her in Ethel Peterson's care.

I had been driven to LaGrange one evening to help launch a new FGBMFI chapter. Merikay had gone to 1015 Pine. Delayed by a fearful thunderstorm, I did not reach home until

3:30 A.M.   About 6:30 I was awakened by an urgent call from Esther, LB's housekeeper. While reaching for early morning medicine, LB had fallen on the hard floor of the butler's pantry and had broken her hip. Already the ambulance had taken her to Evanston Hospital. Worse yet, for me, LB had fallen on Merikay, carrying her along as she fell. Esther was unable to arouse my wife. Didn't know what to do.

I phoned nurse Hellene Westrick, who hurried over to LB's. When she tried to lift Merikay under the arms, Merikay screamed. Sharp pain brought her back to consciousness. Later at the Evanston Hospital the orthopedic surgeon diagnosed a broken collarbone.

LB was heartsick to have caused the accident. It was several weeks before she was discharged home, with nurses day and night. Meanwhile the broken bone in Merikay's neck healed faster than her fear. Again—always it seemed—accidents happened on her right side, the side from which that malignant tumor had been cut off her tongue. This time again fear clutched her heart. Would this latest accident stir the slumbering cancer cells?

Examination revealed a suspicious nodule in her throat on the right side. The doctor wanted to operate, but Merikay was adamant. She refused to go back to Billings. Too many bitter memories. We consulted another doctor who thought an operation not urgent, suggested watching it for awhile. Meanwhile I was desperately trying to find some doctor or hospital in the U.S. who would continue the nontoxic therapy begun by Dr. Nieper. Merikay did not feel strong enough to go to Europe. She did not want to go to Mexico.

Finally someone recommended a doctor in Atlanta. We made reservations and arrived at Doctors' Hospital in early December.

Merikay shared a sunny, spacious room with a divorcee.

During that time Merikay led the woman back into fellowship with the Lord. As the weeks went by, the therapy—intravenous injections—seemed to be working well. Then the doctor wanted an excisional biopsy to determine definitely whether the tumor in Merikay's throat was malignant.

"But we came to you to avoid surgery," I protested.

"This biopsy is simple, nothing serious," he insisted.

So we went ahead. It was Christmas Eve. Late that afternoon the doctor entered Merikay's hospital room with the bad news. It was malignant. The biopsy scar would quickly heal, the doctor went on, almost gaily. We had plenty of time to decide what sort of treatment to have.

I'd been invited to Christmas dinner by Ginny and David Collins. He was dean of St. Phillips' Cathedral. I asked if Merikay could have a pass and go with me.

So busy Ginny Collins came for us Christmas morning. Still stunned by the medical verdict, Merikay sat silently that afternoon in an armchair near the sparking woodfire. Her neck was wrapped in a pink scarf.

"That way," she'd said in the hospital, "nobody can see the blood."

The blood! How many times I had pleaded the precious blood of Jesus over Merikay and rebuked that foul spirit of cancer.

It was an all-family gathering—about twenty in all. Sons and sisters- and brothers-in-law and sisters and the dean's witty eighty-year-old mother-in-law. Merikay and I were the only outsiders. At one point in the conversation, Ginny Collins turned to Merikay. "And what did you get for Christmas, dear?"

Merikay smiled back serenely. "Oh, I got my throat cut." She paused while the group sucked in their breath. "But Jesus is healing me."

"I've got news for you, ma'am," sneered Chris, the nineteen-year-old son. "There just ain't no such animal!"

I turned to Chris. "I suppose you think you're pretty smart?"

"I'm not perfect, but I've got a good brain."

I looked him over carefully. The Lord directed my attention to his legs and impressed me that one was shorter. "You couldn't be more right," I said as gently as possible. My inner impulse was to tell him what I really thought of him. "Your right leg is shorter than the left."

Chris argued, then looked in the mirror. There was a difference.

"Chris," I said with emphasis, "either Jesus is the Son of God like He says, or He's a liar. He healed everybody He touched when He walked this earth in human form. He still does today. I'm going to pray and ask Jesus to lengthen your short leg. When He does, will you accept Him as your Lord and Savior?"

"Yeah, man." Chris laughed. "*If* he does. If he does."

I asked his father to hold up Chris's legs under the ankles as Chris sat on a straight chair. I prayed in tongues. Merikay prayed in tongues softly as she held my hand. I touched Chris's forehead lightly with my other hand. The dean's eyebrows raised as Chris's short leg grew right out in his hands. Try as he would, stamping and jumping, Chris could not make the leg short again.

"Okay, Chris," I said, "how about making good your promise to take Jesus into your life and heart?"

And he did before his parents, relatives and Merikay, whose bright witness had sparked his challenge. That night (I learned later) he gave away his crates of beer in the basement and stopped smoking pot. Jesus does indeed make all things new.

That was only the first of several miracles He performed that Christmas Day. By the time I took Merikay back to the hospital in the early evening, the spine of a young niece, made crooked by an auto accident years before, had been straightened out. And a relative with emphysema, and a hole in his lung as big as a silver dollar, had been perfectly healed (as subsequent X-rays confirmed).

"If only," Merikay sighed in my arms as I kissed her goodnight, "if only Jesus will do it for me again." Our embrace was more tender than ever, because of the doctor's hard words.

On New Year's Eve we were back in Chicago. We'd returned home from 1015 where it had been our custom to watch the new year in, after our church service. Merikay's parents both loved Guy Lombardo. LB would have had to watch the merriment alone for the first time, if we had not come. At midnight bells pealed merrily. Noise makers crackled. Men and women cavorted around in funny paper hats and high spirits.

Now Merikay's green eyes looked deep into mine. "Laurie," she said with a momentous quietness, "this is going to be the last year of my life." She melted into my outstretched arms. "Oh, Buzz, we promised to go together . . . remember?"

Then she cried herself to sleep in my arms, with little half-heard sobs. "I won't even make it to your birthday . . ."

My birthday was July the fifth. So far away and yet so close. I'd tried to laugh it off. Yet in the hollow silence of my heart, I prayed . . . and prayed . . . and prayed . . . "Not yet, Lord . . . please . . . not yet."

We'd often joked about making our twenty-fifth wedding anniversary. A quarter of a century. Sounded so impressive. Yet would we even make the twenty-fourth—September 13, nine weeks after my birthday?

Merikay and I had accepted a week's ministry in Florida.

The night before we were to fly south, the hairdresser came to the house to fix Merikay's hair. Whether she fixed anything else I'll never know. But Merikay took offense at something she fancied I had said. Her green eyes snapped. Next morning she was in no shape to go. At her urging I postponed my plane six hours. She was contrite and sad. But in spite of heroic efforts, she could hardly stagger out of bed to the bathroom. I called Ethel again to stay with her and left, as I had so many times before, with a heavy heart.

"Lord, I passed the test in 1961. Put You ahead of Lance. Put You ahead of Merikay. Do I have to again? And again . . . ?"

This was to be the last time we would be apart, I promised myself. Surely a merciful and loving God would not require . . . *Take up your cross daily and follow Me.*

God confirmed that He wanted me in Jacksonville. One of the leading millionaires received the baptism in the Holy Spirit at the Fellowship banquet. Funds were raised to begin telecasting locally the "Good News" series started by the FGBMFI. Two women who'd wandered into the banquet, invited only by the Holy Spirit, came up as I finished speaking and took Jesus into their lives.

For several days and nights Merikay locked herself inside the house and refused to answer the phone. How many times I started to fly back. Was I serving the Lord, *really?* What about the statement in the Bible that he who does not take care of his own is worse than an infidel? Finally I did break off my schedule to fly back home.

It seemed wise to us both to return to Florida to complete our speaking schedule and, more important, to get Dr. Bill Reed's opinion of her neck. Dr. Bill examined Merikay, after praying and laying hands on her. Many times his patients had been healed by the power of God before he had a chance to operate. In the operating room he always called the team together for prayer first. During the period of his active practice in Michigan, about 40 percent of the patients referred to him were healed without operations.

Dr. Bill thought the operation should be done soon. Merikay had been complaining about difficulty in swallowing. So she checked into the Centro Espanol Hospital in Tampa, where Dr. Bill was chief of surgery. On my pillow that morning (would it be the last we'd ever share together?) I found a note in her precise handwriting, "Already I miss you. And I haven't even left yet."

Room 306 was small, but sunny. There I waited for an eternity, which the clock called only eight hours. Other operations were canceled. Evidently Dr. Bill had found complications. The anticipated time had been only two hours. I hobbled on my crutch down to the main floor just off the operating room. Finally a weary Dr. Bill stumbled out, gave me a big hug.

"She's come through okay," he said. "But we need to pray. She's in the hands of Jesus."

For three endless days Merikay hovered between life and death in intensive care. Now it was I who could only visit for five minutes every two hours. Merikay's head was swathed in bandages. All that showed were her nose and those green eyes, now dull with pain. All around her the little pips on the green screens warned of the failing hearts of patients on either side.

So I could be near Merikay, and also keep what was one of the few private rooms, Dr. Bill had me admitted to the hospital, took some X-rays, and examined my crushed hip area. He expressed amazement that I could put any weight on that leg.

"Only Jesus the Great Physician is enabling you," he said.

What a miraculous recovery I had experienced. New bones regrown in my hip area. New muscles, new nerves. The great Creator is also the Re-Creator. Although limited, I was still alive. I could still maintain an active ministry.

Finally Merikay was rolled into "our" joint room. Wrapped in white bandages, she could make only grunting sounds the first few days. The administrator told me they'd never allowed a cot in any patient's room before. I expressed surprise. Every first class hospital permitted this. Wasn't this a first class hospital?

The cot was moved in, between her bed and the door. Often in the night I'd be awakened by a pricking, as the nurse mistakenly stuck me instead. Sleeping was a problem. It seems as though the entire staff in a hospital conspires to keep patients awake. If it isn't the nurse shaking you awake to thrust a cold thermometer into your sleepy mouth, she's shaking you awake to give you a pill so you can go back to sleep. Or the inescapable orderly. All through the night, every two hours, he'd swtich on the glaring top light, and jiggle his clinking ice. It didn't matter how many times we told him we didn't want ice.

"Remorseless, like *The Iceman Cometh,*" quipped Merikay.

Together, but in beds apart, we encouraged each other during those long nights. Together we watched in childlike glee as each morning the multicolored horses pranced into the pasture just beyond our window. As she became able to mumble a little better, Merikay referred to herself as "Eleanor of Aquitaine." Or, on other darker occasions, as "The Mummy's Return."

Gay cards, letters, and bouquets of flowers flooded our hospital room. Merikay was bathed in the love of the many friends, some of whom came great distances to pray with her.

Dr. Bill warned me that the prognosis was "guarded." It had been a miracle that Merikay had survived this eight-hour, bloody operation. But her heart was sound. Her lungs were good (Thank God, she'd stopped smoking years before). But the tumor was huge, intertwined with veins and muscles. It had been pressing her windpipe out of shape, choking her to death.

"Why didn't you come to me instead of that doctor in Atlanta?" Dr. Bill asked. "I would have removed the entire tumor at that time, instead of spreading the killer cells throughout her body with an excisional biopsy. Now I want you to get her out of the hospital just as soon as possible. This is my practice with every surgical patient. Get'em up and out. A hospital's no place to get well in."

Merikay felt too weak to face the exhausting plane trip home. Besides in late March Chicago often had treacherous weather. Dr. Bill was concerned about possible pneumonia.

"Stay around the area for a couple of weeks at least," he urged. "I want to keep a close eye on her. Bring her back for a check-up at least once a week."

While in El Centro Espanol, Merikay won her final victory in her battle with the bottle. Never again would she be imprisoned by its chains. She received a real deliverance. The temptation was to leave. Free at last!

# 23

# Beyond Tomorrow

Weak as she was, Merikay went everywhere with me, ministering to those in worse shape. Or were they?

We journeyed about the land of sunshine, enjoying its balmy breezes as only those can who have been prisoner behind hospital walls. Merikay drank in each sunrise and each sunset as though it might be her last. Sniffed the fragrance of each flower. Squeezed the last drop of joy out of each fleeting moment. Often I thought about her statement to me on New Year's Day. Could it be prophecy? I broke into cold sweat. Here it was already early April . . .

Eventually we flew back to still chilly Chicago. For once LB found it hard to express herself. "Darling," she said and her voice quavered. "Why did you come back so soon? I'd hoped you'd stay in Florida forever. Well, almost. Things just haven't been the same around here without you. You're my jolly dolly."

LB even tilted her cheek toward me, inviting me to kiss her. Briefly. She abhorred any show of emotion.

The weeks passed more pleasantly than in all the other years of our marriage. Merikay's bright spirit ministered to all who came seeking to comfort and encourage her. I'd had a long-standing date to speak to the Full Gospel Business Men's groups in Cleveland. I determined not to go, unless Merikay felt strong enough. She did. So we went. By the time we had finished driving around spread-out Cleveland after the meeting, it was 2 A.M. We unpacked and got to bed.

"Snuzz," I apologized, "if I'd thought it would be like this, I'd never have asked you to come."

Merikay giggled sleepily. "Oh, it's been fun . . . . Fierce fun. But what can you do? It always seems like the most needy person is the last to come up for prayer."

Yes, it had been that way. We'd finished the public prayer line when this desperate man had come up. It had taken an hour and a half of prayer and counseling. But in the end he'd been delivered from that dark spirit of suicide and baptized into laughter by the Holy Spirit. Yes, it had been worth it all. Merikay sighed again happily.

"Besides I have you and you have me." A little pause. "And we don't have to get up tomorrow morning. Next appointment's at that dinner."

A couple of weeks later, Merikay and I were flying to another consultation with Dr. Bill. Bothered by the slow healing of her neck, and a sharp pain increasing in her hip area, which she felt was her sciatic nerve, Merikay wanted Dr. Bill's opinion.

He gave it gently, sorrowfully. The cancer had come back again. Like a soft flower in the too-hot sun, she wilted. I took her to my brother Ed's where she went to bed.

In desperate hope of getting help somewhere, somehow, I went to the Episcopal Charismatic Conference of clergy and wives. During lunch I was asked to speak. Over the rattle of knives and forks I shared the healing miracles of God in the lives of Merikay and myself.

"We can each meet Jesus in any one or all three ways," I said. "Around the world I've prayed with thousands. Jesus is no respecter of persons. Rich or poor, black or white or yellow, it makes no difference. Whenever we meet His conditions for salvation, we always come to know Him as our Savior. When we yearn to know Him better, have a heart hunger for more of Jesus, then we can always meet Him as the Baptizer with the Holy Spirit."

I paused and took a deep breath. "The doctors tell me there is little hope for my darling wife, Merikay. No matter what happens, I will always believe that when we meet His conditions for divine healing, Jesus is bound by His own unalterable word to bless us. He is still the Great Physician. When our Lord walked the dusty roads of Galilee, He healed every one who came to Him. And Jesus Christ is the same yesterday, today and forever."

I explained that His healing power doesn't mean that we are to live forever on this earth. But when the time to join Him comes, we can fall from the Tree of Life like a ripe apple, not a rotten one. God, the Lord of the Cosmos, doesn't need cancer or kidney disease. All He needs to do is to take away the breath of life He gave us.

Later I was informed I had been elected to the board of directors of the conference. When I told Merikay at my brother Ed's, she forgot the pains long enough to laugh.

"Serves you right for opening your big, fat mouth!" A tear glistened. "You see, you do need me, Big Buzz. I bet you talked too long as usual. How are you going to get along without me?"

That's the question I'd been asking myself time and again during these last few months.

After the luncheon I had spotted Ginny Collins from Atlanta and an old friend, for ten years a faith missionary to Indonesia, Ed Stube. Merikay bloomed when he entered her bedroom.

"Why, Ed, you don't look any older than when we gave that birthday party for you twelve years ago in Seattle."

So Ed, Ginny, a professor from Sewanee and I laid hands on my love. In my heart a silent, rending cry, "Oh God, do it again. Just one more time!"

As we walked through the living room towards the door, my sister-in-law, Agnes, was coughing. That reminded me of the strange fever that had been running her temperature up and down for ten days. The strain also was telling on my brother.

Agnes had never been much for divine healing. But this time she eagerly accepted our offer. The doctors hadn't done very well. As we prayed the fever left her.

"Aggie," I asked, "have you ever been born again?"

I knew she was a life-long Methodist who even managed to drag my reluctant brother along.

"I'm not sure," she said. So we prayed the sinner's prayer together. Like a little child Aggie, whose blonde hair was streaked with gray, came into the kingdom of God. My brother's eyes were closed as he stood at my side. His lips were moving.

"How about you, Ed?"

"Oh, no," he protested quickly. "I'm not ready yet."

I took his right hand in mine. "Pray with me."

Ed and I had never gotten along well. We were opposites in temperament and character. I felt that I was the last person in the world who could lead him to Christ. But through the miraculous power of the Holy Spirit, Ed prayed the sinner's prayer out loud before a bunch of strangers. At the end he gave me a firm handclasp. And I, for the first time in our lives, threw my good arm around his shoulders. Now we were really brothers.

Dr. Bill had urged Merikay to go to the University of Michigan for immediate radiology. But Merikay had had her fill of hospitals. She wanted to go home to her own house and our own bed where we had lived and loved for nearly twenty-four years. So we flew back home.

More desperate medical consultations followed. Some suggested another operation. Dr. Bill was not sure her body could stand that additional trauma. Some urged chemotherapy. Finally on the very day Merikay and I were scheduled to return to Florida for several meetings, a friend and I took Merikay to Evanston Hospital for her first radiation treatment. I was still all for trusting Jesus, but the family felt we should try every medical avenue.

Then the doctors decided to hospitalize Merikay to spare her the pain of the daily twenty-mile round trip to Evanston. When I went to see her, they had so filled her with morphine that she didn't even recognize me. Just as soon as she would begin to fight her way out of the sedation fog, the nurses would inject her again.

The doctors had abandoned radiology. Abandoned hope. As they said to me, "You wouldn't let her suffer, would you?"

I replied that Merikay was a Christian. She did not want to be sedated into eternity. In a lucid moment, I asked her desire.

"Laurie, please," she begged me. "I want to go home. To my own bed."

The doctor said he'd have to discontinue the IV if she did. I'd have to take full responsibility. I'd have to feed her through a nose-tube. God then sent along a Catholic nurse we knew. She volunteered to leave her present case and come stay with us day and night as long as necessary. A week, a month, a year!

God in His mercy had speeded up my healing so I could now minister to Merikay's needs. How poignant it was to be with her . . . to be able to rub her back, to help with the bed pan, to feed her through the tube down that uptilt, saucy nose, to lie beside her praying as she fought for breath.

And all the time searching the depths of my soul. Was there something I hadn't done that was blocking her healing? Was God speaking to me again, as on that distant day at St. Stephens?

To her mother, I wrote a note: "Dear LB, I want you to know how much your friendship and support means to me, especially at this time. For the way you *always* come through . . . in Paris, in New York, in Deming, in Sioux City and St. Joe's Hospital, and in everything. Where would I be now if you hadn't started the ball rolling after the prop accident by phoning the right people? No matter what or who, or when, I *do* love you, dear."

As usual LB had been sending a flood of hot cooked meals, flowers, medical supplies. Came limping in on her walker every day. Dressed up to the hilt. Her heart might have been breaking, but nobody could tell by looking at her. *Really, a woman of iron,* I thought admiringly.

But the Holy Spirit would not let me off the hook that easily. "Confess your sins one to another," He reminded me.

I may have forgiven her. Almost. But I had not asked her forgiveness. So with a friend I faced the redoubtable LB one afternoon at her home at 1015 Pine. Somehow I felt I needed a witness. I asked her to forgive me for every wrong act and every wrong word I'd ever said or done. And for every wrong thought I'd had about her over the past nearly twenty-four years.

She sat stony-faced, as though she hadn't heard a word.

But after we left, Esther told me, LB—who had shed no public tears at her beloved husband's death—had cried for fifteen minutes.

I knew I should have done this long before. "Now, Lord—what next?"

Memories of the past when I had left Merikay to serve as I believed God wanted me to, flooded my mind as I lay beside her in the night hours. Desperately I tried to make up for all those times. How wonderful of Jesus to let me meet her needs now by feeding her through the nose-tube, washing her body, rubbing her aching back.

She never complained. When the pain would get especially severe, she would gaily call, "Hey, Big Buzz, how about some of that old prayer power?"

I'd lay my hands on her tenderly and pray in tongues. The pain would leave. She was taking so little codeine, the doctor couldn't believe it.

Our priest came from nearby St. Elisabeth's to give her communion. As we knelt beside her bed, Merikay fully forgave everyone that had ever hurt her, including the pilot who had hit me. And especially me, for being away so often and so long.

Night after night I prayed as she fought for breath. Played gospel songs. Read aloud the healing miracles of Jesus.

Came an anxious call from Binghamton. Our old friend, Dr. Lall Din, a Pakistani, wanted to come and "comfort" me. I wondered at his use of the word. He had been praying and fasting for me and Merikay, he continued, and that morning the Lord had given him a word. It was from Hosea 6, "Come, let us return to the Lord. For He has torn us, but He will heal us; He has wounded us, but He will bandage us. He will revive us after two days; He will raise us up on the third day that we may live before Him." Beautiful words. Of encouragement?

That same day Merikay nearly slipped away. Her nails turned blue and I overheard the frantic report of the nurse, and the doctor's calm, "Make her as comfortable as possible. Get her head up. Put her back in that hospital bed. Prop her up with pillows. Let me know just as soon as she dies."

We hurried about, neither of us letting the other know we knew. Finally in a few hours color began to return to Merikay's face. The blueish tint faded from her fingernails. The second day she perked up. We resumed the nose-tube feedings, discontinued the day before. "He will revive us after two days . . ."

That night I called in the brethren. The tide was turning. Surely fasting and prayer would complete the healing so obviously begun. A dozen friends from as far as fifty miles away joined hands and hearts in a prayer vigil that lasted until 4:30 A.M. Merikay entered into every prayer our loving friends offered. Even prayed in one of the beautiful tongues God gave her. How we all prayed and believed and praised! It seemed she had been truly healed.

Then the morning light . . . her breath so rapid and shallow. We shared our love for Jesus, all our adventures with Him. We told each other how much we loved each other . . . how love like ours couldn't really be put into feeble words.

Again I asked her to forgive me for my impatience and for leaving her alone so many times. She smiled. So sweetly it tore my heart. She didn't open those beautiful green eyes. But she squeezed my hand so hard my fingers hurt. We kissed. She murmured softly, "I love you . . . always will."

That little chuckle. "You thought you'd get there first. But I'm going to beat you there, Big Buzz . . . and when you come . . . you'll find me waiting there." A sigh. Goodbye to this thing we call "life." Gently she slipped into Jesus' waiting arms.

Yet for my darling . . . Merikay, my love . . . my little Snuzz-Buzz . . . life had just begun. "He will raise us up on the third day that we may live before Him."

Within minutes of my phone call, LB manipulated her metal walker through the doorway. Then she saw Merikay, lying so radiant and still, never so beautiful. LB peered over the rail of the hospital bed for a long moment.

"Leave us alone, please," she snapped.

She took Merikay's soft hand in both of hers. Soft as silk. I hobbled quietly from the room.

When the men came with the stretcher three hours later, she was still sitting there, silent as a shadow, clasping Merikay's slim fingers. So hard to let her go.

Everything at the memorial service was sparkling white. A small cross of flowers came from our many friends in Tennessee-Georgia Christian Camp. St. Elisabeth's modest stone church was packed with those who loved Merikay. Triumphantly the organ burst into "Christ the Lord is Risen Today," introducing the beautiful Episcopal communion service.

All who had been baptized into the Christian faith, regardless of denomination, were invited to the communion rail. Presbyterians, Baptists, Catholics, Methodists, Pentecostals. They came with tear-stained, smiling faces and open hearts. I turned to our son and reminded him that he had been baptized as an infant in a Catholic church in Brooklyn. He came quickly forward and knelt beside me at the altar rail. It was the first time in his life that he ever took communion. And he took it with me. I remembered how often Merikay had said that if her own mother and her brother, and our son would only accept Jesus as their personal Savior, the suffering would be worth it all. And how her self-sufficient brother, Gene Howard, had knelt the night of our prayer vigil and called out to God on behalf of his beloved sister, that her life might be spared.

From the church a caravan of cars swung slowly onto the highway. It was only a few miles to Memorial Park in Skokie. But it seemed forever. Under a bright awning—Merikay just hated black, declared LB defensively—stiff wooden chairs ringed the gravesite. LB and Esther were in the front row, so LB's failing eyes wouldn't miss a move of the priest. He looked impressive in black cassock and white surplice. Father Bill Baar, more friend than priest, was burying the second member of the Howard family. A sight LB had never let herself imagine she would live to see. Tears again glistened in those jet black eyes . . .

"They shall run and not be weary. They shall walk and not faint." The words were like darts in my heart. That passage quoted by the minister was Merikay's favorite verse from the book of Isaiah.

"As I saw her life," he was having trouble with the words, "it was an acting out of this. I have known Merikay for many years through several serious illnesses. I've never seen greater courage or greater strength."

How true. Only the alcoholic knows the inner agony of slavery to the bottle.

"But it wasn't a grim courage. It was a happy courage . . . different. A lightness. And we saw this wonderful combination of goodness, lightness and fun."

*Hey, Big Buzz,* the words echoed in my heart. *Turn on that old prayer power . . . .*

"She was a beautiful spirit . . ."

*You thought you'd get there first . . .*

How that dark fear had choked her will to live.

*. . . and when you come . . .*

"Was and always will be."

*You'll find me waiting there.*

"Unto Almighty God we commend the soul of Merikay, our sister departed. We commit her body to the ground . . ."

What does the Scripture say? Absent from the body, but present with the Lord.

"Earth to earth . . ."

Strange. I know she's not there.

"Ashes to ashes . . ."

Yet every word is a blow to my heart.

"Dust to dust . . ."

Tears trickled slowly from my eyes.

"In the sure and certain hope of the resurrection of eternal life through our Lord Jesus Christ . . . through whose coming in glorious majesty to judge the world . . . earth and sea shall give up their dead and the corruptible bodies of those who sleep shall be changed and made like unto His glorious body . . ."

I thought of my many visions of the heavenly places. No diseased bodies there . . . no missing limbs . . .

"He that raised up Jesus from the dead shall also quicken our mortal bodies by His Spirit that dwelleth in us."

No blind eyes . . . no deaf ears . . . no crippled bodies . . . no pain, suffering . . .

". . . into the fellowship of thy saints through Jesus Christ. Almighty God, Father of our Lord Jesus Christ who is the Resurrection and the Life . . .

"May the angels bring you into Paradise . . . may the martyrs lead you into the Holy City of Jerusalem . . . may the chorus of angels receive you . . ." The priest was now making the sign of the cross. "And may you have eternal rest with Lazarus who watched your suffering. So, for the faithful departed," his voice choked, "Merikay . . . the mercy of God . . . rest in peace."

Fr. Bill's eyes glistened as he closed his prayer book. Was he thinking, like me, of those many warm and loving times Billy snuggled into Merikay's fur coat?   "Do you think you could let me borrow my son for a year, Merikay? I need him in the choir."

On wings of gold a small butterfly danced by. How Merikay had loved butterflies. She had butterflies on her dishes, her glasses, on her earrings . . . I thought of the butterfly emerging from its chrysalis . . .

My thoughts about you, Merikay—my love—seem to come only in poetry . . .

*I remember that sweet melody that every thought of you*
*    brings back anew . . .*
*The pain, the joy when girl meets boy . . .*
*Your lilting smile . . . your laugh, the tender touch, the fra-*
*    grant warmth of you . . .*
*How gallant and how gay . . . through every troubled day and*
*    tortured night . . .*
*The softness and the sweetness that is you . . .*

*We will meet again, on some flower-strewn distant plain.*
*Where we'll have time for all the things for which there was*
*    no time here . . .*
*Because over there . . .*
*Across the million miles, yet close within my soul's grasp, as*
*    near as breath . . . So tender close . . .*
*I feel you still.*
*Because time is no more we'll have all time to do, to say*
*    the tongue-tied words down here below . . . freed from*
*    the chains of flesh.*
*But most of all to share our deepest thoughts, our fragile*
*    dreams, the depth, the length of love that down here*
*    we but just begin to glimpse . . . love beyond our love.*
*Ah, darling mine, how empty is life without you . . . a silent*
*    song, a rose without a scent.*
*And it is raining teardrops in the hollow of my heart.*
*Yet never, never would I wish you back again where all the*
*    trouble and the turmoil is.*
*And so my heart yearns ever to that not-far-distant day when*

*from the chrysalis I too shall burst, butterfly and buoy-*
*ant bright . . .*
*And so from darkness into His perpetual light.*
*And so no goodbye kiss.*
*My love for you is just as long, and just as strong as all*
*eternity . . . my love, my darling, my sweetheart.*
*You who have shared with me my dreams, heart-hurts and*
*joys that know no words . . .*
*Thoughts that never can be captured in the net of words . . .*
*So soft and so steel-strong your faith and love . . . that*
*Gave and gave, beyond all reason towards my need . . .*
*And ever living, still loves on. Its tender touch entraps my*
*heart*
*forever*
*and forever*
*and forever more.*
*All ways and always, your own,*
*Laurie*

# Epilog

God's ways and God's timing are perfect. Only He can transform life's tragedy into triumph, bring life out of death. Because Merikay died, at the precise time that she died, three names were written in God's book of life.

When I bought the tombstone, God turned the business transaction into a redemptive encounter. The salesman came into God's family.

A TV commentator who interviewed me later regarding a FGBMFI matter could not understand my joy. He knew I had just lost my wife. I shared with him that nothing can destroy the joy of knowing Jesus. He wanted to know that kind of Savior.

And the taxicab driver who took me to the TV studio also gave his life to the Lord.

I praised God for glorifying Himself through Merikay's death. Yet, how to fill this empty void in my heart? At times came the agonizing question, "Why, Lord?"

"I gave her the desire of her heart, son."

Through my silent tears I remembered that word of knowledge given by Dr. Lall Din, three days before her homecoming, "He will raise us up on the third day that we may live before Him."

Yes, my darling Merikay is living in His sight. No more pain, no more struggle. Just joy unspeakable and full of glory. I remembered the familiar faces shaped like hearts . . . the radiance of those seen in my visions while I lay dying nearly twenty years before . . . separated only by a thin mist . . . all around us . . . so close it seemed I could reach out and touch them. Just a different dimension.

"Lord, I know You didn't cause Merikay's death any more than You caused that propellor accident."

"Son, I used the prop accident to strengthen your healing ministry even as I am going to use this agonizing experience to develop more compassion and an even greater healing ministry."

New faith flamed in my spirit. I can do all things through Christ who strengthens me. And if I can, anybody can. Nobody's too small or weak or insignificant to be used by God . . . if we're willing to be used where we are, in the condition we're in, in the way He wants to use us. And to His glory.

I glanced at what the world calls Merikay's grave. *But you, the real you,* I thought, *you're not there.* That heavy stone is warmed by those lovely words, *"I am the resurrection and the life; he who liveth and believeth in me shall never die."*

As passersby look down, these words will make their hearts look up.

Yes, Merikay, my love, I know that we shall meet again in heavenly places . . . where all sorrow and sighing have fled away . . . and He will wipe away all tears . . . so I rejoice in that love of Jesus that knows no depth, no height, no length, no end . . .

apart . . . but not for long . . .

until we meet again . . .

beyond tomorrow.